Natural Law Liberalism

Liberal political philosophy and natural law theory are not contradictory, but – properly understood – mutually reinforcing. Contemporary liberalism (as represented by Rawls, Gutmann and Thompson, Dworkin, Raz, and Macedo) rejects natural law and seeks to diminish its historical contribution to the liberal political tradition, but it is only one defective variant of liberalism. A careful analysis of the history of liberalism, identifying its core principles, and a similar examination of classical natural law theory (as represented by Thomas Aquinas and his intellectual descendants), show that a natural law liberalism is both possible and desirable. Natural law theory embraces the key principles of liberalism; it also provides balance in resisting some of its problematic tendencies. Natural law liberalism is the soundest basis for American public philosophy, and it is a potentially more attractive and persuasive form of liberalism for nations that have tended to resist it.

Christopher Wolfe is professor of political science at Marquette University. He received his PhD from Boston College and has been teaching at Marquette University since 1978. His published books include *The Rise of Modern Judicial Review* (1986), *Judicial Activism* (1991), and *How to Read the Constitution* (1996). His edited volumes include *Liberalism at the Crossroads* (1994); *Natural Law and Public Reason* (2000); *That Eminent Tribunal* (2004); *The Family, Civil Society, and the State* (1998); *Homosexuality and American Public Life* (1999); and *Same-Sex Matters* (2000). Dr. Wolfe has published articles in many scholarly journals and in *First Things*, as well as book reviews and various opinion pieces. He is the founder and President of the American Public Philosophy Institute.

Natural Law Liberalism

CHRISTOPHER WOLFE

Marquette University

CAMBRIDGE
UNIVERSITY PRESS

CAMBRIDGE UNIVERSITY PRESS
Cambridge, New York, Melbourne, Madrid, Cape Town, Singapore, São Paulo, Delhi

Cambridge University Press
Avenue of the Americas, New York, NY 10013-2473, USA

www.cambridge.org
Information on this title: www.cambridge.org/9780521140607

Christopher Wolfe 2006

First published 2006
First paperback edition 2009

Printed in the United States of America

catalog record for this publication is available from the British Library.

Library of Congress Cataloging in Publication Data

Wolfe, Christopher.
Natural law liberalism / Christopher Wolfe.
    p.   cm.
ISBN 0-521-84278-6 (hardcover)
    Liberalism. 2. Natural law. I. Title.
JC574.W65 2006
320.51–dc22   2005027578

ISBN 978-0-521-84278-5 hardback
ISBN 978-0-521-14060-7 paperback

Contents

Acknowledgments

This book would not have been possible without the very generous support I have received from a number of foundations. The National Endowment for the Humanities and the Randolph Foundation provided support for a 1993–94 sabbatical in which the work on the book was commenced. The book took final shape during my 2000–01 sabbatical, with the support of the Lynde and Harry Bradley Foundation, the Earhart Foundation, and the Lehrman Institute.

The Earhart Foundation and the Bradley Institute for Democracy at Marquette University also kindly supplied funds for summer work.

Portions of the book were presented at various conferences, including the International Foundation for Human Rights conference on "Natural Right and Liberty" in Rennes, France (December, 1994); a conference on "Practical Reason and Multiculturalism" at the University of Navarra, Pamplona, Spain (November, 1996); the Center for Economic and Policy Education conference, "Public Morality, Civic Virtue, and the Problem of Modern Liberalism," at St. Vincent's College (April, 1999); a Sacred Heart Major Seminary/Ave Maria Law School conference on "St. Thomas Aquinas and the Natural Law Tradition" (June, 2000); and the conference "Catholic Perspectives on American Law," Catholic University of America (March, 2001). I am grateful to the organizers of these conferences for their support, and to the participants for their comments and suggestions.

Chapter 2 is based on "Natural Law and Public Reason," which appeared in the *American Journal of Jurisprudence*, Volume 42 (1997) and in *Natural Law and Public Reason*, edited by R. George and C. Wolfe (Georgetown University Press, 2000). Chapter 4 was published as "Liberalism and Paternalism: A Critique of Ronald Dworkin" in *The Review of*

Politics, Volume 56, No. 4 (Fall, 1994). The author gratefully acknowledges the summer grant from the Bradley Institute for Democracy and Public Values at Marquette University which made preparation of that article possible. Chapter 5 appeared as "Being Worthy of Trust: A Response to Joseph Raz" in *Natural Law, Liberalism, and Morality*, edited by R. George (Clarendon Press, 1996). Chapter 6 is based on a review of Stephen Macedo's *Diversity and Distrust*, in the *American Journal of Jurisprudence*, Volume 46 (2001).

Most important are the debts I owe to various people with whom I have discussed portions of the manuscript or who have read and commented on it. Paul Carrese of the Air Force Academy, Jim Stoner of Louisiana State University, Kevin Miller of Franciscan University of Steubenville, and Joe Reisert of Colby College provided valuable reactions (not all favorable) to a paper in which I developed some of the main ideas of the book. Gerry Wegemer of the University of Dallas and Fred Freddoso of Notre Dame provided comments and assistance on a variety of points. A conference presentation by Peter Berkowitz of George Mason Law School played an important role in helping me to see how close my own thinking was to the broad tradition of liberal political philosophy. John Tryneski of the University of Chicago Press provided valuable advice that helped me to take certain steps in reformulating the book's thesis.

The members of the core group of the American Public Philosophy Institute, including Robert George of Princeton, Gerry Bradley of Notre Dame, Michael Pakaluk of Clark University, Russ Hittinger of the University of Tulsa, and Hadley Arkes of Amherst College, have helped provide the intellectual support and friendship that have made this project so enjoyable and worthwhile.

Finally, I owe a deep debt of gratitude to Lew Bateman of Cambridge University Press, who has been as supportive an editor as one could hope to have.

Introduction

Should liberals ground their liberalism in classical natural law? Should those who take their orientation from natural law theory necessarily be liberals?

Many liberals and natural law theorists will regard each other as distinctly unlikely (and uncomfortable) bedfellows. They will feel, in fact, that if they wake up and find themselves in bed with each other, it must have been the result of some improbable Shakespearean plot in which one's expected bedfellow has been switched and the difference has not been noticed until the following morning.

The proponents of natural law, tracing their roots to Thomas Aquinas, and in many ways back beyond him to the classical Greek natural right tradition, maintain that it is possible for human beings to recognize a wide range of objective human goods. They believe these goods provide a necessary framework for political life, for understanding and pursuing the common good. Liberals, tracing their roots through John Stuart Mill back to John Locke, and in certain ways further back to Thomas Hobbes, are more skeptical of the possibility of agreement on what is good for human beings, and would limit the object of political life to defending the rights of individuals to pursue their own ideas of the good. Natural law theorists defend "regulating morality," while liberals generally oppose it. Can there be fundamental agreement between such apparently distinct traditions of thought?

I want to argue that the relationship between liberalism and natural law is – or at least can be – more like the ordinary relationship between other kinds of bedfellows: namely, good spouses. In a good marriage, there is underlying agreement on fundamental matters, combined with some genuine complementarity – that is, differences – that may cause tensions but that also contribute to their mutual personal improvement. Often it takes years to see that the differences and tensions are not just a source of difficulty but an opportunity for growth. That has certainly been the case with the rocky relationship between liberalism and natural law.

It is interesting to play with this analogy (although in the end, like most analogies, it has its definite limits). Not the least of the difficulties is that the stories of the relationship of natural law and liberalism vary so greatly, depending on whether the story describes continental, English, or American liberalism. The story line I follow focuses on Anglo-American liberalism: born and developing in England, but eventually coming to have its center of gravity in America, more democratic and more free of the vestiges of pre-liberal social structures.

Natural law and liberalism were, after all, originally "married," in the classical liberal political philosophy of John Locke. From the beginning, there were problems with the marriage. Perhaps the brash young man had married the daughter of an old and declining family only to buttress his own reputation, and the young woman had been misled by the young man's veneer of respectability. Perhaps, too, the young lady was too tied to her old family ways, and insufficiently open to some of the new ideas and practices of her consort. The partners increasingly believed that their apparent similarities were superficial and that, in fact, they didn't have much in common. Although they had used the same words (especially "natural law"), they had meant different things by them. Their growing recognition of their differences led to bitterness and recrimination, terrible fights, irreconcilable differences, separation, and a bitter divorce.

Only after many years did the former partners – spurred in part by a growing realization of their own defects – take another, deeper look at each other and recall the genuine good in the other person that had been lost sight of amidst the fighting. As their feelings toward each other softened, to their own surprise it seemed possible that reconciliation might be possible, and the marriage once again consummated.

The happy ending to this story, however, requires that both parties come to the realization of their compatibility and even their need for each other. But the achievement of that happy ending is more than a little doubtful. The process by which natural law has come to appreciate the strengths of liberalism, in recent times, has moved at a much more rapid pace than liberalism's recognition of its need for natural law. And, in fact, liberalism today seems intent on "going it alone," without the need for any support outside its own commitment to autonomy, which entails the permanent revisability of all personal commitments.

For years it has been said that there is a "crisis of liberalism," but it is really an *intellectual* crisis of *contemporary* liberalism. Liberalism, understood broadly, is generally triumphant around the world, in the wake of the collapse of communism, and for good reasons. Those reasons were brought home with particular force on September 11, 2001. Liberal democracy offers people a measure of freedom, prosperity, and well-being that no other form of government seems able to provide as consistently. Whatever the faults of liberalism – and liberal democracy, like every other form of government, has its own characteristic weaknesses – it is by far the best game in town, and we should want to preserve and strengthen it. But preserving and strengthening it may mean moderating it, and the vice of contemporary liberalism is to place such a great emphasis on the chief animating principles of liberalism, liberty and equality, that insufficient attention is paid to other human goods, including truth, family, and piety.

The way to deal with the crisis of contemporary liberalism is to embrace what I will call natural law liberalism. The principles of natural law philosophy provide a more solid foundation for liberalism and moderate its more problematic tendencies. They secure the strengths of liberalism while mitigating its defects. Above all, they provide a ground for liberalism that rests on a confidence that human beings can and do know the truth about the human good (in its great variety of forms) rather than a skepticism about such knowledge or a despair that human beings can ever agree on it. It grounds liberalism positively in the truth about the human person rather than negatively in various forms of agnosticism, about man as much as God.

This natural law liberalism cannot be billed simply as a "return" to some past form of liberalism, one that was still influenced by medieval natural law before that influence became attenuated in the course of time. Contemporary natural law thinkers have to confront the plain fact that liberalism arose precisely as a reaction *against* a society in which natural law thinking seemed dominant. For much of the last four centuries, classical natural law and liberalism have been perceived (by people on both sides) as opponents, or even deadly enemies.

This perception is wrong, for several reasons. First, some of what passed as "natural law principles" in pre-liberal societies was not in fact an essential part of natural law philosophy, but merely one particular application of it, and even, in some cases, an actual distortion of it.

(The failure to protect a sufficiently broad form of religious liberty was especially notable.) Second, while it is true that liberalism was a reaction against a society in which natural law principles played a role, it is also true that from the beginning liberalism retained important elements of natural law thought.

Natural law liberalism, then, depends on moderating both traditions. Classic natural law has to be separated from its original historical, political, and social context, purified of elements that are inconsistent with its most important principles, and adapted to modern circumstances. In this process, the fundamental harmony between natural law and reasonable forms of liberty and equality will become apparent.

Liberalism has to be freed of its insensitivity to the fact of the deep influence of the "regime" – including liberal democratic political communities – on the formation of people's ideals and character: their thoughts, desires, attitudes. Moreover, certain perennial substantive tendencies of liberalism, which tend to be exacerbated in contemporary liberalism, have to be overcome: the tendency of toleration to evolve into forms of skepticism and relativism (at least about the human good) and principled religious indifferentism, and the tendency of equality and freedom to evolve into an egoistic individualism that undermines the family and commitment to human goods beyond consumeristic well-being.

Another way to say this is that liberalism must be moderated so that when it shapes its citizens – as it inevitably will, even in its milder way[1] – it does so in ways that are more fully compatible with important intellectual and moral goods: with reason and faith, and with the moral virtues that regulate the passions and promote individual and social well-being. Natural law, without disturbing its convictions that there is a truth, that human beings can know it, and that their well-being lies in finding and living in accord with it, has to be so formulated as to recognize, in ways that its historical representatives have sometimes failed to do, the intrinsic importance – the necessity – of human freedom and the limits of coercion and law.

The goal of this book is to make a modest start at developing a fuller statement of natural law liberalism. My first task will be to identify key inadequacies of contemporary liberalism, which provides us with an incentive to look more closely at natural law liberalism as an alternative.

---

[1] On the shaping power of liberal regimes, see Martin Diamond "Ethics and Politics: The American Way" in *The Moral Foundations of the American Republic*, R. Horwitz, Ed. (Charlottesville, VA: University Press of Virginia, 1977), pp. 39–72, especially pp. 62–68.

To this end, in the first part of the book I examine contemporary liberal doctrines of public reason and reciprocity and autonomy.

The inability of these major theorists to establish plausible cases for the doctrines of liberal public reason and liberal autonomy should induce us to look elsewhere, to some source other than contemporary liberalism, for an adequate ground for our public philosophy. In the second part of the book, I try to develop a basic notion of "natural law liberalism" as that more adequate alternative. I show why it is plausible to believe that, despite the appearances of history, liberalism and natural law are not only compatible, but mutually reinforcing. Liberals should ground their liberalism in natural law philosophy, and natural law thinkers should be liberals (albeit "moderate" liberals, unlike most representatives of contemporary liberalism).

In the final substantive chapter, I present an example of how natural law liberalism "cashes out" – what its distinctive approach would be – by examining the topic of religious liberty. I argue that its approach is different from classical natural law, in that it embraces a broader and more robust form of religious liberty (including the right to proselytize), and also different from contemporary liberal theory, in its refusal to celebrate religious diversity as a good in itself, because of its commitment to pursue religious truth.

A brief conclusion outlines what a natural law liberal public philosophy would look like. In a future work, I hope to develop natural law liberalism further, by developing its substantive content (and contrasting it with contemporary liberalism) on a variety of important issues: the foundations of human dignity, religious truth, freedom of thought and discussion, marriage, family, and sexuality, property and economic life, and political life.

The conclusion of my analysis of liberalism is that it greatly benefits precisely from elements derived from natural law that contemporary liberals most wish to eliminate on the grounds that those elements are inconsistent with the principles of liberalism. If we want to have a healthy liberalism – and my argument is that Americans, including those oriented toward natural law (despite historical tensions between liberalism and classical natural law), should want precisely that, as should others around the world – we need to attend to the fundamental compatibility between and reciprocal support of liberalism and natural law. We need a natural law liberalism.

PART I

CONTEMPORARY LIBERALISM

RAWLS'S POLITICAL LIBERALISM

Rawls begins with conceptions he considers implicit in our political culture. The first is that of citizens as free and equal persons, who have a capacity to understand and act on principles regulating a scheme of social cooperation and a capacity to develop, revise, and pursue rationally a conception of the good. The second conception is that of society as a fair system of cooperation among free and equal citizens, an idea which is developed to arrive at a "political" conception of justice, which applies only to the broadest social framework of the nation and the way that persons relate to one another politically within that basic structure. This political conception seeks to avoid philosophical controversies, in order to advance its strictly practical task of securing fair terms of social cooperation. (Partisans of different comprehensive philosophical, moral, and religious views will find fuller justifications within their own theories, providing Rawls's theory of justice with an "overlapping consensus.")

The fair terms of social cooperation turn out to be two principles of justice: first, "each person has an equal right to a fully adequate scheme of equal liberties, which scheme is compatible with a similar scheme of liberties for all" (including freedom of thought and conscience, political liberties, freedom of association, liberty and integrity of the person, and the rule of law) and, second, "social and economic inequalities must satisfy two conditions, (i) they are to be attached to offices and positions open to all under conditions of fair equality of opportunity; and (ii) they are to be to the greatest benefit of the least advantaged members of society."

The justice of these principles is arrived at by a certain procedure, namely, a thought experiment of putting citizens in an "original position," behind a "veil of ignorance" (not knowing their status in society or their conceptions of the good). These citizens are to choose principles of justice, in light of their recognition of certain primary goods (basic rights and liberties, freedom of movement and occupation, power and prerogatives of office, income and wealth, and the social bases of self-respect). Given a choice between justice as fairness and utilitarianism, Rawls says that people in the original position will choose the former, on the basis of the "maximin" rule: where there is uncertainty about a choice, but one knows that the worst outcome of one choice is satisfactory while the worst outcome for the other is unsatisfactory, it makes sense to select the alternative that results in the best worst case. People in the original position, not knowing their status and their conceptions of the good, will choose justice as fairness over utilitarianism, where the worst-case scenario is very great: loss of one's liberties as part of a social calculus.

Rawls says, in *Political Liberalism*, that *A Theory of Justice* did not sufficiently distinguish between moral and political philosophy: "a moral doctrine of justice general in scope is not distinguished from a strictly political conception of justice."[3] In his revised work, the distinction between comprehensive philosophical and moral doctrines, on one hand, and political conceptions becomes fundamental. Justice as fairness is held to embody certain (partial) conceptions of the good, but Rawls denies that it entails any comprehensive conception of the good. At the same time, he does not describe it as "neutral," recognizing that it tends to foster some ways of life (e.g., those that value tolerance, civility, a sense of fairness, the ability to compromise), while undermining others (e.g., those based on intolerance).

Political Liberalism[4] and later articles[5] develop at some length the concept of "public reason":

> when constitutional essentials and questions of basic justice are at stake, citizens are to be ready to justify to one another their political actions by reference to the public political conception of justice, and so by conceptions and principles, values and ideals that they sincerely believe other citizens may reasonably be expected to endorse. The thought is that citizens, finding themselves living together in political society, and exercising the coercive power of government over one another, should, at least on fundamental political questions, justify their opinions and deeds by reference to what they may suppose others could accept consistent with their freedom and equality.[6]

That is, citizens ought to appeal to public reason rather than simply to their own comprehensive views. Moreover, "[w]e add to this that in making these justifications, we are to appeal only to presently accepted general beliefs and forms of reasoning found in common sense, and the methods and conclusions of science when these are not controversial."[7] Rawls grants that arguments based on comprehensive views can be introduced into public discourse, but only on condition that other arguments,

---

[3] *Political Liberalism*, p. xv.

[4] Part Two of *Political Liberalism* discusses "Three Main Ideas" of which two – the idea of an overlapping consensus and the priority of right over good – were discussed extensively in *A Theory of Justice*. Public reason is the third main idea.

[5] Especially "The Idea of Public Reason," In *Rawls, Political Liberalism*, expanded edition (New York: Columbia University Press, 2005).

[6] From "The Idea of Public Reason: Further Considerations" (manuscript on file with the author).

[7] *Political Liberalism*, p. 224.

acceptable to those with different reasonable comprehensive views, are used as well.

In his later work, Rawls was pursuing a new goal (beyond replacing utilitarianism as the foundation for liberalism). He wanted to answer the question: "How is it possible that there may exist over time a stable and just society of free and equal citizens profoundly divided by reasonable though incompatible religious, philosophical, and moral doctrines?"

Why *this* question? We must look at Rawls's thumbnail sketch of European political philosophy (in the preface to *Political Liberalism*) to discover why. Rawls argues that the problems of political philosophy in the modern world derive from the special nature of democratic political culture, due to the historical context of modern politics. The ancient world experienced no tension between religion and politics because Greek religion was a civic religion rather than a religion of salvation with a class of priests dispensing necessary means of grace and with ideas of immortality and eternal salvation. The Greek civic religion contained no alternative idea of the highest good to be set against the Homeric epics at the core of Greek politics (the ideal way of life of the early Greek warrior class). Greek philosophy rejected the Homeric ideals and "had to work out for itself ideas of the highest good for human life, ideas acceptable to the citizens of the different society of fifth-century B.C. Athens." Moral philosophy was "the exercise of free, disciplined reason alone," not based on religion, "as civic religion was neither a guide nor rival to it."[8]

All this was changed by the arrival of Christianity. Medieval Christianity was quite different from ancient civic religion. It was authoritarian, salvationist, creedal, priestly and sacramental, and expansionist. This medieval world gave way eventually to a modern world shaped by three historical developments. First, the Reformation fragmented the religious unity of the Middle Ages and led to religious pluralism, which in turn led to other kinds of pluralism. Second, the modern state, with its central administration, came into existence, initially ruled by monarchs with great powers. Third, the early seventeenth century saw the emergence of modern science (Copernican astronomy, Newtonian physics, calculus).

The ancient world never knew "the clash between salvationist, creedal, and expansionist religions" that arose only with the Reformation. The Reformers were like those they attacked, in that they were dogmatic and

---

[8] *Political Liberalism*, p. xxii.

intolerant. Neither side had doubts about the nature of the highest good or the basis of moral obligation in divine law. Their problem was

> How is society even possible between those of different faiths? . . . For many, [toleration was] acquiescence in heresy about first things and the calamity of religious disunity. Even the earlier proponents of toleration saw the division of Christendom as a disaster, though a disaster that had to be accepted in view of the alternative of unending religious civil war.[9]

> What is new about this clash is that it introduces into people's conceptions of their good a transcendent element not admitting of compromise. This element forces either mortal conflict moderated only by circumstance and exhaustion, or equal liberty of conscience and freedom of thought.[10]

Political liberalism assumes the fact of a pluralism of comprehensive doctrines (religious and nonreligious) and sees this, not as a disaster, but as the natural outcome of the activities of human reason under enduring free institutions. "To see reasonable pluralism as a disaster is to see the exercise of reason under the conditions of freedom itself as a disaster."[11] Only with the success of liberal constitutionalism did it become clear that social unity and concord was possible without agreement on a general comprehensive doctrine (religious, philosophical, or moral). "Perhaps the doctrine of free faith developed because it is difficult, if not impossible, to believe in the damnation of those with whom we have, with trust and confidence, long and fruitfully cooperated in maintaining a just society."[12]

Thus, the historical origin of political liberalism (and of liberalism more generally) is the Reformation and its aftermath. For with it, the problem of the essential conditions of a viable and just society, among people who are divided by profound doctrinal conflict, moved to (and continues to occupy) center stage. (Rawls asserts that focusing on these long-standing classical problems will at least provide guidelines for the problems of contemporary life, such as race, ethnicity, and gender.)

Rawls points out the developments in moral philosophy that paralleled the rise of political liberalism. Men like Hume and Kant sought to "establish a basis of moral knowledge independent of ecclesiastical authority and available to the ordinary reasonable and conscientious person" and then to "develop the full range of concepts and principles in

---

[9] Ibid., p. xxiv.
[10] Ibid., pp xxv–xxvi.
[11] Ibid., pp. xxiv–xxv.
[12] Ibid., p. xxv.

but as a mis-use or abuse or failure of reason (the evaluation of which is completely unaffected by how "natural" an "outcome" it is considered to be, in Rawls's sense of "natural").[22]

Better Than a Modus Vivendi?

Rawls argues that political liberalism is superior to a "modus vivendi." A modus vivendi is a relation analogous to a treaty between two contending nations, which is adhered to by each, not because there is a common law and legal authority that each party accepts and that can enforce this law, but because the treaty's provisions are in the interests of each; but either party may withdraw from the treaty if its view of those conditions changes.

A modus vivendi is a settlement in which people and groups with different comprehensive views are willing (as a second-best alternative) to live peacefully in a pluralistic society that is regarded as something less than the ideal precisely because it is pluralistic, because the true comprehensive opinions on fundamental issues are treated on a par with erroneous views. The reason for such a willingness to live peacefully – to accept the principle that the state will not adopt, or promote, or enforce one of the contending positions – is that none of the contenders has sufficient power to make its own views the basis for society. (This insufficiency of "power" is ambiguous: it may refer either to raw coercive power or to sufficient political support to have its way through peaceful political processes.) This could imply that, as soon as one of the parties had sufficient political power, the pluralism would be dispensed with. The standard example is the post-Reformation wars stand-off between European Catholics and Protestants in the seventeenth century, in which each side became willing to tolerate the other because it lacked sufficient coercive power to impose itself (at an acceptable price in bloodshed), but in principle believed that rulers should uphold true religion and suppress heresy, and would do so if circumstances made that policy possible. Nineteenth century Catholic teachings on the confessionally Catholic state as the ideal state, and religious pluralism as a necessity under less desirable circumstances, could be, and in American history often have been, regarded as a later instance of this approach. The social unity in such a modus vivendi, Rawls says, "is only apparent, as its stability is contingent on circumstances remaining

---

[22] See Lief Wenar, "*Political Liberalism*: An Internal Critique" in *Ethics*, Vol. 106, p. 32 (October, 1995), especially pp. 42–48.

such as not to upset the fortunate convergence of interests."[23] Political liberalism (based on an "overlapping consensus") is more stable, because it is itself a moral conception affirmed on moral grounds, and will not change with a shift in the balance of power in society.

At the same time, Rawls – especially in *Political Liberalism* – recognizes that an explicit grounding of liberalism in a *comprehensive* philosophy entailing pluralism – either on the grounds that the "truth" about fundamental issues in principle cannot be known, or on the ground that the "truth is that there is no truth," or on the grounds that the truth is somehow best approximated by a melange of pluralistic opinions – was likely to exclude too many people (especially a large number of politically active Christians) from the consensus required for a stable political order.[24] So his strategy required that liberalism be able to convince firm adherents of comprehensive views that there are *principled* reasons – compatible with their adherence to the truth of their own comprehensive views – for accepting a liberalism that *politically* subordinates their comprehensive views to the necessary conditions of social cooperation. Above all, this meant their willingness to abide by the requirements of "public reason," according to which they cannot simply appeal to their comprehensive views to justify their political positions, but are limited to arguments that others could considerable "reasonable" (in the narrower, Rawlsian sense of that term).

The problem for Rawls is that serious American religious believers who do not consider pluralism good in itself find a modus vivendi perfectly plausible, and not necessarily unstable.[25] As long as the conditions of widespread pluralism prevail – for as long as the facts bear out Rawls's contention that the burdens of reason lead ineluctably to the fact of reasonable pluralism – a modus vivendi is, for them, perhaps a lamentable necessity, but it is also *what political morality, under those circumstances,*

---

[23] *Political Liberalism*, p. 147.

[24] Recall John Courtney Murray's observation that, if the First Amendment is understood to make pluralism an article of *faith*, "there are immediately in this country some 35,000,000 dissenters, the Catholic community"; see *We Hold These Truths* (Image Books, 1964), p. 63. If it is less clear that Catholics today are quite so monolithic (if many of them are willing to join in the general celebration of pluralism, treating it as an article of faith), that is because contemporary liberalism has made successful inroads into the Catholic community, in ways that may only reinforce the ambivalence serious Catholics feel about Rawlsian liberalism and its tendency to undermine certain articles of faith – that is, its tendency to advance a particular comprehensive philosophical position.

[25] For arguments on behalf of a modus vivendi, see Part 5, "Modus Vivendi?," of *The Idea of Political Liberalism*, V. Davion and C. Wolfe, Eds. (Rowman and Littlefield, 2000).

demands. What John Courtney Murray called the post-Reformation "articles of peace" accepted political pluralism as a "second-best" situation, but – putting it more strongly – also viewed it as *the morally choiceworthy* policy to pursue. (Even if the specific theological or philosophical reasons given for embracing the modus vivendi were somewhat different, the modus vivendi benefited from its own "overlapping consensus.") Therefore, a modus vivendi need not be unstable.

A political liberal might argue that a modus vivendi is still undesirable, even if temporarily stable, because it preserves an order in which religious minorities (or other minorities uncompromisingly committed to the truth and political relevance of their comprehensive views) can harbor intentions of gaining political power and imposing their views. (This fits nicely with Rawls's maximin strategy: the chance of a hostile minority gaining such power might be slim, but the worst case scenario of oppression is so bad as to make avoiding it a high priority – high enough to justify the acceptance of political liberalism as a principled alternative, and one that would, moreover, by inculcating political liberalism in the citizenry, actively undermine the likelihood of that worst care scenario.)

This argument against a modus vivendi is not persuasive, however. To begin with, the long-term dangers of a modus vivendi – harboring groups that intend to impose their will if they become politically dominant – are not as great as some consider them to be.[26] This argument presumes that the groups resistant to political liberalism are potentially very dangerous, because they harbor the desire to *impose* their will, should political circumstances ever permit that. But those who prefer a modus vivendi today generally would not want to "impose their views" on others in the political community, even if they became politically dominant. To make the point in a simple way, religious believers today who regard pluralism as intrinsically undesirable might reject the Establishment Clause, but they strongly believe in the Free Exercise Clause of the U.S. Constitution, because they recognize that even true opinions on fundamental issues must be accepted freely, rather than imposed.[27] They reject *principled* acceptance of pluralism as a good in itself, and they refuse to put their deepest comprehensive views off-limits in present political discourse – which political liberalism would demand of them – yet they are opposed, in principle, to imposing

---

[26] Ibid., chapter 11, Bernard Dauenhauer, "A Good Word for a Modus Vivendi," p. 214.

[27] One of the most significant examples of this approach is the teaching of the Catholic Church in the Second Vatican Council's "Declaration on Religious Liberty." *Vatican Council II*, Austin Flannery, Ed. (Northport, CT: Costello, 1996), p. 551.

their views on others. This makes the "worst case" scenario look considerably less bad, and shifts the balance of the argument significantly.

Rawls's Conventionalism

Finally – a more radical theoretical criticism – Rawls's political philosophy is surprisingly "conventional." It assumes too much to be regarded as a solid foundation for a public philosophy. Pierre Manent, writing in *First Things,* focuses on the questions "how did our democracy come into being?" and "how did our democracy go, so to speak, into nonbeing and evolve into totalitarianism or at least open itself to what has been aptly called 'the totalitarian temptation'?"[28] In a response to a critic of the article, he subsequently wrote that answering these questions requires being able to give "a thorough analysis of political life within an account of the human world." But, Manent comments, American thinkers do not aspire to so broad a goal: "I understand that Americans are different from Europeans in that they take the democratic regime for granted."

One consequence of these remarks is that John Rawls does *not* qualify as a political philosopher. He certainly is a citizen in good standing of the American body politic, and a very commented upon teacher and writer. He contributed to a revival of the debate about our social arrangements not only in the English-speaking world, but in the whole democratic world. But he *presupposes* the validity, truth, and excellence of our democratic principles and institutions, and so cannot do more than ingeniously tinker with parochial details.[29]

While Rawls and others represent a recent "explosion of philosophical writing analyzing and justifying such matters as justice, democracy, rights, freedom, and equality,"[30] Manent says, "Who needs one more justifier for what he or she already believes? I need someone who is able to free me from the bondage of present conventions."[31] But Rawls cannot get to the most fundamental issues of political philosophy because that would entail a comprehensive theory, which is too divisive, in his own view, to serve as the basis for a public philosophy.

Isn't it enough that Rawls's conventional assumptions correspond to those of the community for which he writes, namely, Western constitutional democracies? I think not. First, from a short-term perspective,

---

[28] *First Things* Number 103 (May, 2000), pp. 15–22.
[29] *First Things* Number 106 (October, 2000), p. 9.
[30] Quoting from the letter to which Manent is responding, from J. L. A. Garcia of Boston University, *First Things* (October, 2000), p. 7.
[31] Ibid., p. 9.

it might appear to be adequate, but short-term perspectives are inadequate to ground a public philosophy. We cannot simply assume that there will be no challenges to democratic assumptions, even in the relatively foreseeable future. For example, if American society were subject to dramatic stresses, such as severe economic depression or a successful terrorist assault of great magnitude (perhaps through biological or chemical weapons), would challenges to democratic principles emerge, and could they be successfully resisted?

Second, the answers to more particular questions of public philosophy cannot be separated from the answers to the initial and broader questions. Free speech, for example, would be an essential part of any American public philosophy. But virtually no one believes that speech can never, under any circumstances, be prohibited or punished. What are the *reasonable* limits to free speech? The answer to that question will depend naturally on the *purpose* of free speech,[32] and that, in turn, will require a much broader political philosophy that does not simply assume democratic institutions and practices (e.g., free speech).

Third, we should be more alert to the need for such a broader political philosophy, given the rise of international terrorism and aggressive anti-Western, anti-liberal democratic movements, governments, and cultures. For many years, the confrontation with Soviet communism was a considerable stimulus to Western political theory, which required something more than assumptions of Western superiority – arguments were needed. With the fall of communism, liberal democracy temporarily appeared to be the only game in town, having vanquished its enemies. Now, liberal democracy confronts a more difficult opponent, rooted in a form of religious fanaticism that seems impervious to reason.

No amount of argumentation will "persuade" a religious fanatic. But it matters a great deal what people in such cultures – who are invited to become religious fanatics – see as the alternative to it. If the alternative to religious fanaticism is a political community in which their deepest convictions about reality and human life are said to be false (as in comprehensive liberalism) or one in which those convictions are required to be put to the side and treated as politically irrelevant (except to the extent that they happen to harmonize with political liberalism) – if the political community is one in which the ideals of truth and goodness most

---

[32] See Francis Canavan, *Freedom of Expression: Purpose as Limit* (Durham, NC: Carolina Academic Press, 1984).

important in their lives are thoroughly relativized or privatized – religious zealotry may appear to be the only tolerable option. If the alternative is a more classic form of liberalism as "articles of peace" – a modus vivendi – which would permit them to retain and to deploy in political argument their comprehensive views, while demanding that they accept the social ground rules of freedom of conscience for all citizens, the likelihood of "converting" them to liberalism would be much greater.

Only if liberalism is able to put forward a face that makes public appeals to ultimate standards of truth and goodness possible will it be able to compete for the hearts and minds of many people in the world who are not simply raised with conventional Western ideas and attitudes. The challenge facing even this moderate liberalism – the challenge of convincing many people that freedom of conscience is good, even if moral relativism or privatization of comprehensive views is not – will still be a great one. But I believe that there is a much greater possibility of successfully meeting that challenge than there is of persuading them to accept comprehensive or political liberalism.

Contemporary Liberal Exclusionism II

Rawls, Macedo, and "Neutral" Liberal Public Reason

Classical Greek political philosophy maintained that all political regimes profoundly shaped the character of their citizens. This was not simply a choice, but a fact. The way of life of the polis or the political community – which was the framework for everything, including religion – was the broadest horizon for most people in the Greek and Hellenistic and Roman worlds. The rise of Christianity and its social dominance during the post-Constantinian era changed that perspective profoundly. Christian political thought, especially as found in the work of Augustine, dramatically expanded the human horizon by making men citizens of a "heavenly commonwealth," one that transcended this world, and by so doing it "demoted" politics from its preeminent role in classical thought. Nonetheless, Christian political thinkers – following St. Paul,[1] and especially with the embracing of Aristotle by Thomas Aquinas – continued to recognize an authority to foster virtue and punish vice in those who had charge of the political common good (albeit a more limited one, subject to a higher authority, the Church). If the earthly city was confined to dealing with temporal goods, those goods still included important religious and moral goods.

Liberalism brought with it a new understanding of the purpose of political life. As initiated in important respects by Thomas Hobbes and developed more fully in John Locke, liberalism maintained that the purpose of

---

[1] In his *Letter to the Romans*, XIII:3–4 ("For rulers are not a terror to good conduct, but to bad. Would you have no fear of him who is in authority? Then do what is good, and you will receive his approval, for he is God's servant for your good. But if you do wrong, be afraid, for he does not bear the sword in vain; he is the servant of God to execute his wrath on the wrongdoer.").

civil society and the state – a human invention to escape the difficulties of life in the state of nature – was quite limited: the protection of self-preservation and the rights essentially required for it, including liberty and property. If morality and character formation were not entirely off limits to government – and they weren't – they were a proper concern of the state only to the extent that they were instrumental to the protection of natural rights. And those natural rights, as Thomas Jefferson rightly understood the implications of Locke, included the right to "pursuit of happiness," the choice of the way of life that one would pursue to achieve happiness.

Classical liberals like Locke and Jefferson were not insensitive to the character formation that liberal regimes themselves effected. Among the great benefits of liberalism were the qualities of tolerance and self-reliance and humanity that it fostered. But the range of legitimate social and political character formation was more limited in liberal societies, and the virtues encouraged by liberalism were those that facilitated social life, leaving to individuals and the private sphere the choice of the particular way of life – including the choice of virtues or human excellence – that would be pursued.

This sense of the right to choose one's own way of life is powerful in liberal societies, and its importance is undeniable. This should be true not only of people who see autonomy as an end in itself, but also of those who are deeply committed to some substantive vision of morality. Any proper understanding of a good human life should recognize that moral goodness lies in the human will, not just external actions. We all know that a person who is coerced into performing good actions or does them for bad reasons is not praiseworthy. Who would admire the "generosity" of a person who gave a great deal of money to a charity – but only because he is being blackmailed, or only to make people think well of him and increase his business profits? The only actions that are morally praiseworthy are those that are done freely. This line of reasoning powerfully supports the idea that government should not dictate or impose a way of life, but should leave that choice to individuals (with the exception of those choices that clearly redound to the harm of others, which can legitimately be proscribed).

In contemporary liberalism, this idea has been expressed – by the early Ronald Dworkin, for example – especially in the idea that government should be "neutral" as to moral choices:

the first [or liberal] theory of equality supposes that political decisions must be, so far as is possible, independent of any particular conception of the good life, or of

what gives value to life. Since the citizens of a society differ in their conceptions, the government does not treat them as equals if it prefers one conception to another, either because the officials believe that one is intrinsically superior, or because one is held by the more numerous or powerful group.[2]

Michael Sandel has characterized the political regime based on this understanding as "the procedural republic" and maintains that powerful forces are pushing American life in this direction:

> With a few notable exceptions, such as the civil rights movement of the 1950s and 1960s, our political discourse in recent decades has come to reflect the liberal resolve that government be neutral on moral and religious questions, that matters of policy and law be debated and decided without reference to any particular conception of the good life.[3]

John Rawls, the central figure of contemporary Anglo-American political philosophy since the publication of *A Theory of Justice* over three decades ago, also embraced this view of liberal neutrality, but with qualifications. In his later *Political Liberalism*, he cautioned that the term "liberal neutrality" is easily misunderstood. He said that justice as fairness "is not procedurally neutral," since "its principles of justice are substantive and express far more than procedural values," and then went on to argue that

> we may distinguish procedural neutrality from neutrality of aim; but the latter is not to be confused with neutrality of effect or influence. As a political conception for the basic structure justice as fairness as a whole tries to provide common ground as the focus of an overlapping consensus. It also hopes to satisfy neutrality of aim in the sense that basic institutions and public policy are not to be designed to favor any particular comprehensive doctrine. Neutrality of effect or influence political liberalism abandons as impracticable, and since this idea is strongly suggested by the term itself, this is reason for avoiding it.[4]

Political liberalism may affirm the superiority of certain forms of moral character, but it does so as part of a political conception of justice, and "does not lead to the perfectionist state of a comprehensive doctrine."[5]

---

[2] Ronald Dworkin, "Liberalism," in *A Matter of Principle* (Cambridge, MA: Harvard University Press, 1985), p. 191. Dworkin later retracted this view of liberal neutrality, as he noted in his "Foundations of Liberal Equality," In *Tanner Lectures on Human Values*, Vol. 2 (Salt Lake City, UT: University of Utah Press, 1990), p. 7.

[3] Michael Sandel, *Democracy's Discontent: America in Search of a Public Philosophy* (Cambridge, MA: Harvard University Press, 1996), p. 24.

[4] John Rawls, *Political Liberalism* (New York: Columbia University Press, 1993), pp. 193–94.

[5] Ibid., p. 194.

For example, strengthening the virtues of tolerance and mutual trust (e.g., by discouraging religious and racial discrimination) does not create a Platonic or Aristotelian perfectionist state, nor does it establish a particular religion (like early modern Catholic and Protestant states). "Rather, it is taking reasonable measures to strengthen the forms of thought and feeling that sustain fair social cooperation between citizens regarded as free and equal. This is very different from the state's advancing a particular comprehensive doctrine in its own name."[6]

One of the key new concepts developed by *Political Liberalism* was that of "public reason." Public reason is an important Rawlsian doctrine, because it provides a more developed argument for the "bracketing" of fundamental and controversial moral, philosophical, and religious issues in politics – removing these issues from the political agenda of liberal democratic societies, and leaving them in the sphere of private decision making.

In this chapter, I would like to examine more closely the Rawlsian idea of public reason, because I think that its inadequacies help to demonstrate the illusory character of even the qualified liberal neutrality that Rawls is willing to subscribe to. The specific form of Rawlsian public reason I wish to subject to analysis is the form defended by Stephen Macedo, in his *Liberal Virtues* and, later, in *Diversity and Distrust*.[7]

Natural law liberals can respond to the idea of "public reason" in two somewhat different ways, depending on how it is understood. If public reason is interpreted broadly (perhaps I could even say literally), natural law theorists would argue that natural law is *the* philosophy of public reason. Acting according to right reason – for good reasons – is, after all, precisely what natural law is all about. Natural law theorists believe that their views are based on "political values everyone can reasonably be expected to endorse" – again, taking "political" and "reasonably" in their broad senses.

In contrast, if public reason is interpreted in a more narrow, Rawlsian sense of the term – above all, a sense in which public reason generally excludes reliance on comprehensive moral, philosophical, and religious doctrines – natural law theorists would reject it, precisely because it attempts to put the grounds, and often the substance, of people's deepest moral convictions off-limits in public discourse. Rawlsian public reason

[6] Ibid., p. 195.
[7] Stephen Macedo, *Liberal Virtues* (Oxford: Clarendon Press, 1990) and *Diversity and Distrust* (Cambridge, MA: Harvard University Press, 2000).

would thereby exclude a significant portion of what we can know by reason – which is relevant to and valuable for the common good – and in doing so this truncated public reason becomes unreasonable.

MACEDO'S RAWLSIAN PUBLIC REASON

In *Liberal Virtues*, Stephen Macedo defended a notion of liberal public reason, one that he considered a fair statement of Rawls's concept of public reason.[8]

According to Macedo, liberalism asks us to consider principles of justice from an impartial point of view, one capable of discerning reasons that should be acceptable to everyone concerned. This requires reasoned arguments that are (1) publicly stated, (2) openly debated, and (3) widely accepted.[9] The requirement of public justification requires that we filter out reasons and arguments whose grounds are (1) private, (2) too complex to be widely understood, and (3) otherwise incapable of being widely appreciated by reasonable people.[10]

The grounds of public justification are three. First, there is the fact of pluralism – people typically and "reasonably" disagree on important issues, largely for reasons described by Rawls as the "burdens of reason." Second, public justification is required by our respect for people as free and equal moral beings (if they pass certain threshold tests of reasonableness). And third, public justification makes it possible to distinguish intractable moral and philosophical issues from other, practical problems, which are more urgent (from a liberal perspective) and easier to grapple with, for example, securing basic liberties and establishing fair principles of distribution.[11]

There is much that is attractive in Macedo's public reason. For example, a political theory that elevates common, reasoned deliberation above

---

[8] The main difference between Rawls and Macedo is that Macedo is much more definite – and unapologetic – about political liberalism's fostering of a particular way of life that is incompatible with other ways of life. Public policy, moreover, can fairly attend to fostering the essential prerequisites of this way of life. At points, therefore, I think that Macedo may cross the line into a form of comprehensive liberalism, though he would likely deny this. Macedo develops the idea of public reason further in *Democracy and Distrust*, which will be discussed later.

[9] *Liberal Virtues*, p. 12.

[10] Ibid., pp. 63–64. Rawls says that "in making these justifications [according to public reason], we are to appeal only to presently accepted general beliefs and forms of reasoning found in common sense, and the methods and conclusions of science when these are not controversial."

[11] Ibid., p. 47.

mere struggles over interests, power, and desires is valuable. Macedo's form of public reason also, more than some other forms (including Rawls's, I think), accepts the public accessibility of arguments which reflect a genuine concern for human character or virtue (albeit in a rather truncated form).

But, in the final analysis, Macedo's attempt to articulate and defend public reason provides us with an excellent example of the fundamental inadequacy of the liberal conception of public reason.

SOME BASIC PROBLEMS WITH LIBERAL PUBLIC REASON

Public reason requires that arguments providing public justification not be (1) private, (2) too complex to be widely understood, and (3) otherwise incapable of being widely appreciated by reasonable people. Accepting for the moment the requirement that they be public, let me ask what it means to say that an argument cannot be either "too complex to be widely understood" or "otherwise incapable of being widely appreciated by reasonable people," which together presumably make up (at least part of) the requirement that they be "publicly accessible."

When is an argument "too complex"? When is an argument "incapable of being widely appreciated by reasonable people"? When is an argument not "publicly accessible"? Macedo seems to rely on common-sense notions of what these mean, without explaining them in any detail, but, as is often the case, that won't do.

Does an argument have to be "simple" enough (presumably the opposite of "complex") so that *all* the citizens understand it? So that *most* of them do so (and does that mean a large, rather than a mere, majority)? So that the "educated citizenry" does so?

If *all* the citizens have to understand it, liberal public reason is in trouble, because it's hard to imagine many arguments that all citizens would understand. Some people are not very intelligent, and many more have not been well educated. It's even hard to imagine very many substantive arguments that *most* citizens would understand, if you mean actually existing citizens, with all their warts. Keep in mind that most public political debate these days probably occurs in roughly 15 second "sound-bites" – and while some of this may be blamed on the perpetrators of the sound-bites, it's hard to deny any responsibility to the consumers of them.

Are we to construct some idealized figure – something like the law's "reasonable man" – perhaps a person of "average" intelligence with an "average" education (whatever that would mean)? What are the standards according to which such idealized figures should be constructed? Or is it that the arguments should be intelligible to well-educated people, who then serve as representatives of all those who share their views, though perhaps in wide-ranging forms of sophistication? If so, how should we define "well-educated"? And then we might ask whether the well-educated people of a given society or era can accept as rational some pretty irrational positions. And, if we go down the road of relying on educated people, haven't we, at that point, established a pretty latitudinarian conception of what is *publicly* accessible, since we'd probably be taking pretty atypical people as the standard? (Although, perhaps it is not unreasonable to indulge a suspicion that, if public reason is adopted as a standard, those who are most adept at manipulating language and symbols – what some have called the "chattering classes" – are going to end up with a disproportionate share of the power to define what can and cannot be admitted into public discourse and decision making.)

Whether an argument is publicly accessible certainly *cannot* be evaluated simply on the basis of whether people happen to agree with it (making it accessible) or disagree with it (leading to the conclusion that it is inaccessible). That would make any conventional view *ipso facto* publicly accessible, irrespective of how irrational it was, and any widely rejected view *ipso facto* not publicly accessible, irrespective of how rational it was – which would make reform and improvement of public views (an important liberal desideratum) excessively difficult.

Does public accessibility have to do only with the logical quality of the argument itself? Should we consider the rhetorical effectiveness of arguments put forward on behalf of a position? That is, might most people in a society resonate with an argument – giving it the appearance of public accessibility – for irrational motives, e.g., on the basis of an effective rhetorical appeal to prevailing prejudices? Do we factor in (either positively or negatively) the "customary ways of thinking" in a society? Does the existence of a custom provide an argument that the judgment embodied in the custom is publicly accessible, or does its being "merely a matter of custom" undermine its claim to being a genuinely rational judgment?

And must the argument that public arguments be "publicly accessible" itself be publicly accessible?

For a start, then, there are a whole series of ambiguities about the meaning and measure of liberal public reason – enough to doubt that it is a very useful concept.

I want to turn now to raise another set of questions by looking at Macedo's critique of natural law from the viewpoint of public reason.

MACEDO'S CRITIQUE OF NATURAL LAW

Macedo's primary, but not his only, critique of natural law is that it fails to meet the requirements of public justification. This is due, he says, to the "large gap between the first principles of the natural law and actual moral norms."[12] To get from one to the other requires much work by a process of moral inference, which requires a wisdom or reasonableness not found in everyone or even in most people. Therefore, relying on such arguments is contrary to the equality of respect embodied in liberal canons of public justification. Or – he holds out the possibility – natural law can save itself from elitism by appealing to popular prejudice about how human beings should behave, making it an "unreasoned populism."[13]

In the natural law theory of Thomas Aquinas, there is a progress of some sort from first principles of the natural law ("good is to be done and evil is to be avoided," "act according to reason") to general moral norms ("do not steal") to more specific moral norms ("borrowed goods should be returned") to actual moral judgments ("this gun should be returned to this person from whom I borrowed it"). The first, most general precepts are known to everyone, at least in the abstract, though they may not always be applied to particular cases because of the distorting effects of passions.[14] The more general moral norms are normally known to all, but they can be blotted out by evil persuasions and by vicious customs and corrupt habits. (Aquinas gives the example of theft not being considered wrong among the Germanic tribes, on Caesar's account.[15]) As one moves on to more specific moral norms and actual moral judgments, there is more room for failures both as to the knowledge of the moral norm and also with respect to how generally the norm holds – that is, there are more likely to be exceptions. For example, borrowed goods should be returned, but if someone who is betraying his country asks for a borrowed weapon to be returned, one might be justified in refusing to return the goods.[16]

Now this is not a deductive process. One doesn't logically "deduce" a more specific moral norm from a general moral norm. The first principles

---

[12] Ibid., p. 211.

[13] Ibid., p. 212.

[14] Thomas Aquinas, *Summa Theologiae*, I–II, Q. 94, a. 6: "As to those general principles, the natural law, in the abstract, can nowise be blotted out from men's hearts. But it is blotted out in the case of a particular action, in so far as reason is hindered from applying the general principle to a particular point of practice, on account of concupiscence or some other passion...."

[15] Thomas Aquinas, *Summa Theologiae*, I–II, Q. 94, a. 4.

[16] Thomas Aquinas, *Summa Theologiae*, I–II, Q. 94, a. 4.

and the general moral norms (which roughly correspond to the Decalogue[17]) are generally known to all because they are self-evident. More
specific moral norms are also self-evident, but they require more knowledge and are therefore in some cases – especially as cases involve more
detail or specificity – self-evident only to those who have reflected more
deeply on them.[18] (In Macedo's terms, the "gap" between first principles
and concrete moral norms is greater.)

According to this view, basic moral norms are widely known, though in
some cases they may be obscured by passions or corrupt customs or habits.
The ability to construct effective arguments explaining moral norms, however, it must be noted, can vary quite a bit. *That is, many people may
know that something is wrong, but not necessarily be able to articulate
that knowledge very well.*

Take a simple example: the proposition that "murder is wrong." Few
people would object to that proposition. But the simple experiment of
playing "devil's advocate" for the contrary proposition will reveal that
most people's efforts to "prove" that murder is wrong are usually not very
impressive. Their inability to articulate a very well-reasoned argument
does not mean that they are wrong, but it does suggest that there is a
difference between "inarticulate knowledge" and "articulate knowledge."

Now the question that must be posed is this: when advocates of public
reason contend that liberalism requires reasoned arguments that are or can
be "widely accepted," arguments that "should be acceptable to everyone
concerned," is it sufficient that arguments be "acceptable" to people on
the basis of what I have called "inarticulate knowledge"?

If the answer is "no" – that is, if more developed and articulate knowledge is required – then I believe a political theory's requirement of public
reason is self-destructive, because it is a demand for something that is
hopelessly utopian. If the answer is "yes" – that is, if arguments can be
considered publicly accessible even if they can be accepted only on the

---

[17] Thomas Aquinas, *Summa Theologiae*, I–II, Q. 100, a. 3. Some have argued that only the
second table of the Decalogue is part of the natural law. See Ernest Fortin, "Augustine,
Aquinas, and the Problem of Natural Law," in *Mediaevelia*, Vol. 4 (1978), p. 179. Thomas
says more generally that the moral precepts of the old law are reducible to the *ten* precepts
of the Decalogue, though he does indicate that these may be known through reason or
faith. The first table of the Decalogue, however, should be understood as part of the
natural law in the sense indicated in Thomas's discussion of the virtue of religion: that it
commands "that man should do something through reverence for God," not in the sense
that it commands "this or that determinate thing" II–II, Q. 81, a. 2, ad 3. See also his
discussion of the precepts of justice, II–II, Q. 122, a. 1, a. 2, and a. 4, ad 1.

[18] Thomas Aquinas, *Summa Theologiae*, I–II, Q. 94, a. 4.

basis of inarticulate knowledge – then natural law arguments meet that (lower) standard of public accessibility. In fact, it is one of the great strengths of natural law theory that it can account for the fact that people in general, not just intellectual elites, are able genuinely to know fundamental moral principles – being "reasonable" in that sense – even when (as is often the case) they are not capable of much in the way of rational arguments for particular ethical positions (especially as the questions get more complicated).

Note, too, that if the only realistic standard is adopted – the one which admits inarticulate knowledge – Macedo's simple distinction between natural law teachings that are too complex and popular prejudices about how human beings should behave tends to break down. What he calls "popular prejudices" may or may not be genuinely prejudice, that is, irrational. They may be inarticulate, and therefore appear to be "prejudice," while actually being quite rational (as in the case of popular beliefs that murder is wrong).

In contrast, another implication of the natural law teaching described above is that sometimes popular prejudices – very widely shared prejudices and even widely shared prejudices that receive sophisticated (though specious) rational defenses from certain intellectuals – may be the result of corrupt customs, and quite wrong, despite their widespread acceptance and defense by intelligent spokesmen. This gives us an occasion to examine issues that particularly highlight the difficulty of establishing a plausible form of liberal public reason, namely, slavery and abortion.

SLAVERY AND ABORTION

Macedo strives valiantly to differentiate between abortion and slavery. For the moment, let me put to the side important questions about public reason in respect to the religious foundations of much abolitionist thinking and activity. I want simply to ask this question: does Macedo give us any reason to believe that the arguments against slavery and the arguments against abortion are essentially different, in that one of them (the antislavery argument) meets the demands of public reason and the other (the antiabortion argument) does not? I think that the answer to that question is clearly "no."

Macedo's position is that abortion "comes down to a fairly close call between two well-reasoned sets of arguments" and therefore "the best thing for reasonable people to do might be to acknowledge the difficulty of the argument and the burdens of reason, to respect their opponents, and to compromise with them, to find some middle ground which gives something to each side while the argument goes forward."[19] Macedo explicitly rejects arguments by John Finnis and Robert George that abortion is not usually even a close call.[20] He specifically denies George's argument that the development from zygote to adulthood occurs without "substantial change."[21] He more or less simply asserts that it is "unreasonable to deny that there are reasonable grounds for ascribing substantial moral weight to the development of basic neural or brain functions – the development of some sort of sensory capacity, consciousness, or sentience – and perhaps viability."[22]

The substantive correctness of Macedo's argument is not my primary concern here, but I must digress for a moment to say a few words about it. Macedo misunderstands George's argument in at least one important respect, and fails to come to grips with it in another. First, he seems to understand George's argument about "substantial change" to mean "a lot of change," when in fact George's key argument is that there is no *essential* change; that is, the "something" that the zygote is never at any point becomes, in the course of developing into a human being, some other kind of thing (some other substance) than it is as a zygote. It changes in many ways – as in the example of developing basic neural or brain functions or becoming viable outside the womb – but those changes never at any time involve a change from its being one thing to another, different thing – as occurs, for example, when the sperm and the egg unite and those two things become one new essentially or substantially different thing. The ball is still in Macedo's court: what is the substantial or essential change that occurs after conception, such that before that point, the thing is not the same human being it is after that point, and possessed of the same fundamental rights?

Macedo does not *argue* that it is "unreasonable to deny that there are reasonable grounds for ascribing substantial moral weight" to certain developments (neural or brain functions, viability) – he just asserts it.

---

[19] Stephen Macedo, "Are Slavery and Abortion Hard Cases?," in *Natural Law and Public Reason*, R. George and C. Wolfe, Eds. (Washington, DC: Georgetown University Press, 2000), p. 29.

[20] See Finnis, "Is Natural Law Theory Compatible with Limited Government?," in *Natural Law, Liberalism, and Morality*, R. George, Ed. (Oxford: Clarendon Press, 1996), pp. 1–27, especially pp. 17–18, and "Abortion, Natural Law, and Public Reason," in *Natural Law and Public Reason*, R. George and C. Wolfe, Eds.; and George, "Public Reason and Political Conflict: Abortion and Homosexuality," 106 *Yale Law Journal* 2475 (1997).

[21] George, "Public Reason and Political Conflict," p. 2493.

[22] Macedo, "Are Slavery and Abortion Hard Cases?," p. 32.

George's principle is simple and straightforward: the "thing" in the womb is a human being, from conception onward. As a human being, it shares with other human beings certain fundamental rights, including a right not to be killed. If there are reasonable grounds for saying that more developed human beings should not be killed, but less developed human beings can be killed, Macedo ought to give them. But, frankly, I doubt that any argument about the moral quality of a human life that turns, for example, on lung capacity – as the viability argument does – will meet the most minimal standards of reason or public accessibility (however much that specious distinction may appeal to certain persons).

This is not to say that the proponents of the pro-abortion rights position have no legitimate concerns on their side. And therefore, as Macedo argues, "the best thing may be to try and give something to both sides," to find some middle ground. But *Planned Parenthood v. Casey*[23] (contrary to his suggestion) is not the middle ground, since it attends to the innocence and right to life of the unborn child hardly at all. A proper middle ground would be something more like this: prohibiting abortion, in order to give fair weight to the unborn child's right to life; providing assistance (financial, medical, emotional) to women with difficult pregnancies, in order to minimize the costs of carrying through such pregnancies; promoting easier adoption laws, to provide for children whose biological parents are not able or willing to care for them (and to minimize the long-term costs of carrying an unborn child to full term); educating people (especially young people) to the enormous costs (especially human costs) of irresponsible sexual activity and also to the equal responsibility of men for the children they help to conceive; and focusing penalties for abortion not on pregnant women, but on those who provide them with abortions.

Now some people (including most academics) will probably find this "middle position" frankly outrageous, on the grounds that it simply represents the position embraced by the pro-life movement in this country – and on that they would be right. This experience of outrage may be useful, however, if it gives them some inkling of how their opponents feel when *Casey,* and a variety of other purported "compromises," are described as "middle ground" in this debate.[24]

---

[23] *Planned Parenthood of Southeastern Pennsylvania v. Casey* 505 U.S. 833 (1992), cited in Macedo "Are Slavery and Abortion Hard Cases?" at p. 30.

[24] See, for example, Eileen McConaugh, *Breaking the Abortion Deadlock: From Choice to Consent* (Oxford: Oxford University Press, 1996), and Roger Rosenblatt, "How to End the Abortion War," *The New York Times Magazine*, Vol. 141 (January 19, 1992), p. 26.

But let me return to the question of public reason. We have seen Macedo's position on abortion. What is his position on slavery? The question arises, of course, because of some of the striking similarities between the two issues. Macedo says, but does not explain why, that "there is something a little slick in drawing quick analogies between slavery and abortion in order to impugn public reason."[25] But that analogy is, in fact, a very defensible one. If antiabortion arguments fail to meet the test of public reason today, would antislavery arguments have met the test of public reason in the 1850s? I think the answer is clearly "no."

Macedo's argument is:

projecting myself back to, say, 1857, it seems quite doubtful to me that the merits of the arguments for slavery would have appeared in as reasonable a light as do both sides in today's abortion debate. . . . I suppose there were some whose defense of slavery, coupled perhaps with opposition to "wage slavery" in the North, amounted to a reasoned public case, worthy of some sort of respect.[26]

He then goes on to deny that this is grounds for principled compromise, citing George's argument that "respect may sometimes be owed to persons who in general exhibit reasonableness and good will, but not to some position they have adopted, which one regards as so deeply misguided and wrong as to be unworthy of respect."[27]

The difference between abortion and slavery is simple: Macedo thinks that both sides of the abortion debate really have reasons (so a "principled compromise" – which he considers *Casey* to be, although, on its own terms, it reaffirms "the central holding" of *Roe v. Wade* – is appropriate), while even decent people who supported the slavery position had no reasons, but were merely the victims of circumstances and traditions that were indeed morally perverse (so public reason would not have required some sort of principled compromise – such as Stephen Douglas's position of leaving slavery to the states, perhaps).

The problem is that there were lots of Americans – and, yes, even decent ones – who believed that slavery was just and good for everyone concerned, and there are lots of people today who believe that the pro-abortion rights position Macedo finds reasonable is "so deeply misguided and wrong as to be unworthy of respect," even though people of general reasonableness who happen to hold that position should be respected.

---

[25] Stephen Macedo, "Are Slavery and Abortion Hard Cases?," p. 42.
[26] Ibid., p. 42.
[27] R. George, "Law, Democracy, and Moral Disagreement," 110 *Harvard Law Review* 1396 (1997).

So where has the requirement of meeting conditions of public reason gotten us? Nowhere.[28]

PUBLIC REASON AS ARGUMENTATIVE SLEIGHT-OF-HAND

Justice William Rehnquist wrote an interesting opinion analyzing the use of the equal protection clause, in *Trimble v. Gordon* (1977). In that opinion, Rehnquist argued that the equal protection clause authorized such broad second-guessing of legislative decisions that it could be viewed "as a cat-o'-nine-tails to be kept in the judicial closet as a threat to legislatures which may, in the view of the judiciary, get out of hand and pass 'arbitrary,' 'illogical,' or 'unreasonable' laws."[29]

Public reason is a similar "cat-o'-nine-tails" that can readily be dragged out of the closet as a convenient all-purpose "stopper" in debate. A good example of this can be found, I think, in Macedo's debate with Robert George and Gerry Bradley and with Hadley Arkes on the issue of homosexuality.[30]

Macedo's original position on natural law theory, in *Liberal Virtues*, as we saw above, was that it failed to meet the requirements of public justification, because the work of drawing moral inferences from general natural law principles may be beyond the capacity of most people, and such inferences are not an appropriate basis for law. But later, in his response to John Finnis's defense of a right of the law to discourage homosexual conduct (within the limits of the subsidiarity principle), he

---

[28] Rawls himself was somewhat ambivalent about the relationship between public reason and abortion. In *Political Liberalism*, he suggested that any prohibition of abortion, at least in the first trimester, would fail the requirements of public reason, but he retracted this assertion in the introduction to the later paperback edition of the book. In "The Idea of Public Reason Revisited," 64 *University of Chicago Law Review* 802 (1997), Rawls contended that it is a "misunderstanding" that "an argument in public reason could not side with Lincoln against Douglas in their debates of 1858." He simply asserts that "[s]ince the rejection of slavery is a clear case of securing the constitutional essential of the equal basic liberties, surely Lincoln's view was reasonable (even if not the most reasonable), while Douglas's was not." But whether blacks were fully human beings and appropriate subjects of "equal basic liberties" was precisely *the point of contention* in the slavery debate of that time – as it is the point of contention, in our time, regarding very young human beings still in the womb. Rawls is right about Lincoln and the rights of blacks, in just the same way as those who seek to protect the rights of the unborn today.

[29] 430 U.S. 777 (1977).

[30] 84 *Georgetown Law Journal* 261–337 (1995). See also the Finnis–Macedo exchange on the same subject in *Natural Law, Liberalism, and Morality* (Oxford: Clarendon Press, 1996).

seemed to change directions somewhat. In his conclusion, Macedo argued that

The best way of thinking about political power in a democratic constitutionalist regime such as ours is as the shared property of reasonable citizens, who should be able to offer one another reasons that can publicly be seen as good to justify the use of that power. *Many natural law arguments (including those discussed above [i.e., Finnis' arguments about homosexual acts]) are indeed acceptably public, as Finnis asserts: the reason and evidence on which they are based are not overly complex or vague, and they can be shared openly with fellow citizens.* The vice of the new natural law position described above is not its vagueness, complexity, or lack of public accessibility but, as we saw, its unreasonable narrowness and arbitrary extension.[31]

It is worth noting that Finnis's arguments were not the stuff of everyday conversation. If not "overly complex or vague," they were still arguments requiring some serious intellectual ability to follow.

But then Macedo extended his critique of current conservative thought on homosexuality in a *Georgetown Law Journal* article, to which George and Bradley and Arkes responded at length. In Macedo's article, there is some ambivalence about the relationship between conservative moral arguments and public reason. In a footnote early in the argument, he seems to take back his concession that natural law arguments "are indeed acceptably public," when he says:

There may be something appropriate about the limited depth in which we can consider the new natural law arguments. As Rawls has recently argued, the reasons offered for justifying and shaping our basic rights and liberties ought to be ones whose force can be appreciated by people lacking specialized intellectual sophistication and by people proceeding from a variety of abstract, not unreasonable, philosophical assumptions.[32]

So natural law is back to being regarded as too complex to meet the requirements of public reason.

But, in another reference to public reasonableness at the end of the article, Macedo seems to reverse positions once more. His criticism of conservative arguments against legitimizing homosexuality (both "moralistic" arguments and arguments based on the need for "social norms" that curb sexual license) is that they fail the test of public reasonableness. This is not

---

[31] Stephen Macedo, "Sexual Morality and the New Natural Law" in *Natural Law, Liberalism, and Morality*, p. 44 (emphasis added).

[32] Stephen Macedo, "Homosexuality and the Conservative Mind," 84 *Georgetown Law Journal* 264 n.15.

because they are overly complex or inaccessible to the ordinary citizen, but because they fail to provide "adequate public justification," i.e., they are simply not reasonable persuasive arguments.[33]

As I indicated above, Macedo's argument drew a lengthy and powerful response from his opponents. Macedo's subsequent reply argued both that the response was not adequate philosophically and also that

> it now seems to me even clearer, moreover, that insofar as it is not possible to defend the value of some homosexual relationships in natural law terms, this is true for reasons that are neither understood nor accepted by the vast majority of the public. These reasons are too open to reasonable disagreement to furnish a basis for demarcating fundamental rights and liberties in a regime properly dedicated to the authority of public reason.[34]

In his concluding remarks on George and Bradley's response, Macedo repeats this argument:

> If our disagreements indeed lie in these difficult philosophical quarrels, about which reasonable people have long disagreed, then our differences lie precisely in the territory that John Rawls rightly (on my view) marks off as inappropriate to the fashioning of our basic rights and liberties. It is . . . inappropriate to deny people fundamental aspects of equality based on reasons and arguments whose force can only be appreciated by those who accept difficult to assess claims about the nature and incommensurability of basic goods, the relationship between intrinsic and instrumental value, and the dispute over whether pleasure is a reason for action. I submit that if the new natural law does not fail for the fairly straightforward reasons I have offered . . . then the new natural law argument fails as a basis for fashioning basic liberties and the principles of equality on grounds of its esotericism.[35]

So Macedo has come full circle to his original position that natural law is unable to meet the demands of public justification.

Now, in all honesty, doesn't it seem pretty clear that Macedo has established a Catch-22 situation for natural lawyers? If advocates of natural law do not put forward a powerful and intellectually sophisticated argument for their positions regarding political life and moral issues, they fail the requirement of reason per se (they lack an adequate public justification). Their positions become nothing more than the popular prejudices – the "unreasoned populism" – criticized in *Liberal Virtues*.

In contrast, if natural law theorists *do* provide powerful and intellectually sophisticated reasons for their positions, then *ipso facto* they are going

---

[33] Ibid., p. 299.
[34] Stephen Macedo, "Reply to Critics," 84 *Georgetown Law Journal* 329.
[35] 84 *Georgetown Law Journal* 355.

beyond the limits of public justification, because their arguments become too complicated and inaccessible and controversial. "Public reason" is the ever-convenient cat-o'-nine-tails that can be dragged out as soon as the argumentative going gets tough. In fact, the *more* sophisticated the natural law argument, the *easier* it becomes to dismiss it.

Note also in the argument about homosexuality one of the enduring and characteristic features of liberal argumentation. "Equality" is assumed to be the undifferentiated "default" position for society – it doesn't require being established by an argument, and it's nothing if it's not simple. Having arbitrarily established this as the starting point, the burden of proof is thereby placed on the opponents of liberalism to justify any departure from the equality principle – and if they don't come up with a *compelling but simple* response, liberalism wins.[36] But this is not much more than playing a game with loaded dice.[37]

If, on the other hand, advocates of homosexual rights, for example, were subject to the same requirement of establishing a satisfactory philosophical basis for their position – and if their simple assertion of a radical equality principle were (rightly) dismissed just as easily as conservative positions on the grounds that it is a mere "prejudice" (although an elite prejudice rather than a popular prejudice) – their arguments quickly would have to become more sophisticated, and thereby become inaccessible to "people lacking specialized intellectual sophistication."[38]

---

[36] This seems to me an enduring quality of liberal argumentation. I noted the same mode of argument in Bruce Ackerman's *Social Justice and the Liberal State* in a review written more than 20 years ago; see *The Public Interest*, Number 62 (Winter, 1981), pp. 127–28.

[37] While it is less clear in the earlier discussion of abortion, I think the same principle operates there. The burden of proof is placed on antiabortion advocates to prove that life begins at conception and that such life is entitled to all the normal protection accorded at least innocent human life. The battle rages, with arguments put forth on both sides, and then a draw is declared – and a "moderate compromise" that substantially reaffirms abortion rights is put forward as the appropriate resolution. Complex moral argumentation is always considered to be inconclusive, and as "ties go to the runner" in baseball umpiring, the resultant "ties" on civil liberties issues always go to the side favoring more "freedom," which is assumed to be the liberal position. This approach is particularly questionable in a democracy, as it usually involves judicial overruling of legislative enactments, despite the "antimajoritarian problem" implicit in that disposition. In a democratic republic, one would think that "ties" ought to result in upholding legislative acts.

[38] In this regard, note Macedo's own efforts to prevent his rejection of natural law principles regarding sexuality from becoming a defense of promiscuity (Macedo, "Homosexuality and the Conservative Mind" 84 *Georgetown Law Review* 261.) Even apart from the question of whether Macedo makes an adequate intellectual case against promiscuity (which is doubtful – a case merely for "moderation" doesn't rule out anything other than "immoderate promiscuity"), it seems likely that the same kinds of objections Macedo

PUBLIC REASON AND RELIGION

Much might be said about public reason and religion, but I will make only a few observations.[39] By emphasizing the "reason" of public reason, it is possible for liberals to circumscribe significantly the role that religion plays in liberal public discourse, when religion is considered to be nonrational. And the "public" part of public reason can further this process, if religion is understood as essentially a form of private revelation. Rawls and Macedo both adopt this general approach, at various points in their writing. But both elements of this approach are problematic. Religion claims, in at least some forms, or at least up to some point, to be quite rational, and it also typically claims to be quite public.

To take one example from current controversies: suicide. There are various grounds for opposing suicide and assisted suicide on moral grounds. I suppose that some of these might pass muster before the requirements of public reason. But let me suggest a straightforward theological ground for opposing suicide, and ask if it meets the requirements of public reason.

But though this be a State of Liberty, yet it is not a State of Licence, though Man in that State have an uncontroleable Liberty, to dispose of his Person or Possessions, yet he has not Liberty to destroy himself, or so much as any Creature in his Possession, but where some nobler use, than its bare Preservation calls for it. The State of Nature has a Law of Nature to govern it, which obliges everyone: And Reason, which is that Law, teaches all Mankind, who will but consult it, that being all equal and independent, no one ought to harm another in his Life, Health, Liberty, or Possessions. For Men being all the Workmanship of one Omnipotent, and infinitely wise Maker; All the Servants of one Sovereign Master, sent into the World by his order and about his business, they are his Property, whose Workmanship they are, made to last during his, not one anothers Pleasure.[40]

This argument comes from "the greatest liberal of them all,"[41] John Locke. Is it compatible with public reason?

uses against the accessibility of natural law arguments could be used against his own arguments.

[39] On this topic, see Patrick Neal "Political Liberalism, Public Reason, and the Citizen of Faith" In *Natural Law and Public Reason*, R. George and C. Wolfe, Eds. (Washington, DC: Georgetown University Press, 2000), pp. 171–201.

[40] John Locke, *Two Treatises of Government*, Peter Laslett, Ed. (New York: Mentor, 1965), p. 311.

[41] Stephen Macedo, "Multiculturalism for the Religious Right? Defending Liberal Civic Education," 29 *Journal of Philosophy of Education* 231 (1995).

Before 1947, and *Everson v. Board of Education*,[42] I think that it is fair to say that American public philosophy took the political relevance of a providential God for granted. Perhaps the greatest testimony to this was the Declaration's squarely resting men's inalienable rights, the protection of which is government's sole purpose, on a theological foundation: men had these rights because that had been endowed with them by their Creator.

Since *Everson*, separation of church and state has been radically redefined to view public acknowledgment of God as a violation of our fundamental constitutional principles. This has primarily been the work of intellectuals and other elites, whose religious beliefs and practices are dramatically out of line with most Americans' beliefs and practices.[43]

In this area, as in the area of morality, I would argue that one must distinguish between different levels of knowledge: what might be called "inarticulate knowledge" and more fully developed and articulated knowledge. Most people believe in God, although they could not get very far with a Harvard or Oxbridge intellectual in arguing on the subject. I would nonetheless contend that what they have is genuine knowledge – less sophisticated than the positions of many intellectuals, but possessed of the considerable virtue of being right, on rational as well as revelational grounds. Is the existence of a providential God (i.e., a God who creates and attends to his Creation), therefore, defensible at the bar of public reason (broadly and properly defined – not Rawlsian public reason), and "publicly accessible"? Like the American founders, I think it is.

Some religious believers (perhaps especially certain evangelicals) might go further. They appeal to the Bible, and argue that the Bible is true, and should be recognized as true by any reasonable person. To the extent that "faith" is necessary, they would argue that faith is available to all. (They make no gnostic claim to a body of special, secret knowledge, accessible only to an elite.) And such believers are nothing if not willing to share their "reasons" in public! On what non-theological grounds can liberals deny that such claims are, in fact, "publicly accessible" to all? The simple fact that "some people don't believe" won't do; that's true of virtually all positions (certainly including liberal contentions). Unless "reason," as liberals understand it and its implications, is said to be, in principle, a superior source of knowledge, why should liberal reason be privileged

---

[42] 330 U.S. 1 (1947).
[43] See Robert Lerner, Althea K. Nagai, and Stanley Rothman, *American Elites* (New Haven, CT: Yale University Press, 1996).

over evangelical faith? In a given society, faith might actually be viewed by a large majority as a more, rather than less, "publicly accessible" form of knowledge. Aside from comprehensive liberalism's skepticism, is there a clear reason, other than the conventional beliefs of American elites, why religion – even in the form of revealed religion – should be considered any less publicly accessible than, say, Rawlsian liberalism?

I do not at all deny that religious differences – especially those based on differing views of divine revelation – can make for considerable tensions in the public sphere (and, at the extreme point, as current events show, war), and that dealing with these potential and actual tensions requires a great deal of thought and discussion. I see no reason to believe, however, that public reason will be any more helpful a concept when considering the relation of religion and politics – if we are employing a typically liberal form of public reason – than it is regarding the intersection of politics and morality. In contrast, if public reason is understood more broadly, as it is understood by natural law theorists, it may be a defensible and useful concept, but it will provide little support for the forms of liberalism embraced by Rawls and Macedo.

CONCLUSION

These brief observations indicate that liberal public reason is not a very intelligible or helpful doctrine. Its measures are unclear. It is difficult to square with the complexities of human knowledge. It is easily susceptible to partisan manipulation, especially by the liberals ("political" liberals who also generally have comprehensive liberal philosophical views) who devised it. On the whole, we would be better off without it.

The only alternative that would seem plausible is to expand liberal public reason to a genuine, broad – not arbitrarily truncated – public reason. On the whole, that would be welcome to natural law theorists, who are happy to contend on that level playing field. Natural law liberalism is committed to providing sound and publicly communicable reasons for understanding the common good in certain ways and pursuing it. Those reasons, they believe, necessarily include a substantive conception of the manifold human good. Neutrality is neither possible nor desirable.

3

Liberal Exclusionism III

Gutmann and Thompson on "Reciprocity"

We have seen that some contemporary liberals seek to exclude an important range of arguments from contemporary debate by requiring a form of liberal "neutrality" embodied in the concept of "public reason." In this chapter, I want to turn to another way in which some contemporary liberals attempt to exclude important moral arguments from public debate. Amy Gutmann and Dennis Thompson argue in their *Democracy and Disagreement* that appropriate conditions of public deliberation exclude certain forms of argument.[1] The excluded forms of argument include some that are at the core of natural law arguments for public morality. For reasons similar to those we have seen in previous chapters, I want to argue that Gutmann and Thompson's arguments are not persuasive, and provide no legitimate grounds for putting natural law arguments in favor of public morality off-limits in a liberal democracy.

THE CONDITION OF RECIPROCITY

One of the requirements for democratic deliberation, according to Gutmann and Thompson, is reciprocity:

The foundation of reciprocity is the capacity to seek fair terms of social cooperation for their own sake. Because the results of democratic deliberation are mutually binding, citizens should aspire to a kind of political reasoning that is mutually justifiable. From a deliberative perspective, a citizen offers reasons that

---

[1] Amy Gutmann and Dennis Thompson, *Democracy and Disagreement* (Cambridge, MA: Harvard University Press, 1996).

can be accepted by others who are similarly motivated to find reasons that can be accepted by others.[2]

Deliberative reciprocity involves two requirements. First, there is the moral requirement that when citizens make moral claims "they appeal to reasons or principles that can be shared by fellow citizens" who share their commitment to finding fair terms of social cooperation. This entails seeking "agreement on substantive moral principles that can be justified on the basis of mutually acceptable reasons."[3] Second, there is an empirical requirement that, when moral reasoning invokes empirical claims, they "be consistent with relatively reliable methods of inquiry": claims "need not be completely verifiable, but they should not conflict with claims that have been confirmed by the most reliable of available methods."[4] Moreover, the premises of moral reasoning, even when not explicitly based on empirical evidence, should not be implausible, requiring us to abandon such methods.

Much of what Gutmann and Thompson say about reciprocity is unobjectionable, but what is problematic is their particular elaboration of the requirements of reciprocity, which has the important effect of excluding certain widely (if implicitly) held forms of moral argumentation:

Religious fundamentalists may reply that they accept the requirement of reciprocity because their moral reasons, far from being impervious, are readily accessible to anyone who is willing to live a spiritual life as they do. All those who live such a life can gain similar access to the moral mandates of divine authority. How then, can deliberative democrats claim that these religious appeals are any less accessible than other claims about public policy that draw on the personal experience of some citizens? The answer, which does not exclude religious appeals per se, is that any claim fails to respect reciprocity if it imposes a requirement on other citizens to adopt one's sectarian way of life as a condition of gaining access to moral understanding that is essential to judging the validity of one's moral claims. This requirement stands in contrast to the many moral claims in public life that can be assessed and accepted by individuals who are conscientiously committed to any of a wide range of secular and religious ways of life.[5]

On the face of it, the effect of this requirement might seem to some readers to be the exclusion from the public sphere of democratic deliberation only of a few marginal cranks, as "religious fundamentalists" are regarded among many educated people. In fact, however, the stakes

---

[2] Gutmann and Thompson, pp. 52–53.
[3] Gutmann and Thompson, p. 55.
[4] Gutmann and Thompson, p. 56.
[5] *Democracy and Disagreement*, p. 57.

are much higher: it also excludes anyone who accepts an Aristotelian (and Thomistic) analysis of moral understanding. That is to say, it excludes several of the prominent strands of moral reasoning in Western civilization, which retain considerable influence, especially through their influence on forms of religious morality to which a large number of people still adhere.

WHY LIBERAL RECIPROCITY IS UNREASONABLE

For Aristotle and Aquinas, moral perception is not simply an intellectual act, determined only by abstract reasoning. For classical and medieval moral philosophy, morality required a certain perception of reality – human beings discover morality rather than creating it. Prudence, which is both an intellectual and a moral virtue, guides us to discern the correct moral judgment only when our will is rightly oriented, when our will is truly looking for and disposed to see the right answer.

Just as our physical vision is limited by the well-known phenomenon of "selective perception" – we often see only what we are looking for, or what we are concentrating on, and we can completely miss other objects in plain view – moral perception can be distorted by a certain moral focus – what we *want* to see. These failings derive especially (although not exclusively) from the passions.

What this means in practice is not hard to see. We experience it with some frequency in the form of the human capacity for "rationalization." People can easily be led to find *reasons* for actions they *want* to do. The wish can easily be father to the thought – or, in this case, the desire can shape a convenient moral judgment. For example, a man who wants to dump his long-time spouse for a new trophy wife can easily come up with the necessary rational justification: "marriages in the past were short-term because of early death; in our own society marriages last longer, because of advances in health, but this means that people suited to – and tied to – each other at one stage of their lives are now tied to each other though they are no longer suited to each other; my colleague at work, with whom I have a great deal more in common than with my wife – who perhaps has been out of the workforce for years and who lacks the intellectual vitality of my colleague (and me) – is much better suited to be my spouse; therefore, it is perfectly reasonable to leave behind my old marriage and establish a new one."[6] One can think of many other obvious

---

[6] For the rudiments of this argument, see Philip D. Harvey, "Divorce For the Best," *Washington Post*, Tuesday, July 11, 2000.

examples: what is the likely quality (the accuracy) of the moral perception of a person who is a racist, or a Nazi, or an addict?

But if one's ability to "see" or perceive moral truth is affected by the orientation of one's will, it may be difficult or impossible to perceive the moral truth or rectitude of a certain way of life if one is living a different way of life, a way of life incompatible with the good life. If that is so, it may be right to say that, at least in some cases, there is "a requirement on other citizens to adopt one's sectarian way of life as a condition of gaining access to moral understanding that is essential to judging the validity of one's moral claims."[7] Gutmann and Thompson refer to "the many moral claims in public life that can be assessed *and accepted* by individuals who are conscientiously committed to any of a wide range of secular and religious ways of life" (emphasis added). But there may be some moral claims highly relevant to public life that cannot be so easily assessed and accepted by individuals conscientiously committed to living lives incompatible with those claims. A libertine's capacity to assess *and accept* the moral ideal of fidelity to a spouse, and arguments regarding the social benefits of such fidelity, will be at best attenuated.

Now suppose for a moment that the religious fundamentalists and Aristotelians and Thomists are right – that moral understanding does presume a certain orientation of the will, which is essentially connected with living in a certain way – what would be the "fair terms of social cooperation" in a "deliberative democracy"? Whatever they would be, excluding the arguments of religious fundamentalists and moral traditionalists would presumably not be among them. Gutmann and Thompson's formulation of "reciprocity," then, is based on controversial, unarticulated, and undefended epistemological assumption: that the capacity of the intellect to see reality is not necessarily affected by the moral orientation of the will, and it is therefore unreasonable to require other people to live rightly in order to understand what is right.

This leads me to ask another question, focused specifically on religion: is there built into Gutmann and Thompson's analysis an automatic preference for "sectarian" secular liberalism, with its assumption of the priority of reason over claims of revelation? I think there is, and I don't think they would be apologetic about it. "Fair terms of social cooperation," in their view, simply entails the exclusion of "controversial" religious claims from the public sphere, because, they believe, reason is available

---

7 Gutmann and Thompson, p. 57.

to everyone but revelation is not. But are there "neutral" grounds for making such an assumption, in the face of at least some religious believers' contention that revelation is accessible to all – and perhaps also on the ground that the assignment of priority to reason over revelation itself reflects the positing of "first principles" that are neither neutral nor demonstrable?

Mozert v. Hawkins

Gutmann and Thompson discuss a Tennessee case in which some "born-again" Christians objected to a public school reading program. They mention four parts of the program that were said to be objectionable: (1) a short story describing a New Mexico Indian Catholic settlement (on grounds that it taught Catholicism), (2) a reading exercise showing reversal of sex role stereotypes, with a boy doing the cooking (because it denigrated biblically based sex differences), (3) an excerpt from Anne Frank's *Diary of a Young Girl* (because she writes that nonorthodox belief in God is better than no belief), and (4) a description of the Renaissance's central belief as "the dignity and worth of human beings" (because this belief is incompatible with true religious faith).

I confess that I do not find the fundamentalists' objections (certainly not their formulations) very persuasive – any more than I find it persuasive, for example, that saluting the American flag is equivalent to "worshiping a graven image."[8] But, like the Jehovah's Witnesses' beliefs in *W. Va. v. Barnette*, none of them is so entirely without grounds as to be undeserving of accommodation. If you believe Catholicism is the Whore of Babylon, as some people do, the short story might be viewed as conveying an excessively attractive view of it; if you believe that there are sexual differences that make a sexual division of labor appropriate, you might be irritated at systematic efforts to imply there are no such differences; if you believe in a religious orthodoxy rather than religious individualism, you might object to an attractive portrayal of a young person who represents the latter; if you believe that human dignity comes from being made in the image and likeness of God, you might object to a worldview that seems to detach belief in human dignity from those grounds. Even if you had these beliefs and objections, a fundamentalist parent might be willing to have older children exposed to them, but be reluctant to have them presented to younger children.

---

[8] *West Virginia v. Barnette* 319 U.S. 624 (1943).

Gutmann and Thompson characterize the case this way:

In this case [from the standpoint of the principle of impartiality] two comprehensive moral views face each other in a standoff. On the one side are the parents whose religious beliefs dictate their views about almost all aspects of life, including the way their children should be educated. On the other side stand other parents whose moral views may be no less comprehensive. They believe that their own values, including their religious values, are best served by a school system that chooses textbooks on the basis of the judgment of educational experts. Nor is there any morally neutral position in this case. Neither exempting the children from the reading classes nor upholding the school board's right to require the children to use the textbooks is morally or politically neutral.

While I believe that they are right that no policy is completely neutral, I think they should at least state the differences more clearly. The fundamentalists, it is said, are pitted against other parents who believe that "their religious values are best served by a school system that chooses textbooks on the basis of the judgment of educational experts." It would be more accurate to say that the fundamentalist parents are opposed by "parents who believe that their values are best served not only by a school system that chooses textbooks on the basis on the judgment of educational experts (whose values they happen generally to share), but also one that compels children of other parents, whose beliefs are undermined by those textbooks, to study them."

That is precisely what Gutmann and Thompson themselves believe, as comes out in their discussion of how the principle of reciprocity would handle the problem. They believe that the fundamentalist parents should lose for six reasons. First, because the fundamentalist parents "are trying to prevent schools from teaching their children to make critical judgments, to use their imagination, to exercise choice 'in areas where the Bible provides the answer,' and to consider the merits of the idea that all human beings have dignity and worth," their children "would fail to receive the education that is necessary for developing their capacities as democratic citizens." Since the capacity for critical reasoning "is a prerequisite for making reciprocal claims, its denial cannot itself be the basis for such a claim."[9]

Second, much the same line of argument is used regarding belief in human dignity and worth. This belief is necessary for basic liberty and opportunity and provides moral grounds for the principle of reciprocity. Therefore, opposition to it can be dismissed.

---

[9] Gutmann and Thompson, p. 65.

Third, the empirical claims of the fundamentalist parents are open to objection. If children are required "to read stories describing a Catholic Indian settlement in New Mexico, the effect is not to inculcate belief in Catholicism." For "[t]here is no reliable evidence that children who are required to read about different religions or different ways of life are likely to convert to those religions or choose those ways of life for themselves."[10]

Fourth, perhaps the picture of the boy cooking while the girl reads is intended to change attitudes and may do so, but again the only purpose here is to eliminate differences in the "basic liberties and opportunities" of boys and girls.

Fifth, more generally, "by going beyond what they teach in their home they [the fundamentalist parents] would have to claim an unconditional authority over the education of some future citizens." But "[t]hat kind of claim cannot be the basis for resolving disagreement about educational policy on fair terms of cooperation. In a democratic society, schools share educational authority with parents" to teach children to become good citizens, and "no citizen can fairly claim that what constitutes good citizenship is whatever happens to conform to his or her particular religion."[11]

Sixth, the fundamentalist parents might reject – on the grounds that it is biased against fundamentalism – the very principle of reciprocity, which requires citizens who seek fair terms of social cooperation for their own sake to offer reasoning that is mutually justifiable, that is, reasons that can be accepted by their fellow citizens who are similarly motivated to find reasons that can be accepted by others. The principle, Gutmann and Thompson concede, is not neutral among religions or ways of life, but it "is not just another morality. It is offered as the morally optimal basis on which citizens who disagree about moralities and religions can act collectively to make educational policy." And "it can be appropriately criticized only by proposing an alternative basis [for those who disagree to cooperate], not simply by reaffirming the moral or religious claim that constitutes the disagreement. The fundamentalists do not offer an alternative."[12] Moreover, their own arguments rely on some form of the principle of reciprocity, because their argument that reciprocity is biased "appeals to a sense of fairness that is assumed to be accepted by other citizens as a basis of social cooperation."[13]

---

[10] Gutmann and Thompson, p. 66.
[11] Gutmann and Thompson, p. 67.
[12] Gutmann and Thompson, p. 67.
[13] Gutmann and Thompson, p. 68.

Having argued that the fundamentalists' argument fails the principle of reciprocity, Gutmann and Thompson then maintain that the school board's policy satisfies it. First, the reasons given are general, in the sense that the policy (no exemptions for children on moral and religious grounds) applies to all parents. Second, the policy is based on the distinction between teaching a religion and teaching about it. Schools do not teach particular values (e.g., the doctrines of Catholicism) but teach public values (e.g., human dignity). Third, "[t]he empirical assumptions on which the board relied also satisfy the standards of inquiry that reciprocity sets." For example, reliable methods of inquiry can determine whether a religion is being taught, or merely taught about. And "[t]hose assumptions that do not lend themselves to empirical inquiry were also plausible in a way that could be generally accepted." For example, the "assumption that all human beings have dignity and worth, though not subject to ordinary empirical investigation, is consistent with an extensive set of social practices that are essential to democracy."[14]

In conclusion, Gutmann and Thompson argue that the fundamentalist parents' claim "is not justifiable to citizens who themselves are motivated to present claims that can be justified to citizens with whom they morally disagree," while the school board claims "come closer to meeting this test."[15]

Virtually every one of the arguments offered by Gutmann and Thompson is subject to reasonable objections. That such an intolerant policy is open to objections on the basis of any reasonable view of reciprocity is not surprising.

First, there is nothing in what the fundamentalist parents state that requires them to be opposed to a reasonable notion of "critical reasoning" per se. They are certainly opposed to a certain *form* of critical reasoning: one that would try to induce the children to assume a supposed Archimedean point from which to judge their own religious beliefs and those of others.[16] But the parents have every right to believe, and act on the belief, that their own religious views are the true Archimedean point, and that education should be directed by those views. They naturally oppose elements of the reading program that subtly undermine their own

---

[14] Gutmann and Thompson, p. 68.

[15] Gutmann and Thompson, pp. 68–69.

[16] On this point, they could derive significant support from Alasdair MacIntyre's work, especially *After Virtue* (South Bend, IN: University of Notre Dame Press, 1981), *Whose Justice? Whose Rationality?* (University of Notre Dame Press, 1988), and *Three Rival Traditions of Moral Enquiry* (University of Notre Dame Press, 1990).

religious views. They oppose the implications of the principle that the children should exercise "choice" where there are biblical answers, as if those answers did not have claims antecedent to their choice.[17] Clearly, the parents want the children to "choose" – to choose the Biblical answers just because they are the Biblical answers, that being (in their view) the ultimate principle that should guide all choice. In that sense, it is also true that religious believers want their children to be capable of critical reasoning – but to do so on the basis of biblical norms. They would oppose consideration of the idea that all human beings have dignity and worth *apart from their being created and redeemed by the Biblical God.*

What about "empirical" evidence of whether fundamentalists can have the qualities of critical reasoning that are essential to democratic citizenship: the ability to justify one's own actions, to criticize the actions of one's fellow citizens, and to respond to their justifications and criticisms? As with citizens whose "religion" is secular liberalism, it seems clear that we can find a range of people in this category, ranging from the very articulate to the relatively inarticulate. Many fundamentalists are certainly ready to justify their actions and criticize those of others and engage in debate about justifications and criticisms. The burden is very much on Gutmann and Thompson to show that fundamentalists as a group lack "critical reasoning skills" relative to – not the faculty of Princeton who share Gutmann and Thompson's sophisticated liberalism – but other Americans in general.

Second, Gutmann and Thompson are bothered by the opposition of the fundamentalists to the Renaissance belief in human dignity and worth. But, as already indicated, what the fundamentalists object to is not the belief itself, but the severing of the belief from fundamentalist grounds for it. In this respect, one might even argue that the fundamentalists have an advantage: they frankly have a more articulate *ground* for believing in human dignity and worth than many non-fundamentalists, who simply assume it.

Third, with respect to the reading about the Catholic settlement the fundamentalists are said to lack empirical evidence "that children who are required to read about different religions or different ways of life are likely to convert to those religions or choose those ways of life for themselves." Do Gutmann and Thompson have evidence that reading *respectful* depictions of Catholicism does *not* have any effect undermining

---

[17] On this point, they could derive support from Michael Sandel's *Liberalism and the Limits of Justice* (New York: Cambridge University Press, 1982).

certain fundamentalist religious beliefs? Such depictions may be desirable according to Gutmann and Thompson, because they make the children more "tolerant" of those who are different from themselves in their religious beliefs. But will that tolerance only extend to respecting the political and legal rights of others to have their religious beliefs – or might it help to inculcate a kind of "moral tolerance," according to which sincerity is the fundamental religious virtue? On this point, I suspect, Gutmann and Thompson have no more empirical evidence than the fundamentalists, and the general drift of American society over time (the movement from tolerance of others' legal rights to a general religious indifferentism, especially among the educated classes – the view that sincerity, rather than substantive religious views, is all that really counts) actually provides more support for the latter.

Fourth, the picture of the boy cooking and the girl reading (especially as part of a systematic campaign of such portrayals) may support the "basic liberties" that Gutmann and Thompson want. But it may also go well beyond that limited effect to undermining beliefs in sexual differences that the fundamentalists believe, based on their reading of the Bible. One can believe that cooking is generally a task more likely to be performed by or more appropriate for women without thinking that women's political or legal rights should be curtailed. If Gutmann and Thompson want to say that the fundamentalists' religious rights to educate their children in their religion (in this case, their views of sexual differentiation) can be overridden on such slender grounds (the attenuated connection between antistereotypical textbook portrayals and women's political and legal rights), one may doubt their sensitivity to genuine religious freedom.

Fifth, Gutmann and Thompson claim that "by going beyond what they teach in their home they [the fundamentalist parents] would have to claim an unconditional authority over the education of some future citizens." But that reasoning is egregiously wrong. The fundamentalist parents do not claim an absolutely unconditional parental authority in education. In this case, their objection was only to certain elements of school curriculum, not to the curriculum generally. Nor do they attempt to say that, as a universal principle, any conflict between parental and school authority must be resolved in favor of the parents. (Is there anything in the record that suggests that these parents would favor parental over school authority if the specific content of the parents' belief were, say, a belief in incest?) What we know is that the parents here argue that they should have precedence over school authority with respect to these particular religious beliefs.

Nor do the parents argue, as Gutmann and Thompson tendentiously phrase it, that "what constitutes good citizenship is whatever happens to conform to [their] particular religion."[18] All they need to argue here is that *their* religious beliefs in this case are perfectly compatible with good citizenship. (They would surely concede that some forms of religious belief would not be compatible with good citizenship, e.g., belief in human sacrifice.)

Sixth, while it is unlikely that the fundamentalist parents would object to some general principle of reciprocity, they might very well object to Gutmann and Thompson's principle of reciprocity, which clearly (see the previous section on "The Condition of Reciprocity") rules out any direct appeal to their religious beliefs in public discourse.

In this case, they appeal to the principle of reciprocity by asking the local political majority to exempt them from certain public school requirements. They do not demand that their religious beliefs be integrated into the curriculum. They only ask the forbearance of those with effective political power, their willingness to recognize that parts of the curriculum favored by the "educational experts" in these schools may have the effect of undermining their religious views, and to accommodate these (minority) religious views. On behalf of the dominant elite attitudes that view fundamentalists as cranks, and probably dangerous cranks, Gutmann and Thompson slam the door in the face of this request, and then allege that it is the fundamentalists who are unwilling to seek out and offer mutually acceptable arguments.

Do the school board's arguments satisfy reasonable demands of reciprocity? Yes, say Gutmann and Thompson, because the reasons given are general, in the sense that the policy (no exemptions for children on moral and religious grounds) applies to all parents. This reminds one of the defense given in the past for miscegenation laws: they apply equally to everyone, because *no one* can marry a person of a different race. Gutmann and Thompson say: not only does the policy of no exemptions apply to the fundamentalists who believe that parts of the public school curriculum undermine their religious belief, it also applies to the much larger part of the population that have no trouble with the school curriculum, and therefore it meets the requirements of reciprocity. Can fundamentalists be forgiven if they have doubts about such a principle of reciprocity?

Second, the school board policy is said to meet the demands of reciprocity better because it is based on the distinction between teaching a

---

[18] Gutmann and Thompson, p. 67.

religion and teaching about it. Schools do not teach particular values (e.g., the doctrines of Catholicism) but teach public values (e.g., human dignity). But even apart from the serious doubts one might have about whether this is true,[19] it is not clear whether this distinction is defensible. What if the schools teach "public values," but the teaching of those values (either because of their content – e.g., minimizing gender differences – or because of the manner in which they are taught – e.g., human dignity *apart from* any relation to God) undermines certain religious beliefs, and the necessity of these particular public values *in these forms* is, at best, doubtful?

Moreover, even the willingness to teach "about" a religion or way of life in a nominally neutral way suggests an underlying normative view. This can be seen by reflecting on whether sex education programs typically include in their "teaching about certain moral views" the view that rape is an unobjectionable activity because all women really "want it." Such a view rightly would be excluded from any laundry list of descriptions of different sexual lifestyles, *because even to mention it in a nominally neutral manner would imply a significant normative position*, namely, that this view is not "beyond the pale." For certain fundamentalists, Catholicism is "beyond the pale," and stories about New Mexican Indian Catholic settlements that fail to recognize this fact are deformative.

Third, the school board position is said to accord better with reciprocity because it is based on satisfactory empirical assumptions (e.g., regarding whether a religion is being taught or merely taught about) or, in cases that do not lend themselves to empirical inquiry, the assumptions are plausible in a way that could be generally accepted (e.g., the "assumption that all human beings have dignity and worth, although not subject to ordinary empirical investigation, is consistent with an extensive set of social practices that are essential to democracy"[20]). But the board's *empirical* assumptions are no better than the fundamentalists,' certainly with regard to the shaky distinction between teaching about a religion and teaching religion, or more accurately and relevantly, distinctions regarding teaching about religions in ways that *do* and *do not* advance some religious views at the expense of others. The assumptions about human dignity and worth are widespread, certainly, but fundamentalists do not deny the principle, and only wish to give it a theological grounding. The striking

---

[19] See the discussion of *Mozert v. Hawkins*, in Chapter 6 (p. 111), especially in regard to the poem in the reading program discussed in Stephen Macedo's *Diversity and Distrust*.
[20] Gutmann and Thompson, p. 68.

fact is this: it is very likely that the reason fundamentalists give to ground human dignity and worth – the relation of the individual person to God – is one that would be shared by *more* citizens than whatever reason secular liberals like Gutmann and Thompson would give. If belief in human dignity is "consistent with an extensive set of social practices that are essential to democracy," it is not hard to argue that belief in human dignity *on religious grounds* is at least equally consistent.[21] This should not be surprising, in light of the American founders' own resting of the doctrine of human rights squarely on a foundation of natural theology: "We hold these truths to be self-evident: that all men are created equal; that they are endowed by their Creator with certain unalienable rights...." At the same time, it is also not surprising that this would be a hard fact to accept for the relatively small group of non-believers in the United States (who are disproportionately concentrated among intellectual elites).

Reciprocity, at least as Gutmann and Thompson understand it, does not seem to be an appropriate requirement of democratic deliberation. A broader form of "reciprocity" might do, however: one that simply asks people to direct reasonable arguments to their opponents – with reason being defined broadly, not in Rawlsian terms – and to be willing to listen and respond to their arguments with civility. This would have the advantage of being a more liberal policy – one that has room in the public sphere for those who do not wish their deepest religious and moral views to be relativized or privatized – rather than the more exclusionary policy implicit in Gutmann and Thompson's form of reciprocity.

In the first three chapters, I have dealt with liberal arguments that are exclusionary. That is, Rawlsian political liberalism and public reason, and Gutmann and Thompson's reciprocity, establish norms that would have the effect of ruling out of order direct appeals to many people's deepest moral and religious convictions in political discourse and decision making. These norms would thereby exclude from public deliberations those whose vision of political morality does not permit such subordination of fundamental principles to the desired aims of political liberals. I want to turn in the next chapters to another prominent feature of contemporary liberalism: the principle of autonomy.

---

[21] I say "at least" because it is not at all clear to me how the dominant nonreligious worldview, i.e., modern science, would ground human dignity. If human beings are simply part of the flotsam of a randomly developing universe, why should they be considered to have any more "dignity" than an ape, or a tulip, or a rock? Human dignity, in such a view, is likely to be simply a human invention, not a principle rooted beyond human will in nature, and it is reasonable to wonder how strong such a concept of dignity will be.

4

Contemporary Liberalism and Autonomy I

Ronald Dworkin

Another central aspect of contemporary liberalism, related to its commitment to a certain form of neutrality, is autonomy. The neutrality of the state is in the service of maximizing the autonomy of individuals, their freedom to choose to live whatever life they consider choiceworthy, consistent with the freedom of others to do the same.

One of the central issues between classical and modern political philosophy is the question of the purpose and scope of government. Classical political philosophy understood the goal of the polity as the fostering of a life of human excellence, for the community and its citizens. Modern (especially Anglo-American) political philosophy has tended to narrow the scope of the political community's concerns, focusing on the protection of human rights to "life, liberty, and the pursuit of happiness." And within modern political philosophy, a tendency over time has been to narrow further the scope of legitimate government concerns, as suggested by the contrast between the political thought of John Locke and John Stuart Mill.

American law has been influenced to some extent by classical political thought and both forms (the earlier Lockean form, and the later Millian form) of modern liberal democratic thought. The common law Americans inherited from England, for example, could not be neatly categorized as reflecting classical or modern political philosophy, but contained elements of both. Over time, however, there has been a tendency among legal scholars to "purify" American law of its less modern elements, either in the direction of a more "neutral" liberal democracy or in the direction of more Marxian or radical thought (e.g., the Critical Legal Studies movement, and other forms of post-modernism).

One element of the liberal purification of American law has been the critique of paternalism, the idea that government can legitimately engage in regulation of individual activity for the sake of preventing individuals from harming themselves, apart from any direct impact such activity may have on others. This line of liberal thought, powerfully expressed in Mill's *On Liberty*, has its contemporary representatives as well, among them Ronald Dworkin. It is an essential part of contemporary "liberal neutrality."

At the same time, Dworkin is an interesting example of the ambiguity of liberal neutrality. His earlier work, especially *Taking Rights Seriously*, represented a distinctly antiperfectionist liberalism that held up neutrality among different ways of living as an essential component of a good society. His later work, beginning with his *Tanner Lectures*[1] (eventually included in *Sovereign Virtue: The Theory and Practice of Equality*[2]) explicitly rejected a straightforward and unqualified antiperfectionism, and based his political theory of liberalism on a particular ethical theory, a particular view of the good life. Yet this particular ethical theory is highly formalistic and still requires of government a certain kind of neutrality, in that it must respect the freedom of people to live the lives that they consider to be the best.

This chapter will examine Dworkin's case against paternalism. It begins with a summary of Dworkin's argument, drawing largely on two of his articles: "Liberal Community"[3] and "Foundations of Liberal Equality." I then try to show how Dworkin's critique works only in the case of less nuanced paternalistic views, while it does not have much force against the more substantial arguments in favor of some paternalistic government action.

VOLITIONAL AND CRITICAL INTERESTS

Dworkin's discussion of paternalism begins with a key distinction between what he calls volitional interests and critical interests. "Someone's volitional well-being is improved whenever a person has or achieves something he wants," whereas "critical well-being is improved only by his having or achieving those things that he should want, that is,

---

[1] Ronald Dworkin, "Foundations of Liberal Equality," *The Tanner Lectures on Human Values*, Vol. 11 (Salt Lake City, UT: University of Utah Press, 1990).

[2] Ronald Dworkin, *Sovereign Virtue: The Theory and Practice of Equality* (Cambridge, MA: Harvard University Press, 2000).

[3] Ronald Dworkin, "Liberal Community," *California Law Review* 77 (1989): 479.

achievements or experiences that it would make his life a worse one not to want."[4]

Dworkin clarifies this distinction in two ways. First, from the subjective viewpoint, a person may want certain things without thinking that his life would be a poorer one without them, such as good food, fewer trips to the dentist, or being a better sailor, while other interests might be regarded as essential to a good life, such as a close relationship with one's children or some success in work. The former are volitional interests, the latter critical ones. Second, from an objective viewpoint, people may fail to see their own critical interests, as one might say that someone has a poorer life because he has no regard for friendship or religion or challenging work, while volitional interests by definition are what a person wants.

Dworkin is at pains to point out that the critical/volitional distinction is *not* a "distinction between what is really in my interests and what I only think is." Volitional interests are genuine, not just present judgments about my critical interests that may turn out to be wrong. A person can want something (a volitional interest) without considering it essential for a good life. In fact, someone who wants only what he considers his critical interests would have "a sad, preposterous mess of a life."[5]

PATERNALISM

These two kinds of interests can be viewed as the basis for two different kinds of paternalism: volitional paternalism, whereby coercion helps people to "achieve what they already want to achieve," and critical paternalism, whereby coercion tries to "provide people with lives that are better than the lives they now think good."[6] An example of the former is seatbelt laws, since "the state makes people wear seat belts in order to keep them from harm it assumes they already want to avoid."[7] This volitional paternalism tries to make people better only against their will, not against their conviction. Dworkin does not seem to object to volitional paternalism in principle, although he does not discuss the matter in detail.

In the same *Tanner Lectures*, Dworkin later notes forms of paternalism that seem to be related to, or forms of, volitional paternalism: a

---

[4] Dworkin, "Liberal Community," p. 484.
[5] Dworkin, "Liberal Community," p. 485.
[6] Dworkin, "Liberal Community," p. 485.
[7] Dworkin, *Tanner Lectures*, p. 77.

"superficial paternalism" that forces people to take precautions that are reasonable within their own structure of preferences, and a deeper paternalism of this sort that, for example, would justify forcing people to high culture, on the grounds that its pleasures, for those trained to appreciate them, are more satisfying than any other form of pleasure, as Mill argued.[8] Again, Dworkin does not discuss the legitimacy of this kind of superficial paternalism in detail, although he says in passing that "it is easily defended."[9] The main focus of his discussion and objections is coercive critical paternalism.

Dworkin is skeptical that much coercion is really based on paternalism, a genuine concern for the well-being of others. In the *Tanner Lectures*, he doubts that the "motive for coercion has ever been of much practical importance" and certainly not in our own time: "theocratic colonizers aim at their own salvation, not the well-being of those they force to convert and sexual bigots act out of hatred, not concern for those whose behavior they find immoral." He concedes, however, that "some political movements do . . . want to compel people to act in civic ways, for example, on the ground that civic minded people lead better lives."[10] By contrast, in "Liberal Community," Dworkin expressly embraces the communitarian view that "a true political community must be more than a Hobbesian association for mutual benefits" – it must be "an association in which each takes some special interest in the well-being of others for its own sake."[11]

ADDITIVE AND CONSTITUTIVE VIEWS OF THE GOOD LIFE

Dealing with critical paternalism forces us, says Dworkin, to confront the important philosophical issue of how to evaluate a person's life. This evaluation can be done in two ways. First, we can look at the components of a person's life (events, experiences, associations, and achievements) and ask whether in our view they – in the combination we find them – make the life a good one. Second, we can ask how the person himself judges those components, "whether he regards them as valuable or *endorses* them as serving his critical interests."[12]

---

[8] Dworkin, *Tanner Lectures*, p. 85.
[9] Dworkin, *Tanner Lectures*, p. 85.
[10] Dworkin, *Tanner Lectures*, pp. 77–78.
[11] Dworkin, "Liberal Community," p. 484.
[12] Dworkin, "Liberal Community," p. 485.

If we take the first or "additive" view, "components and endorsements are separate elements of value."[13] The components of a person's life give it critical value, and if someone endorses those components, that endorsement adds to the value. The endorsement itself appears to be another component, but even without it the value of the components remains. The second or "constitutive" view is that "no component contributes to the value of a life without endorsement."[14] For example, if a misanthrope is much loved, but regards love as worthless, the affection of others for him does not make his life more valuable for himself.

Dworkin argues that the additive view is inadequate and that the constitutive view is the right one. Most importantly, the "additive view cannot explain why a good life is distinctively valuable for or to the person whose life it is."[15] Yet it is "implausible to think that someone can lead a better life against the grain of his most profound ethical convictions than at peace with them."[16] "It seems preposterous that it could be in someone's interests, even in the critical sense, to lead a life he despises and thinks unworthy. How can that life be good *for* him?"[17] "My life cannot be better for me in virtue of some feature or component I think has no value."[18]

One key factor in Dworkin's preference for the constitutive view lies in his conception of a good life, which is developed somewhat in the *Tanner Lectures*. He distinguishes there between two models of ethics: what he calls a "challenge model" and an "impact model." The impact model focuses on the consequences or objective value of a person's action for the rest of the world, whatever the standards of objective value.[19] The challenge model sees a good life as having "the inherent value of a skillful performance,"[20] apart from any consequences it may have (again, whatever the standards of a skillful performance may be).

The impact model, with its insistence on the full objectivity of ethical value, leads to the additive view. Someone can lead a better life even when he thinks that life much worse than some alternative. In contrast, the challenge model leads to the constitutive view rather than the additive

---

[13] Dworkin, "Liberal Community," p. 486.
[14] Dworkin, "Liberal Community," p. 486.
[15] Dworkin, "Liberal Community," p. 486.
[16] Dworkin, "Liberal Community," p. 486.
[17] Dworkin, *Tanner Lectures*, p. 76.
[18] Dworkin, *Tanner Lectures*, p. 77.
[19] Dworkin, *Tanner Lectures*, p. 55.
[20] Dworkin, *Tanner Lectures*, p. 57.

view, because "intention is part of performance."[21] We would not give credit to a performance for some aspect that the performer was trying to avoid or would not recognize as desirable.[22]

Dworkin ultimately argues that the challenge model does justice more fully to our common ethical convictions. The impact model downplays the inherent value of human activities too much, making rather common ethical convictions seem silly and self-indulgent (e.g., the desire of many people to play a musical instrument as a pastime, or to know something about a field of learning without being an expert, which will not add much of value to the world), whereas the challenge model makes odd only convictions that few if any people would actually hold (e.g., the idea that one can improve another's life by compelling him to live against his convictions).[23]

CRITIQUE OF VARIOUS FORMS OF PATERNALISM

If we adopt the constitutive view, says Dworkin, that will lead us to reject paternalism, the view that "it is proper for the state to try to make people's lives better by forcing them to act in ways they think make their lives worse."[24]

Crude Paternalism

First, we can reject the "crude or direct form" of paternalism[25], the idea "that a person's life can be improved just by forcing him into some act or abstinence he thinks valueless."[26] Exponents of this form believe that "coercion is justified on the ground that the behavior implanted is good or the behavior excised is bad for people."[27] Take someone who would like to live a homosexual life but does not do so out of fear of punishment. Since he never endorses the life he leads as superior to the one he would like to lead, his life has not been improved in the critical sense by the paternalistic constraints he hates. Accepting the challenge model, with its emphasis on performance rather than mere external result, requires a

---

[21] Dworkin, *Tanner Lectures*, p. 57.
[22] Dworkin, *Tanner Lectures*, p. 77.
[23] Dworkin, *Tanner Lectures*, pp. 55–58.
[24] Dworkin, *Tanner Lectures*, p. 77.
[25] Dworkin, "Liberal Community," p. 486.
[26] Dworkin, *Tanner Lectures*, p. 78.
[27] Dworkin, *Tanner Lectures*, p. 79.

right motive as well as action, and therefore such a life would actually make a person worse off.[28]

Endorsed Paternalism

A second, more subtle form of critical paternalism tries to get around the initial objection by aiming at obtaining endorsement. For example, the state might deploy "a combination of constraints and inducements such that a homosexual is converted and does in the end endorse and appreciate the conversion."[29] Is this person's life improved? The key question here is the "conditions and circumstances of genuine endorsement."[30] Dworkin argues that the defect in paternalism "can be cured by endorsement if the paternalism is sufficiently short-term and limited that it does [not] significantly constrict choices if the endorsement never comes."[31] A child forced "to practice music is very likely later to endorse the coercion by agreeing that it did, in fact, make his life better; if he does not, he has lost little ground in a life that makes no use of his training."[32] The important point is that the endorsement must be genuine, which is not the case if someone "is hypnotized or brainwashed or frightened into conversion."[33] One minimal requirement for acceptable circumstances of endorsement is that the mechanisms we use to secure the conversion not lessen the person's "ability to consider the critical merits of the change in a reflective way."[34] But "[t]hreats of criminal punishment corrupt rather than enhance critical judgment," so even if they secure sincere conversions, they cannot be counted as genuine ones.

Substitute Paternalism

A third, more sophisticated form of paternalism is "substitute paternalism," which "justifies a prohibition not by pointing to the badness of what it prohibits but to the positive value of the substitute lives it makes available."[35] The example used here is more complex. Suppose those in power consider a life of religious devotion a waste of time, leading them

---

[28] Dworkin, *Tanner Lectures*, p. 78.
[29] Dworkin, "Liberal Community," p. 486.
[30] Dworkin, "Liberal Community," p. 486.
[31] Dworkin, *Tanner Lectures*, p. 78.
[32] Dworkin, *Tanner Lectures*, pp. 78–79.
[33] Dworkin, *Tanner Lectures*, p. 79.
[34] Dworkin, "Liberal Community," p. 486.
[35] Dworkin, *Tanner Lectures*, p. 79.

to prohibit religious orders. Someone who might have been in a religious order therefore chooses to go into politics instead, and is successful and valuable to others in a way that he agrees makes his life a better one – though he still thinks it worse than the life he would have had as a religious person.

If we agree that a religious life is wasted, shouldn't we think that the life of politics he has actually led was better? He has, after all, been responsible for the various acts and decisions within it, even though he has never endorsed – indeed, still denies – the superiority of that life compared with the religious life he would have preferred.

But, Dworkin asks, "how can the life he led be better *for* him when he goes to his grave thinking it has been worse?"[36] If we accept the challenge model, we insist on the priority of "ethical integrity" in any judgment about how good someone's life is. Ethical integrity "is the condition someone achieves who is able to live out of the conviction that his life, in its central features, is an appropriate one for him, that no other life he might live would be a plainly better response to the parameters of his ethical situation rightly judged."[37] Accepting the priority of ethical integrity means more than merely saying that disappointment and regret mar a life. (The benefits of the "substitute life" might outweigh the negative components of disappointment and regret.) The priority of "ethical integrity makes a merger of conviction and life a *parameter* of ethical success, and it stipulates that a life that never achieves that kind of integrity cannot be critically better for someone to lead than a life that does."[38]

Ethical integrity, applied to third parties, requires that I take their settled convictions into account in my judgment about what kinds of lives they should lead. In the example above, I can think it would be better if a person who wanted to live a religious life changed his mind and entered politics. But if his conviction that religious life is the best does not change, I should recognize that his living a religious life that I consider a waste is actually better than his bowing to the advice of others against his own convictions. (If someone had convictions that were terrible or base, we would not encourage him to live in accord with them, but "that is because a wicked life is bad for other people, not because we think a life against the grain would be better for him."[39])

[36] Dworkin, *Tanner Lectures*, pp. 79–80.
[37] Dworkin, *Tanner Lectures*, p. 80.
[38] Dworkin, *Tanner Lectures*, p. 80.
[39] Dworkin, *Tanner Lectures*, p. 82.

Conceptual Paternalism

A final, deeper, more subtle and academic form of critical paternalism is possible. In various forms, it can be called cultural or conceptual paternalism, and it aims not so much at directly controlling actions as indirectly influencing them through control over people's access to knowledge about different options.

Suppose, for example, that critical paternalism is defended in terms of its effects not on the present generation, but on future generations. For example, laws prohibiting homosexual acts could be said to aim at eliminating homosexuality as part of "the conceptual menu" so that future generations will not even be able to imagine such a life. While it is dubious that this attempt could succeed, would it be in the interests of those who would have led such a life if it had been on their conceptual menu? Dworkin concedes that some conceptual paternalism would be in the interests of *justice* (e.g., eliminating genocide or racism from the conceptual menu). But he still considers it "odd to think that a person's *own* life could be made a better life to have lived, in the critical sense, by constricting his imagination."[40] In the *Tanner Lectures*, Dworkin considers "cultural paternalism: the suggestion that people should be protected from choosing wasteful or bad lives not by flat prohibitions of the criminal law but by educational decisions and devices that remove bad options from people's view and imagination."[41] Because people choose lives not in a moral vacuum, but in a cultural environment that makes certain lives available by way of possibility and example and recommendation, why shouldn't we make that environment as sound as we can?

Dworkin acknowledges that circumstances such as the ethical vocabulary and example of our culture affect our ethical responses, so we must ask what these circumstances should ideally be. Paternalists argue that "the circumstances appropriate for ethical reflection are those in which bad or wasted lives have been screened out collectively so that the decisions each individual is to make are from a deliberately restricted menu."[42] But Dworkin denies that this desire for collective screening is compatible with a sensible view of ethical reflection: "a challenge cannot be more interesting, or in any other way a more valuable challenge to face, when it has been narrowed, simplified, and bowdlerized by others in advance,

---

[40] Dworkin, "Liberal Community," p. 487.
[41] Dworkin, *Tanner Lectures*, p. 83.
[42] Dworkin, *Tanner Lectures*, p. 84.

and that is as much true when we are ignorant of what they have done as when we are all too aware of it."[43]

Dworkin imagines a paternalist responding "that the challenge is more valuable when the chances of selecting a truly good life are improved, as they would be if the list of possibilities was filtered by wise collective rulers."[44] The problem with this response, says Dworkin, is that it misunderstands the challenge model by confusing "parameters" and "limitations." Limits are those circumstances that make for a lesser life, while parameters are those circumstances that help to define what life would be right for me. The impact model tends to regard all circumstances as limits on the ideal life of creating as much independent value as a human being conceivably can. The challenge view, which treats living well as responding in the right way to one's situation, treats many circumstances as parameters. "Living well includes defining what the challenge of living, properly understood, is . . . [but we] have no settled template for that decision . . . , and no philosophical model can provide one, for the circumstances in which each of us lives are enormously complex."[45] If one assumes, with Dworkin (see below), that ethics is not transcendent – that is, as Dworkin puts it, if I do not think one life would be the greatest for all human beings who will ever have lived – some of the facts that distinguish my life from others are parameters rather than limitations. Dworkin considers as good candidates "biological, social, and national associations, those I was born or fell into."

The paternalist errs in assuming "that we have some standard of what a good life is that transcends the question of what circumstances are appropriate for people deciding how to live, and so can be used in answering that question, by stipulating that the best circumstances are those most likely to produce the really correct answer."[46] Because, however, living well is responding appropriately to circumstances rightly judged, we would be begging the question if we argued that people will lead better lives if their choices were narrowed. (We would need some independent ground for thinking that it is better for people to choose in ignorance of lives that other people disapprove of.) Dworkin's rejection of conceptual paternalism, then, rests on his rejection of an independent, transcendent picture of ethical value, a picture rejected by the challenge model of ethics.

43 Dworkin, *Tanner Lectures*, p. 84.
44 Dworkin, *Tanner Lectures*, p. 84.
45 Dworkin, *Tanner Lectures*, p. 67.
46 Dworkin, *Tanner Lectures*, p. 84.

To develop this argument more fully, we should note that in the *Tanner Lectures*, Dworkin had earlier argued that the challenge model leads to the view that ethical value is "indexed" rather than transcendent. It seems irresistible, he says, that living well, judged as a performance, means among other things living in a way responsive and appropriate to one's culture and other circumstances. Dworkin uses the analogy of artistic value, arguing that part of the challenge of art is defining as well as securing success; likewise, part of the challenge of living well is to define what it is to live well. There is no settled view of what artistic achievement is, and likewise there is no settled canon of skill in living. It is implausible to think that artistic value is transcendent (that there is one absolutely greatest way to make art), for an artist's circumstances enter into the parameters of the challenge he faces. Living well is similarly a response to one's situation: it requires a personal response to the full particularity of situation, not the application, to that situation, of a timelessly ideal life.[47]

A "PATERNALIST" RESPONSE

I want to defend one particular form of paternalism against Dworkin. That is, I do not want to give an unqualified defense of paternalism, as many forms of paternalism are misguided. In particular, I want to dissociate myself from connotations of the word "paternalism" which suggest that people in general are in a sort of state of permanent childhood, with the state as the tutoring adult. But I believe that collective decisions to foster some ways of life at the expense of others are perfectly legitimate, and that paternalism of this sort can be desirable, as the thrust of certain aspects of Dworkin's own argument reveals.

Volitional Paternalism

Dworkin appears to accept the possibility of what he calls volitional paternalism without much difficulty. He says that "superficial paternalism – forcing people to take precautions that are reasonable within their own structure of preferences – is easily defended even from the perspective of volitional interests."[48] From the same perspective, he says, a deeper form of paternalism might be defended, "that people should be forced to high culture, for example, because the pleasures of art are more satisfying to

---

47 Dworkin, *Tanner Lectures*, pp. 63–66.
48 Dworkin, *Tanner Lectures*, p. 85.

those trained to appreciate them, than any other form of pleasure."[49] Dworkin does not specifically say what he thinks of this deeper sort of volitional paternalism argument, though one assumes that there must be some significant prudential limitations to it.

The distinction between volitional and critical paternalism seems somewhat slippery, at best, and I am a bit puzzled that Dworkin seems to accept the former so readily. Volitional paternalism seems to say that a person wants a certain end, and that he *should* therefore want certain means, which the community (but not the person) considers necessarily related to the achievement of that goal. For example, drivers want to survive, and the community believes that seatbelts are a desirable way to accomplish that, while certain individuals either disagree that seatbelts are the best means or even believe them to be counterproductive, or believe that seatbelts interfere with other goals that are as important as somewhat higher chances of survival, or think at least that the balance of different goals – inconvenience included – favors not wearing them. It seems to me that arguments available against critical paternalism would apply also to volitional paternalism, unless we only care about freedom in the choice of ends and not of means. But, then, most "ends" can be considered as "subordinate ends" (or means) in some sense (e.g., people may seek "survival" as a "means" to happiness) and most means can be considered to involve subordinate ends (e.g., a certain degree of comfort or convenience – not wearing seatbelts – may be considered a subordinate end in itself, to be weighed against other subordinate ends such as slightly higher statistical odds of not being killed in a car accident.)

The same problem is even clearer in Dworkin's example of "deeper" volitional paternalism: forcing people to higher culture. If higher culture can be forced on people because the pleasures of art are more satisfying to those trained to appreciate them, doesn't that line of reasoning justify imposing marital fidelity on people on the grounds that the pleasures of a permanent and exclusive love are more satisfying to those trained to appreciate them? Yet one can confidently assume that Dworkin would not accept that line of reasoning, since it would seem to justify a great deal of the critical paternalism he opposes.

One would like to see a fuller discussion of volitional paternalism by Dworkin. I assume that he would place fairly significant limitations on it, but it is hard to know at this point precisely what the limits would

---

[49] Dworkin, *Tanner Lectures*, p. 85.

be, and how they would essentially differentiate it from critical coercive paternalism.

Crude Paternalism and Critique of the Additive View

Let us quickly rid ourselves of the straw man case for paternalism that Dworkin rightly rejects: the view that a person's life is better simply because he is compelled to act (or not act) in a certain way. If Hitler wanted to kill all the Jews, but were locked in jail, he would not be a better person simply because he had been prevented from killing anyone. No amount of regulating the external behavior of human beings can make them necessarily better human beings. Only if the external behavior flows from free will can it be a factor in evaluating the moral quality of someone's life. At best, then, regulation of external activity, which is all that laws may accomplish, can only have an indirect effect on the quality of a human life. But there *is* an indirect effect of some importance (discussed below).

Dworkin argues that the additive view (that a person's approval of a component in his life adds more value to his life – in effect, is another component – but that the value of the other components still exists independent of the person's approval) cannot explain why a good life is valuable *for* or *to* the person whose life it is. It is implausible, he says, that a person can lead a better life against the grain of his most profound ethical convictions than at peace with them.

Dworkin makes his argument here more plausible partly by the extreme terms in which he casts it. Living against the grain of one's *most profound ethical convictions* does seem pretty awful. Moreover, there is no doubt that whatever efficacy paternalistic laws have in achieving their ends would be diluted considerably in the case of people who have strong, deep, settled convictions.

But when sophisticated paternalists make laws, they do not think only of that case. In fact, in many areas, the more common case may be that of people with convictions – or, better, beliefs – that are rather superficial. For example, with respect to the question of pornography, one might ask what the "convictions" of most people are. A certain number have deep and settled convictions about pornography: either that it is an evil (e.g., because it goes against some natural end of sexuality and undermines important social institutions such as the family, or because it undergirds a system of oppression of women) or that it is good, or at least unobjectionable (e.g., because it provides a desirable outlet for perfectly natural and healthy desires). But one wonders whether it is fair to say that most Americans have deep, settled convictions of either kind. Many women evince little interest in pornography – either in indulging in it or in interfering with others' indulgence in it – and many men seem to have ambivalent attitudes toward it, perhaps indulging in it sometimes, but with reservations manifested especially in the feeling of shame, a sense that it is not an admirable pastime.[50]

On so many issues, people have opinions that are difficult to characterize as deep convictions. Human beings are so often "conventional" in their opinions, adopting half-formed opinions from the environment in which they live, with relatively little sustained thought or reflection on issues. Oftentimes, it seems, others are impelled by powerful passions that lead them to adopt opinions that conform to these passions, again with limited thought and reflection. How many racists adopt their opinions about races on the basis of careful study and reflection? How many 18-year-olds arrive at opinions about pre-marital sexual activity unaffected by raging hormones or current infatuations? For Dworkin, to qualify as "convictions," do opinions need only to be strongly held, or do they require some reflection? Or does it matter?

I think it matters, because one reacts differently to the following two propositions: (1) "it is implausible to think that a person can lead a better life against the grain of his most profound ethical convictions," and (2) "it is implausible to think that a person can lead a better life when compelled to live in ways contrary to ambivalent or unreflective opinions, or to powerful passions." The first formulation sounds attractive. The second is obviously dubious: it seems rather plausible that a person may lead a better life in those cases, especially in the long run. (See the discussion of endorsement below.) Even from the standpoint which recognizes the ideal of people acting freely on their well-thought-out convictions, one can argue that forcing people to live contrary to unreflective opinions or powerful passions may be justifiable.

If many people in society hold opinions that are not deep and settled and reflective, but shallow and ambivalent and unthought-out, laws that restrict living in accord with these opinions could conceivably help people to live better lives. The unthinking racist may be forced by laws that make him live in a society where he has to deal more often with people of different races to change his opinions and actions, and thereby to live a

---

[50] Public opinion polls notoriously fail to measure intensity much of the time, so that they often fail to capture the ambivalence of many members of the public on various questions.

better life.[51] It is at least plausible to think that a man who feels at the same time both a certain attraction and repulsion toward pornography may end up living a better life against the grain of his powerful passions, if laws restrict objects that fuel those passions.

Why a person may be better off if certain passions are restricted becomes more apparent when we see that Dworkin states the goal of conceptual paternalism too narrowly. It is not just a case of removing options from a *conceptual* menu. It is also a question of removing opportunities that have a distorting influence on the will and passions. A significant component of the paternalist anti-pornography argument, for example, is that pornography is important not primarily because of its influence on the intellect, but because of its influence on the will and passions. Paternalistic legislation aims not simply at removing some *ideas* from people's *minds*, but at removing *stimuli* to certain *passions and desires*. This protection of people from harmful stimuli – the assistance to them in controlling their passions – is important, among other reasons, because it has an impact on the likelihood that people so controlled will eventually endorse those controls.

Future Endorsements

Dworkin argues that the defect in paternalism "can be cured by endorsement if the paternalism is sufficiently short-term and limited that it does [not] significantly constrict choices if the endorsement never comes."[52] For example, a child forced "to practice music is very likely later to endorse the coercion by agreeing that it did, in fact, make his life better; if he does not, he has lost little ground in a life that makes no use of his training."[53]

But what if the time spent practicing music prevented him from developing a hobby that *would* have brought him either a great deal of satisfaction or improved his capacities to respond to the challenge of living? Why isn't that a very significant loss? And how can one ever say the child will "very likely" endorse the imposition or constraint? Parents are

---

[51] Of course, Dworkin might allow for some government attempt to overcome racist thinking on the grounds that racists injure the rights of others. My argument here is the paternalistic one: that it might be desirable, in principle, for government to suppress racist thinking – or perhaps better, racist expressions – because the racists themselves would be better off. (Whether government ought to do this involves other, prudential questions, of course.)

[52] Dworkin, *Tanner Lectures*, p. 78.

[53] Dworkin, *Tanner Lectures*, pp. 78–79.

continually frustrated trying to discern *any* "likely" result of their actions. On this analysis, it might be difficult to justify *any* paternalism.

On the other hand, if the endorsement is the thing that cures the problematic character of paternalism, why does it have to be short-lived? And shouldn't we throw in as one factor the magnitude of the benefit derived from the paternalism? Perhaps Dworkin's formula for legitimate endorsed paternalism ought to be:

Paternalistic action is legitimate if it comes to be endorsed. Given our uncertainty about whether it will be endorsed, however, paternalistic action is justified in direct proportion to the importance of the benefit to be gained (as it is ultimately endorsed) and to the likelihood of ultimate endorsement, and inversely as to the length of time before endorsement, the degree of coercion, and magnitude of short-term costs and of opportunities foregone.

The problem, for Dworkin, is that this set of principles could plausibly justify a great deal of paternalistic action.

Dworkin says that the important point about future endorsements is that they must be genuine, which is not the case if someone "is hypnotized or brainwashed or frightened into conversion."[54] One minimal requirement for acceptable circumstances of endorsement is that the mechanisms we use to secure the conversion not lessen the person's "ability to consider the critical merits of the change in a reflective way."[55] But "(t)hreats of criminal punishment corrupt rather than enhance critical judgment," so even if they secure sincere conversions, such conversions cannot be counted as genuine ones.

Dworkin is right, I think, in stating that a person who is brainwashed or hypnotized has not had his life improved, since his free will seems permanently impaired by such forms of coercion. But it seems an overstatement to assume this about all threats. One is curious, for example, as to how the parents who "force" their children to practice music do so. If it is by threats of punishment, does that mean that subsequent endorsement is not genuine?

If an alcoholic were forcibly "dried out" against his will by threats of punishment, would a subsequent endorsement be sincere but not genuine on the grounds that his critical judgment had been corrupted rather than enhanced? Dworkin might be able to provide another reason why such coercion was inappropriate, (or perhaps he would justify it as a form of volitional paternalism), but it does not seem subject to the complaint that

54 Dworkin, *Tanner Lectures*, p. 79.
55 Dworkin, "Liberal Community," p. 486.

critical judgment is corrupted. It is altogether likely, in fact, that the former alcoholic's critical judgment had been *enhanced* rather than corrupted by the threats of punishment, by the removal of an important obstacle to rationality.

That obstacle is not just drunkenness itself, which is an obvious form of irrationality or at least an attenuation of rationality, but also the more subtle but deep *inclination* to drink that distorts judgment about many other things (for example, an alcoholic's evaluation of the force of his job responsibilities, or his attitudes toward people based on their support or opposition to his habit).

Likewise, a paternalist might argue that homosexual acts are an obstacle to critical judgment, since they involve an orientation of the will that obscures critical judgment with respect to use of the sexual faculty (and whatever supports or opposes a desired use of it), and that indulgence in pornography is an obstacle to critical judgment, since it involves an orientation of the will that similarly obscures such critical judgment (e.g., about women). Dworkin simply does not consider the relationship between habits and judgment and choice. This is also a problem in his treatment of the next form of paternalism.

Ethical Integrity

Dworkin's case against what he calls "substitute" paternalism – which is based not on the evil of what is prohibited but on the positive value of the substitute it makes available – turns on the principle of "ethical integrity." According to this principle, a person should be able to "live out of the conviction that his life, in its central features, is an appropriate one for him, that no other life he might live would be a plainly better response to the parameters of his ethical situation rightly judged."[56] This "makes a merger of conviction and life a parameter of ethical success," and a life without ethical integrity cannot be critically better than a life lived with integrity.

Are there many paternalists who actually argue for paternalistic action on the grounds that a person could be doing something better, even though what he is doing now is not bad in some way? If "substitute paternalism" abstracts from any argument that the life now lived by a person is somehow wrong (even apart from the question of subjective culpability),

[56] Dworkin, *Tanner Lectures*, p. 82.

I think not many people hold such a position. Paternalists usually seek, not to create higher levels of virtue, but to eliminate vice.

Is a life of ethical integrity always better than the alternatives? Dworkin doubts that a person made to live a life other than the one he considers best has a life that is better *for him*.

On one level what Dworkin says seems unobjectionable. Certainly most people, including paternalists, would view it as desirable that people act according to their convictions. Paternalists are simply concerned in a different way about their having *good* convictions and they have a different perspective on the formation of convictions. Nonetheless, a paternalist can (and should) acknowledge that moral principle demands that one always act on the basis of one's conscience, even an erroneous conscience (one that sincerely believes that something evil is in fact good and choiceworthy). Of course, as Dworkin acknowledges, society may stop someone from acting on his ethical convictions on the grounds that this will lead to harm to others, no matter how sincere he may be. Paternalists would differ from Dworkin in accepting a much less direct form of harm as a basis for legitimate regulation of a person's activity.

The salience of the requirement of ethical integrity is also affected by short-term/long-term considerations. One can imagine, for example, a case in which forcing a person to live a life opposed to ethical integrity in the short run may conduce to a life (*with* ethical integrity) that is better even *for him* in the long run, namely, the case where the person comes to endorse the higher life he has been forced to live.

A deeper objection to Dworkin's reliance on ethical integrity to undercut arguments for paternalism is his failure to attend more closely to considerations of how convictions are formed, and the role for law that a paternalist might see in that process. Dworkin focuses on the case where the merger of conviction and life is brought about by accommodating life to conviction: with the cessation of paternalistic acts, the person can act on what his convictions are. But where do these convictions come from, and can the law play a role in the formation of convictions?

What about the reverse case of ethical integrity, one might ask: where paternalism forces a person to engage in good acts, or more typically to refrain from engaging in bad acts, in order to facilitate his developing different and better convictions about what acts are good and bad? We are back to the question, touched upon above, of the sources of convictions and the role the law can play in shaping them.

The main argument for paternalism is not that people should be forced to refrain from bad acts so that they will be good. Rather, it is that they should be forced to refrain from bad acts so that it will be easier or more likely that they will be good. Law does not create virtue, but it can remove obstacles. How? First, by prohibiting bad acts that create habits or dispositions that are serious impediments to the formation of good convictions. And second, by contributing to the formation of good convictions themselves.[57]

For example, laws that prohibit the sale of certain drugs create obstacles to drug use and abuse, and some people – especially those not deeply committed to drug use – will not use drugs for fear of legal punishments. Those who refrain from it simply because of the punishments are not virtuous – their will is still disposed to perform the act. But if they are not permitted to engage in those acts over a long period of time, they will not form the habits or dispositions that would make it much more difficult to arrive at the conviction that such acts are wrong.

Dworkin does not seem to consider that the way people live may affect their convictions, that there is a reciprocal influence between our ideas and our acts: not only do our ideas help to shape our acts, but our acts also may affect our ideas. Paternalistic laws aim not only at preventing acts, but also at nourishing convictions.

The success laws achieve in forming convictions in particular cases varies. The paternalist hopes that his laws will foster ethical integrity, by providing conditions that support decent convictions. To the extent that the laws sometimes only prevent acts, without successfully fostering in them the corresponding convictions, the paternalist can still hope for endorsement at some time in the future, and can view the absence of ethical integrity as an unfortunate condition, occasioned by the failure of these individuals to embrace proper convictions, and justified by the requirements of the common good. That is, even if the individuals are not "better off" themselves, a paternalist might believe that the restrictions are justified by society's desire to avoid the indirect harms the prohibited acts would entail, among which are the encouragement and support they would give to others to act in that way.

Influencing the Conceptual Menu

Dworkin also considers "critical paternalism," which is defended in terms of its effects not on the present generation, but on future ones. For

---

[57] A fine discussion of the utility of law for establishing the conditions of a decent life is Harry Clor's *Obscenity and Public Morality* (Chicago, IL: University of Chicago Press, 1969), chapter 5. See also Yves Simon, *The Philosophy of Democratic Government* (University of Chicago Press, 1951), pp. 110–12.

example, laws prohibiting homosexual acts, he says,[58] could be said to aim at eliminating an active homosexual life as part of "the conceptual menu" so that future generations will not even be able to imagine such a life. Dworkin puts it somewhat more moderately (and accurately, I think) when he characterizes this form of paternalism in the *Tanner Lectures*: "people should be protected from choosing wasteful or bad lives not by flat prohibitions of the criminal law but by educational decisions and devices that remove bad options from people's view and imagination."[59] (Of course, the use of the criminal law and the use of educational devices are not incompatible.)

Critical paternalism can place certain ways of living so at the margins of what is a conceivably good life that few people would give them any serious consideration. Until recently, for example, the vast majority of Americans would not have considered an active homosexual life as an imaginable way of life for themselves or any decent person.

Moreover, there is no reason, in principle, why a policy of critical paternalism cannot also seek to educate citizens, to give them sound reasons *why* certain lives ought to be so disfavored, in accordance with their intellectual abilities. For example, it might allow adults and college students to study arguments in favor of a disfavored life, while making such study off-limits at lower educational levels, and while maintaining legal prohibitions. (Of course, the given mores of a community will place limits on what form of critical paternalism citizens can agree upon.)

Dworkin argues that a life is less well lived if it is based on simple acceptance of conformity to social conventions, rather than on serious reflection. Obviously, we would prefer a society in which people refrained from, say, torture for well thought-out reasons. But given a choice between a society in which people rather unreflectively opposed torture and another in which people embraced it with considerable ethical integrity, it would be at least reasonable to choose the former. The reasonableness of such a choice would be based not merely on the rights of the tortured, but on what would be good for the torturers themselves. Moreover, the superiority of unreflective nontorturing to reflective torturing would exist even if there were a certain *subjective* superiority of the "ethically integrated" torturers, arising from their dedicated pursuit of what they think is good according to their invincibly deformed consciences.

---

[58] Dworkin, "Liberal Community," p. 487.
[59] Dworkin, *Tanner Lectures*, p. 83.

Nor should one prefer the society of reflective torturers on the grounds that they could more easily be brought to see the objective evil of what they are doing than unreflective nontorturers could be brought to have convictions (rather than mere beliefs) about not torturing people (i.e., more easily brought to live ethically integrated lives). A habit of reflection might make the reflective torturers more open to change, but a habit of torturing might make them less sensitive to the desirability of change. And there are ways short of tolerating evil acts to induce people who unreflectively reject evil to be more reflective about that rejection – classical education along the lines of the Platonic dialogues or scholastic disputations, or even traditional catechisms, are examples. Ethical integrity hardly requires an unrestricted conceptual menu.

Moreover, all conceptual menus are limited, since there are infinitely varied ways of life and no one could reflect on them all. (The limits of what can be studied are especially obvious at the lower educational levels.) Doesn't it seem strange to say that not considering *every* possible way of life means that a person's life is worse off?

Nor does it seem enough to assert in response that the conceptual menu ought to include at least those ways of life that are considered or have been thought in the past to be good ways of life. That response concedes that a restricted conceptual menu is not per se bad. If our choice, then, is between restricted menus why should mere convention dictate which restricted menu is best, as opposed to a judgment regarding which menu emphasizes and gives greatest support to the objectively best way of life?

Dworkin considers it "odd to think that a person's *own* life could be made a better life to have lived, in the critical sense, by constricting his imagination."[60] But one can easily imagine useless or dangerous uses of the imagination, and ask why constriction of these (not so much punishing them, as preventing or reducing the likelihood of them) would be bad, especially given the potential costs, if the imagining opens one to living a bad life.

"A challenge cannot be more interesting, or in any other way a more valuable challenge to face, when it has been narrowed, simplified, and bowdlerized by others in advance, and that is as much true when we are ignorant of what they have done as when we are all too aware of it," says Dworkin[61]. But would skiing be a greater challenge, and skiers' lives better lived, if some ski resorts contained ski runs so difficult and dangerous as

---

[60] Dworkin, "Liberal Community," p. 487.
[61] Dworkin, *Tanner Lectures*, p. 84.

to be life-threatening, and skiers had to find out which ones were and how so? Does cutting unsafe ski resorts out of the menu for skiers make life less interesting and valuable, whether or not skiers know that this restriction has been imposed?[62] The assertion that restricted menus are necessarily inferior ones does not hold up, unless one operates with a skeptical assumption about our capacity to distinguish what is desirable or undesirable to have on the menu.

Transcendent Standards

Dworkin ultimately has recourse to the proposition that ethics is not based on a transcendent standard.[63] The real error of the conceptual or critical paternalist, Dworkin thinks, is that he "assumes that we have some standard of what a good life is that *transcends* the question of what circumstances are appropriate for people deciding how to live, and so can be used in answering that question, by stipulating that the best circumstances are those most likely to produce the really correct answer."[64] But the skillful performance demanded by the challenge model includes not only producing a product, he says, but also defining the very meaning of what the good life means. Just as there is no one absolutely greatest way to make art, but artistic value must be judged in relation to the historical circumstances in which it was produced, so there is no one best way to live, and living well must be judged in relation to the full particularity of a person's circumstances.

---

[62] Perhaps Dworkin would respond: since life is threatened, we can call this prohibition of unsafe ski-runs volitional paternalism, since we can assume skiers have a preference for enjoying skiing, and not ending life this way. But that simply returns us to the ambiguity of volitional paternalism. We could just as easily say that those who are searching for the best way of life have a preference for a good way of life, and so they do not need to consider immoral ways of life.

[63] It might be objected that if Dworkin takes a rejection of a transcendent standard as a starting point, much of what I have said in response to his criticisms of paternalism so far is irrelevant, since it assumes the possibility of such a standard. But I do not think that Dworkin's rejection of a transcendent standard is his starting point. He does not begin by saying "we have no transcendent standard" and then show that "therefore we should not be paternalists." The order of my argument here more or less follows Dworkin's own order, in which he starts out by describing different forms of paternalism and then subjects them to critical analysis. The rejection of a transcendent standard, then, is not an assumption from the start, but a factor that arises within his subsequent analysis and critique.

[64] Dworkin, *Tanner Lectures*, p. 84.

But can Dworkin himself avoid employing a transcendent standard? He says that the paternalist errs in imagining that we have a standard of a good life "that transcends the question of what circumstances are appropriate for people deciding how to live." But why does Dworkin assume that people *ask* the "question of what circumstances are appropriate for people deciding how to live?" Why do we bother to try "deciding how to live?" Dworkin's assumptions here indicate that he too has a transcendent standard, one that somehow tells him that human beings are "choosing beings." Moreover, his emphasis on "the central, constitutive role the model of challenge assigns to reflective or intuitive *judgment*"[65] also seems to commit him to the notion that human beings are "reasoning beings." A transcendent standard is implicit in his characterization of the challenge model. His transcendent standard – a certain form of rationality – is admittedly at a very high level of generality, but that does not exempt him from his own criticism.

Dworkin is right to have that transcendent standard: I think that human beings do inevitably – if not always articulately – ask what the best life they can live is, and do answer that question by employing their intellects and wills. But he thereby assumes that there is some criterion for distinguishing between right and wrong answers, that human beings have some capacity for knowing the truth about how to live, and that they ought to respond to this challenge of defining what the best life is.

The error here is not the paternalist's, but Dworkin's. He seems to assume that he has some Archimedean point from which he can criticize the paternalist for assuming that there is a transcendent standard before our engaging in the challenge of living. He is *asserting* that the only way to live well is to define for yourself what it means to live well. But from what vantage point can he make that assertion, unless he has smuggled in a transcendent standard of his own?

Impact and Challenge Models

While most of the preceding arguments deal with Dworkin's more particularized contentions, I should briefly raise questions about his dubious dichotomy between the impact and challenge models. It is hard to resist the inclination to think that the impact model is a straw man. Certainly there are those who believe that the quality of a person's life is affected

---

[65] Dworkin, *Tanner Lectures*, p. 86, emphasis added.

by extrinsic products of that life, such as great art or social works. But who believes that a life could be considered good *simply because of* certain products? Does anyone believe that someone leads a good life simply because he does things that are good for some people, even if he has no desire to be good, or in fact desires to be bad to people? Does anyone believe that a criminal forced to make good things for people in prison leads a good life? (It may be *less bad* than a life of crime itself, of course, in the very limited sense that accomplishing an evil adds to the evil of desiring it.) People in general instinctively understand that virtue or goodness lies not *simply* in certain results of action, but in an orientation of the will toward certain human acts.

When Dworkin suggests that the impact model supports ethical paternalism, he gives the following as an example of that thinking: "people's lives would go better if they were forced to pray, because in that case they might please God more and so have a better impact, even though they were atheists."[66] It is astonishing that Dworkin would use such an example, as if the "prayer" (compelled utterances) of an atheist would of itself be pleasing to God, according to any contemporary ethical model.

The real opposition lies between two forms of the challenge model, which emphasizes "skillful performance": one that stresses objective, substantive criteria for skillfulness (there are acts that are good and those that are bad, by virtue of their objects) and another that denies that there are such objective, substantive criteria, focusing purely on "procedural" qualities of skillfulness (e.g., whether someone has really reflected on a problem seriously, grappling with its difficulties, arriving at a personal judgment). In both cases, it is true that virtue does, in some sense, lie in skillful performance in the meeting of some challenge, but Dworkin has a very reductionistic and formalistic view of the criteria for skillfulness.

CONCLUSION

What I hope to have shown in the course of this chapter is merely that Dworkin's critique of paternalism is not a persuasive one, except with respect to relatively crude forms of it, which imagine that coercion is able to accomplish more than it can. I do not contend that I have made a case for paternalistic government policies, which would take a more substantial showing and an effort to deal with many more objections.

[66] Dworkin, *Tanner Lectures*, p. 78.

I do think that such a project would be a valuable and necessary one. Paternalism, from one point of view, is simply unavoidable. It would be an illusion to believe that the form and content of the law – all law, in liberal regimes as well as others – do not have a powerful influence on the lives of many human beings, subtly shaping their attitudes about what a good human life is. Only a relatively artificial and abstract view of human beings, divorced from an adequate sociology of knowledge and ethical life, would fail to see the connections. Unfortunately, that artificial and abstract view of human beings tends to have considerable influence among liberal intellectuals, from Mill on down. If government and law inevitably shape human beings, it makes sense to be aware of the tendencies of any given regime and to foster what is good and resist what is bad in it.

This general defense of paternalism does not justify any particular paternalistic policy, and it may be that there are large areas of human endeavor that it is prudent to leave free, or relatively free, of government control. (In fact, I think that is the case.) It is also true that paternalism always poses dangers of various kinds. Paternalism can obviously go askew when it is put at the service of bad ideals or employs bad means to a good end. It also has to overcome a certain kind of negative presumption: it is much more desirable for a person freely to choose good and reject evil than to be constrained to do so. The goal of paternalism should be, ultimately, to facilitate free choice of the good, not merely to constrain people to engage in (or refrain from) some external act. Moreover, when government acts to achieve a paternalistic objective, it ought to do so in accord with the principle of subsidiarity (i.e., the principle that a given function ought to be exercised by the lowest level of community that can perform that function adequately).

Much remains to be done to articulate the grounds and conditions of intelligent paternalistic policies in modern, pluralistic liberal democracies. But that complicated task can only be undertaken when the fallacies of principled arguments against paternalism, such as Dworkin's, are properly understood.

5

Liberalism and Autonomy II

Joseph Raz

I want to turn now to an argument of a distinguished contemporary liberal political theorist, Joseph Raz of the Oxford, that moral paternalism[1] is inadmissible because it denies people full citizenship and undermines the necessary trust of citizens. This chapter takes up the critique of Raz on autonomy begun in Robert George's critique of Raz's earlier work on autonomy.[2]

Raz is a liberal. However, he is unlike many other liberal theorists (e.g., Ronald Dworkin) in his straightforward assertion that autonomy is not an unqualified good. He says that "the good life is a *successful* autonomous life, that is life consisting in the successful pursuit of *valuable* activities and relationships largely chosen by the person involved."[3] The assertion that autonomy is successful only if used for valuable activities makes Raz a distinctly atypical liberal.

Raz is also, however, firm in his adherence to the "harm" principle: he is opposed to coercive moral paternalism. Government should not coercively restrain moral autonomy even when it is used to pursue activities that are not morally valuable, as long as other people are not relatively directly harmed. His argument in "Liberty and Trust" is another part of

---

[1] By "moral paternalism," Raz seems to mean laws whose justification is the good of the person involved, rather than other persons who are affected by his action, where the "good" at issue is his moral good, rather than, say, his merely physical well-being. Pornography laws would involve moral paternalism, seatbelt laws would not.

[2] See Robert George, "The Unorthodox Liberalism of Joseph Raz," in *Liberalism at the Crossroads*, C. Wolfe and J. Hittinger, Eds. (Lanham, MD: Rowman and Littlefield, 1994).

[3] Joseph Raz, "Liberty and Trust," in *Natural Law, Liberalism, and Morality* ed. R. George (Oxford: Clarendon Press, 1996), p. 113 (emphasis added).

his effort to defend this combination of perfectionism and contemporary liberal commitment to the harm principle.

COERCION

Raz begins by indicating some serious reservations about coercion. Coercion, says Raz, "violates a person's independence by subjecting him to the will of another." And while in all our actions our options are shaped by others,

only when manipulated or coerced are we tools in the hands of others. Only then are we affected not only by the actions of others but by actions intended to dictate ours, and to do so not by persuasion but by overriding our will. People enjoy personal autonomy only to the extent that they are authors of their own actions. When subjected, either by coercion or by manipulation, to the will of another that condition is flouted.[4]

This statement is puzzling, given the previous definitions laid down by Raz, and it is unsatisfying for other reasons as well.

Personal autonomy may require that people be the authors of their own actions, but being the authors of their own actions does not mean that people have *valuable* personal autonomy. Raz has explicitly said that "not all the constraints imposed by coercion are a restriction of the autonomy of the coerced," since "[a]n autonomous life is valuable only to the extent that it is engaged in *valuable* activities and relationships."[5] A person deprived of the opportunity to murder has not lost "autonomy, in the sense of a capacity for valuable autonomous life."[6] So the conditions for genuine autonomy are not flouted, even when a person's actions are coerced or his will overridden, except in cases that would have involved autonomy in the valuable sense; that is, autonomy for valuable activities and relationships. Coercion that inhibits or prevents activities and relationships that are not valuable (because, for example, they are morally bad) does not deprive anyone of valuable autonomy.

Nor is it correct for Raz to say that when we are manipulated or coerced we are "tools in the hands of others."[7] The key feature of a tool is that it is simply a means to an end. The person using the tool does not aim at

---

[4] Raz, "Liberty and Trust," p. 120.
[5] Ibid (emphasis in the original).
[6] Ibid.
[7] Ibid.

the good of the tool, but simply at the good for which the tool is a means. But coercion of a person does not necessarily reduce him to a means.

This is shown in the first place by the example of ordinary coercion of acts that violate the rights of others. Non-paternalistic coercive regulation may receive its *primary* justification from the duty of society to protect people's rights against the actions of those who would violate those rights, but there is an important secondary purpose as well: the well-being of the offender. The coercion of those who would infringe the rights of others in no way suggests that society does not regard them "as people who matter in their own right, whose fate is of intrinsic value." What is best for the well-being of those who would infringe on others' rights is precisely that they should not be permitted to do so, or that they should be punished for doing so, as this will prevent them from engaging in immoral behavior and/or will teach them the wrongness of such acts and also prevent habituation in that immoral behavior.

Nor does coercion reduce a person to a means when it is exercised in the cause of moral paternalism (or, for that matter, other forms of paternalism), which aims precisely at the good of the coerced person. Paternalists – at least thoughtful ones – make no claim that they can "make" the coerced people "good" by coercing them (preventing bad actions or commanding good ones), since virtue requires an act of the will. But they do argue that coercion can foster the *conditions* of virtue by preventing the formation of bad habits.[8] The argument that coercion necessarily reduces one person to being the tool of another is, therefore, clearly unwarranted.

TRUST

Raz then turns to an argument against moral paternalism based on the requirements of trust. He starts by pointing out that "there is nothing wrong in loss of autonomy when it occurs in the right circumstances,"[9] as the story of Ulysses and the Sirens shows. (Ulysses, in order to get by the isle of the Sirens – whose beautiful singing lured sailors to their death on the rocks – filled his sailors' ears with wax but, wanting to hear the music himself, he kept his ears open, but had himself tied to the mast.)

---

[8] See Yves Simon, *The Philosophy of Democratic Government* (Chicago, IL: University of Chicago Press, 1951), pp. 110–12, and Robert P. George, *Making Men Moral: Civil Liberties and Public Morality* (Oxford: Clarendon Press, 1993).

[9] Raz, "Liberty and Trust," p. 121.

Ulysses' temporary loss of autonomy was justified not by the fact "that he did it to himself, but that it was done for good reasons."[10] Had he been tied to the mast by his best friend that would have been a friendly and justified act, Raz points out.

Raz notes that various reasons may justify coercion: "to protect another, or to protect the coerced person's own long-term autonomy, or another of his interests, or to make him do his duty, etc."[11] He goes on to argue that independence "is not all or nothing. While significant loss of independence may be hard to justify, trivial loss of independence hardly calls for justification."[12]

Raz gives an example of "innocent coercion": when "[m]y best friend is about to walk into the room where a surprise party is being prepared for him, and I bodily block his way and force him to go to another room to look at a book."[13] Raz says that the significant feature of cases such as this (paternalistic ones, not involving duties of justice or rights of others) is that "coercion is normally justified only if used by friends or others whose good intentions are beyond doubt (e.g., the person's doctor)." It's not just that there are greater chances that the real motive for coercion is benevolent. Even if that were not in doubt, "one may well object if a stranger, let alone a potentially hostile stranger, takes it upon himself to coerce one for one's own good."[14] The point, Raz says, reflects the nature of trust, which involves the relaxation (though not complete abandonment) of the "normal standard of vigilance and independence."[15]

Raz summarizes:

paternalistic coercion is justified when it meets two cumulative conditions: First, it is undertaken for a good reason, one sufficient to make reasonable a partial

---

[10] Ibid.

[11] Ibid.

[12] Ibid, "Liberty and Trust," pp. 121–22. It is unclear to me whether by "trivial" in this sentence Raz means only the magnitude of the limitation on a person's independence (the extent of the constraint), or includes consideration of how *valuable* the autonomy limited is (so that substantial constraint might be a trivial loss of independence if what is lost is an opportunity to do things of little or no value). From the perspective of the latter, for example, antipolygamy laws might involve substantial constraint – men are limited to marriage with one wife, out of all the women in the world, or even in "their world" – but the loss is trivial, given the good of monogamy and lack of worth of polygamy.

[13] Raz, "Liberty and Trust," p. 122.

[14] Ibid.

[15] Ibid.

loss of independence. Second, barring emergencies, it comes from the hands of someone reasonably trusted by the coerced.[16]

Raz's discussion of trust, however, does not make a persuasive case against moral paternalism. Let me begin my questions here by looking at three of Raz's examples in this section. With respect to the example of Ulysses and the Sirens, one might ask "what if a benevolent *stranger* had tied Ulysses to the mast?" (Imagine, perhaps, that as Ulysses stands in the back of the boat, his men facing the other way as they row, a stowaway – not a personal friend of Ulysses – who knows about the danger of the Sirens, comes out of hiding and overpowers Ulysses and ties him to the mast.) Wouldn't that too have been "a friendly and justified act," even in the absence of "trust"? Indeed, isn't it the absence of trust that makes the direct reliance on coercion especially plausible – since a relationship of trust might make persuasion, *instead of* coercion, a preferable tactic?

With respect to the surprise party, one must ask whether we're really dealing with coercion here. Put yourself in the position of the person who is unknowingly about to spoil his own surprise party. As you head to the door of the room, a friend bodily blocks your way and suggests that you go to another room to look at a book. It is conceivable, I suppose, that you say "no," engage in a physical fight with your friend about whether you can go into the room you want to enter, and be physically compelled to go to the other room. But that's not a very likely scenario. Precisely if there is a relationship of trust, you would *defer* to your friend, *obviating* the need for "coercion." It's not that trust "justifies" coercion – it's that it simply makes coercion unnecessary.

The third example is Raz's reference to the fact that coercion is "normally justified only if used by friends *or others whose good intentions are beyond doubt (e.g., the person's doctor),*"[17] an example that raises all sorts of interesting questions. Again, one must ask: in what sense is the doctor using "coercion"? It seems clear that people are *not* coerced by doctors – they trust them and therefore coercion is unnecessary: they choose to follow their advice willingly (although, as a matter of fact, in many cases, they choose to ignore the advice). At the same time, they trust doctors though they are *not* friends. Doctors (just as such) seem to be somewhere in between "friends" and paternalistic public officials. They are more like the former, in that they are freely chosen by the patient, who

---

[16] Ibid. This is the way consent can be relevant to the justification of coercion, Raz says – it can express or establish a relationship of trust.

[17] Ibid (emphasis added).

can walk away from them. They are more like the latter in being "impersonal doers of good," trusted more for their technical than their personal qualities.

Moreover, it may be an exaggeration to say that the intentions of doctors are "beyond doubt." Raz puts it well later, when he says that trust occasions a relaxation of vigilance though not a complete abandonment of it. Part of the problem with the doctor analogy – the way it skews the question somewhat – is that it ordinarily involves the relatively uncontroversial character of health as an end, and trust in the technical competence of doctors in the means to achieve that end. But what if the end of doctoring were less clear, for example, if the practice of involuntary euthanasia spreads (as it has in the Netherlands, for example); that is, what if doctors aim, at least in some cases, at something other than health?[18] What might happen to the doctor–patient relationship in those circumstances?

The trust in technical competence that contributes to trust of non-friends, such as doctors, may also be a factor in acceptance by some people of certain kinds of non–moral paternalism by public officials, such as seatbelt laws, anti-smoking regulations, and food and drug restrictions on alleged carcinogens. But other people might resist this kind of paternalism, even if they have no doubt about the technical competence and good intentions of such public officials (i.e., even if they were similar to friends in having good intentions, as Raz suggests about doctors). People might still object to coercion by them, for example, because, while they admit the technical competence in the statement that "seatbelts save lives" and the good intentions of those who pass the laws, they disagree with the non-technical assumption that "decreasing the statistical likelihood of death in an accident is worth the inconvenience of putting seatbelts on all the time."

The whole relation, then, between trust and coercion and good intentions and technical competence is more complicated than Raz's discussion suggests.

---

[18] See Wesley J. Smith, *Culture of Death* (Encounter Books, 2000) pp. 109–10. Nor is it simply a question of substituting "the control of pain" for "health" in the scenario I'm invoking. Pain control is so effective today as to eliminate it as a ground for euthanasia in almost all cases. Euthanasia is based on a much more fundamental question about the "meaningfulness" of a given human life, and the involuntary euthanasia practiced in the Netherlands usually has nothing to do with pain. In these cases, the actual goal of the doctor is not so much "the health of the patient" as it is "rationing limited medical resources." This may be viewed as a net utilitarian increase in overall health – but this view raises serious questions about trust by an individual of a doctor's intentions with respect to *his* health.

Raz goes on to say that even if reasons for paternalistic coercion are solid, one might object if a stranger took it upon himself to coerce one for one's own good. But, if the reasons for the coercion were good and were serious enough, would one indeed object (or at least *reasonably* object)? Raz is correct, I think, when he says at another point that it depends on whether it is as important that the person do something himself as it is that he do the right thing.[19] But Raz's discussion does not give us any clear criteria for answering that question.

I do not mean to say that trust should never be a factor in evaluating the desirability of adopting a policy of paternalistic coercion. Most obviously, a paternalist should take into consideration the likelihood of the benevolent coercion being successful if it were employed by someone the coerced person does not trust. That would certainly be an important *prudential* consideration, since distrust would magnify the difficulties of achieving successful paternalistic coercion.

What I don't see in Raz's argument is any *principled* argument as to the need for trust as he sees it: as a separate and necessary requirement, over and above good reasons, to justify moral paternalism.[20] This is the key question.

In the beginning of the last section of his paper, Raz makes some trenchant observations about the limits of arguments based on trust. He argues that trust is not a condition of legitimate authority. The main justifying aim of authority is rather, that "it improves conformity with good reasons."[21] There are cases where authorities should intervene to seek social coordination which it is the duty of all to seek. If it does secure the required coordination, then "the absence of trust is a fault with the people and not necessarily with the institution."[22] And, "[n]aturally, trust is not a condition of the legitimacy of an authority in stopping people from violating

---

[19] Raz, "Liberty and Trust," pp. 119–20, and also p. 123.

[20] Raz does concede the possible legitimacy of "paternalistic coercion" without meeting the condition of trust in cases of "emergencies." He does not give examples. There are obvious examples of the necessity of emergency coercive action without trust in cases of a danger of immediate physical harm to a person (e.g., a person who sees a car coming and pushes out of its path a complete stranger who doesn't see it). But it is difficult to imagine "emergencies" involving only moral harm, and so it seems likely that in this instance Raz is using the term "paternalistic coercion" more broadly, to include any coercive action against a person's will for his own good (physical as well as moral), not just moral paternalism (where it is specifically the person's moral well-being that is at issue).

[21] Raz, "Liberty and Trust," p. 123.

[22] Ibid.

the rights of others or unjustifiably harming them."[23] For example, one need not seek the trust of violent offenders as a precondition of having jurisdiction over them.

But Raz wants to say that the legitimacy does require trust in the case of coercive moral paternalism, for the jurisdiction of legitimate authority "does not run to matters regarding which it is better that people decide for themselves, unguided by authority[,] than that they improve their compliance with reason."[24] Coercive paternalism, he says, is a case in point. (He seems to assume that his previous examples – Ulysses, the surprise party, the doctor – have somehow demonstrated this, though, for reasons given above, I think that is not so.) Therefore, "[o]nly those trusted by the coerced can have the authority to use paternalistic coercion."[25]

It is true that it is sometimes better for people to decide some matters for themselves rather than have them decided by authority, even if the authority would make a better decision. For example, decisions about whom to marry, about what occupation to pursue, or how large a family should be are generally best left with the individual or couple involved. But at the same time, all these decisions can be, and often have been, limited by law. Sometimes they are limited in order to prevent direct harm to others, as when a person is prevented from choosing burglary as his occupation. At other times, people can be limited for reasons involving much less direct harm to others or on frankly paternalistic grounds: for example, a man can be prevented from marrying his sister, or his dog, or (at the same time) two women both of whom he loves, or another man; or a couple can be prevented from decreasing the size of their family by aborting a child they have conceived. Such paternalistic legislation may be wrong, of course: *but if it is wrong, it is wrong because it is not based on good reasons.* Whether the authority imposing the limits were trusted would be simply irrelevant.

TRUST AND CITIZENSHIP

After noting a relationship between trust, respect for government, and a disposition to obey the law, Raz goes on to discuss an aspect of trust that is related to citizenship. The citizenship that Raz is concerned with is not legal citizenship but "the status of citizenship which makes it rationally

---

[23] Ibid.
[24] Ibid. For clarity, I have added the comma that the context seems to demand.
[25] Ibid.

possible for people to regard themselves as fully belonging to the political community, and similarly to regard its law as their law, and its government as their government."[26] (Note that this appears to overlap with citizens' sense that they are objects of equal concern and respect.) Full citizenship he defines – and this is a very key point for my analysis of Raz's argument below – as belonging to those

> who either feel, where their feeling is not unreasonable, or who would be unreasonable to deny, that the state or the government recognizes them as people who matter in their own right, that their fate is a matter of intrinsic value in the eyes of the state and its government.[27]

Raz describes this as a "semi-objective" condition. Its objectivity lies in the fact that "[i]t turns not on how people actually feel, but on how it is reasonable for them to feel."[28] People may be deluded that government considers their interests, when it doesn't, or they may feel discriminated against, when they aren't. But there is a subjective component as well – it turns not on how governments actually treat people, but on how the people feel about it, as long as the feeling is not unreasonable. This partial subjectivity means that "[g]overnments should not only act justly, they should also be seen to act so, at least by all those whose beliefs on the matter are not unreasonable."[29]

I think there is substance to Raz's contention on this point, although I am unsure as to how much we agree on the reasons. I would put it this way: government's obligation to pursue the common good requires not only that government actually do so, but that, at least ordinarily, it take reasonable steps to make it clear to its citizens that it is doing so.[30] Several reasons for the latter requirement can be given: first, the failure of government to offer its citizens reasonable grounds to believe that it is pursuing the common good will likely obstruct its ability to obtain their cooperation in pursuing it; second, "civic friendship" is part of the common good, and would seem to entail, at least ordinarily, a communication of respect – in the sense of a commitment to pursue their

---

[26] Ibid., "Liberty and Trust," p. 124.
[27] Ibid.
[28] Ibid.
[29] Ibid., "Liberty and Trust," pp. 124–25.
[30] I say "at least ordinarily" because I can imagine unusual circumstances in which short-term failure to do so might be justified. I think an example might be constructed which is analogous to a military tactic that seems like a blunder (to fool the enemy) and which is justified even if it also fools one's own troops (assuming that the latter will obey anyway, as a matter of discipline).

good – to one's fellow citizens. I presume that this latter reason is similar to the principle of citizenship that Raz invokes.

PROBLEMS WITH RAZ'S CITIZENSHIP

Raz indicates that he assumes "that it is good that all residents within the jurisdiction of a political community should be full citizens of the community."[31] It is unclear how he would regard the status of two classes for whom this might be problematic, and these examples also suggest problems with some of Raz's definitions. First, what about resident aliens – especially those who remain aliens of their own volition, as opposed to those who are precluded from a citizenship they desire? Presumably they are not "full citizens," in the ordinary sense of the term. They don't "regard themselves as fully belonging to the political community."[32] On the other hand, they should be able to have the feeling that "the state or the government recognizes them as people who matter in their own right, that their fate is a matter of intrinsic value in the eyes of the state and its government."[33] Not only citizens, but every human being can demand that every other human being (not just the state or government) view them in that way. Among other conclusions one might draw from this is that even if "full citizenship" requires government to treat a person as someone with intrinsic value, treating someone as a person with intrinsic value does not require granting them full citizenship, if the latter is understood to include rights as elementary as voting.

Second, what is the status of imprisoned felons in a political community? They do belong to the political community and should be able to feel that government recognizes them as people in their own right, whose fate is of intrinsic value, and in that sense they have "full citizenship." But their participation in the political community is problematic and is frequently and reasonably curtailed. For example, it seems reasonable to deny voting rights to imprisoned murderers and rapists and embezzlers, on the grounds that their actions have demonstrated a will sharply and substantially opposed to the common good and a willingness to act on it. If this is so, do they lack "full citizenship"? One could probably answer that question in different ways, depending on one's definition of "full" citizenship.

[31] Raz, p. 125.
[32] Ibid., p. 124.
[33] Ibid.

My own preference would be to say that they are full citizens, but that full citizens may sometimes legitimately be deprived of certain rights, if there are reasonable grounds for so doing.[34] Others might prefer to say that governments may sometimes reasonably deny certain citizens full citizenship. Either way, an important point is that "full citizenship for all" is more complicated than Raz's discussion of it suggests.

CITIZENSHIP, SELF-RESPECT, AND MUTUAL RESPECT

Raz goes on to give good reasons for the importance of citizenship. Denial of full citizenship to a group can be destabilizing to the community, if it creates estranged people or groups who regard the government as alien and potentially hostile. Moreover, since human beings are political animals, an essential ingredient of their well-being is feeling part of a larger community. Being second class citizens forces a flawed life on people, he says.

Of course, there are people who might be considered "second class citizens" by some (it is not clear whether this would include Raz), who have a flawed life in this respect not because of the action of the government, but because their own actions have called down upon them legitimate restrictions on their status and participation in society, such as imprisoned felons.

Another problem of citizenship raised by Raz flows from the objective character of the condition for full citizenship, that is, that the belief that one is a full citizen be reasonable. One can imagine circumstances in which lack of self-respect or self-esteem (perhaps fostered by hypocritical government propaganda) leads people to think that they deserve second class status. To identify with one's own state on such terms is to compromise one's own self-esteem and self-respect, says Raz.

How would Raz apply this to the case of the imprisoned felon? Presumably he *deserves* his second class status. His sense of "belonging" to the political community should be qualified in some sense, that is, the sense that he has set himself apart from the community by his own actions attacking it. It might even be argued, paradoxically, that government would promote his self-respect best by punishing him. Self-respect – like

---

[34] This would have to be elaborated more fully, by distinguishing between rights that are so fundamental that they can never be taken away and others that are not so fundamental that they cannot be conditioned in some way. The right against compelled religious belief or worship, for example, would fall in the first category, the right to vote in the second.

the sense of belonging that constitutes citizenship – must have (at least in part) an "objective" character. One's self-respect and self-esteem ought not to rest, unreasonably, on the belief that one ought to have self-respect and self-esteem *with respect to* acts that are the proper object of censure, by oneself and by others. The self-respect that derives from being a person *capable* of a rational and morally upright life is, of course, compatible with recognizing and experiencing the guilt that flows from failure to live up to this capacity – indeed "appropriate guilt" is a testimony to our freedom, which is so intimately tied up with the foundations of our self-respect.[35] To the extent that punishment helps a person to *see* himself more clearly and to evaluate his acts properly, it conduces, in the long run, to a *legitimate* self-respect and self-esteem.

Raz argues that one important factor in citizenship (which requires having reasonable grounds to believe that one's worth is recognized by one's political society and its government) is

mutual respect between groups within the society who have diverse cultures and ways of life. To feel part of a society, to be a full citizen of it one must be able to profess one's basic beliefs, and conduct one's life in accordance with them and with one's deepest feelings without fear of criminal sanctions, legal or social discrimination, or social ridicule or persecution.[36]

The example he chooses to illustrate this point is that of gay men and lesbians. Homosexuals do not enjoy full citizenship when aspects of their conduct are criminalized, when they face public and private employment discrimination, where portrayal of the culture is censored (legally or voluntarily), and when they are not free to display affection in public as heterosexuals do. "Such manifestations of bigotry, where officially sanctioned or socially widespread, condemn gay men and lesbians to second class status in their own society."[37]

Raz then ups the ante when he goes on to argue that "[i]n considering this case it is important to remember that the case I am making does not depend on the fact that homophobia is an unfounded prejudice," as

---

[35] I resist any temptation to say that freedom is *the* foundation for our self-respect. It is precisely the Achilles' heel of modern philosophy that it has been able to find a foundation for human dignity only in human freedom – the will – and not in the capacity of human beings to know the truth – intellect, which is the proper guide to the will. (Where reason is considered, it generally is understood only as some form of *instrumental* rationality, admitting rational knowledge of means, but denying the capacity to know objective human ends.)

[36] Raz, p. 126.

[37] Ibid.

groups with misguided and worthless beliefs and ways of life have the same claim to be admitted as full citizens as do gay men and lesbians.[38] The most fundamental way that political societies protect and promote people's well-being is to extend full citizenship to all their members. Raz notes that some circumstances might override this duty, "but it is difficult to envisage situations in which someone capable of enjoying full citizenship (i.e., excluding cases of severe mental illness, serious retardation or the like) should be denied it for his own good."[39]

It is not clear to me exactly how broad a claim Raz is making when he says that his case does *not* depend on the view that "homophobia is an unfounded prejudice." Does this mean that *any* case arguing for legal or social restrictions on homosexual activity – even if it were a reasoned moral position rather than an unfounded prejudice – would violate Raz's requirement that members of all groups be treated as full citizens? If so, his claim will not bear analysis, in my opinion.

If Raz's argument does not depend on the contention that homophobia is an unfounded prejudice, let us take him at his word and assume for the moment that legal and social sanctions on homosexual activity are reasoned moral positions, and in fact are true. Let us assume, for example, that homosexual activity is harmful to individual well-being and harmful to social well-being.[40] Raz accepts the perfectionistic principle that society ought to promote the well-being of its members. If

---

[38] Ibid.

[39] Ibid.

[40] For example, the case might be made that (1) homosexual acts are physically dangerous (cf. Jeffrey Satinover, *Homosexuality and the Politics of Truth* [Grand Rapids, MI: Bakers Books, 1996], Chapter 3, which helps explain the striking difference in male heterosexual and homosexual mortality rates); (2) homosexuality is correlated with higher levels of various psychological problems (cf. Sandfort, Graaf, Bijl, and Schnabel, "Same-Sex Sexual Behavior and Psychiatric Disorders: Findings from the Netherlands Mental Health Survey and Incidence Study [NEMESIS]," Archives of General Psychiatry, Vol. 58, pp. 85–91 [2001]); (3) active homosexuality deprives people of the possibility of heterosexual marriage and thereby having biological children of a conjugal union (engendering children with the person you love); and (4) that homosexual acts are morally wrong and therefore society ought to prohibit them as a way of promoting, directly and indirectly, the moral good of those who might be tempted to engage in them. Or one might argue homosexual activity undermines the well-being of *society*, because society depends on certain institutions, such as the family, and these institutions in turn depend on certain moral dispositions in the citizenry, which are incompatible with the acceptance of the case for the active homosexual lifestyle. On these kinds of issues, see Christopher Wolfe, *Homosexuality and American Public Life* (Dallas, TX: Spence, 1999) and *Same-Sex Matters* (Spence, 2000).

active homosexuality undermines that well-being, then society has reasonable grounds to discourage or even prohibit that lifestyle. The validity
of this argument turns on the truth or falsity of the allegations about the
unrepentant homosexual lifestyle, that is, on whether "homophobia" (in
the sense of moral objections to homosexual conduct) "is an unfounded
prejudice."

Now Raz has asserted that the demand for "full citizenship" somehow
makes the argument about the worth or value of the unrepentant homosexual lifestyle irrelevant, but nowhere does he justify this assertion. The
earlier argument about the status of imprisoned felons suggests that it is
wrong. It is true that imprisoned felons (e.g., murderers, rapists, embezzlers) differ from active homosexuals, in that the former directly assault
the rights of others, while the latter harm others indirectly or only themselves. But where has Raz shown that such a distinction is relevant, much
less crucial, to the point at issue, that is, the legitimacy of government
intervention? The argument respecting imprisoned felons, to the extent
that it is valid, demonstrates one of two things: either (1) full citizenship is
perfectly compatible with prohibiting people from acting in certain ways,
and punishing them, or (2) the granting of full citizenship is not always
good. It is open to Raz, to show why it is appropriate for government to
deny full citizenship (or to subject those who are fully citizens to some
punishment or civil disability) in cases involving direct assault on the rights
of others and not appropriate to do the same in cases "merely" involving
the well-being of citizens themselves (and society less directly). But I do
not see that he has made (or even tried to make) any such argument in
this chapter.

For the record, I would concede the prudent public policy demands
that a government that tries to restrict homosexual acts and to educate its
citizenry as to the disorder implicit in the homosexual orientation ought
to make it clear to its citizens that this involves no depreciation of the
intrinsic value of those who have a homosexual orientation or, for that
matter, those who actively practice a homosexual lifestyle. In fact, the
basis for the government's action is an intense concern for the well-being,
moral and otherwise, of *all* its citizens, including homosexuals. Such a
government should give no reasonable ground for any citizens, including
active homosexuals, to believe that it depreciates them. Naturally, active
homosexuals, disagreeing with the government's assessment of the moral
character of their actions, are unlikely to believe in the benevolence of the
government. But then neither do many people who break the law and are

punished for it. What counts is whether there are *reasonable grounds* for their "lack of trust" – and that turns precisely on whether "homophobia" is, or is not, an "unfounded prejudice."

LIBERAL TYRANNY

I want to conclude by observing that Raz's argument may be an invitation to a form of liberal tyranny. According to Raz, it is not only criminalization of homosexual acts that constitutes a denial of full citizenship and is therefore wrong. He says that this denial of full citizenship extends also to "manifestations of bigotry" that are "socially widespread," such as (1) discrimination against active homosexuals in private as well as public employment, (2) voluntary (as well as legal) censorship of media portrayal of gay conduct and its culture, and (3) social hostility to public displays of homosexual affection.

On Raz's analysis, therefore, it appears that parents (to avoid employment discrimination) must tolerate active homosexuals teaching their children in public schools, and perhaps even in private schools. Their opposition to this – not so much with respect to possible seduction, but primarily and much more importantly with respect to the formation of their children's moral ideals[41] – is itself intolerable in Raz's liberal state.

Even *voluntary* censorship – not just "officially sanctioned" censorship – of gay conduct and culture in the public media is contrary to the requirement of according "full citizenship" to gays and lesbians. This seems to translate, practically, into an *obligation* of the media to portray gay conduct and culture favorably – or at least neutrally, in a way that "normalizes" such activity.

---

[41] The mention of seduction usually brings complaints of "bigotry" (see, e.g., the letters in *The Wall Street Journal* of March 3, 1994), but the danger of seduction, given the existence of groups like the North American Man–Boy Love Association who *call for* "intergenerational intimacy" cannot be dismissed out of hand. (But the ground for discrimination in such cases would not be homosexual orientation per se.) The stronger argument against school employment of active homosexuals, in my opinion, is the likelihood that many active homosexuals, far from being predators, will be "nice guys." And parents with traditional moral views reasonably oppose the hiring of such people in a school for precisely the same reason they would oppose hiring racists or Nazis who were "nice people": children's views of morality are affected by the superficially attractive qualities of people they meet and like, and therefore moral education can be seriously deformed if children develop personal relations of respect and affection with people who have immoral opinions or publicly support immoral conduct. And, for the same reasons, parents could also reasonably object to the hiring of teachers who support homosexual conduct, or who engage in or support immoral heterosexual activity, e.g., cohabitation.

Any lack of freedom of gays and lesbians to engage in public displays of homosexual affection similar to those employed by heterosexuals (presumably things such as kissing and holding hands)[42] is likewise seen as intolerable. The fact that it does not matter whether this "manifestation of bigotry" is "officially sanctioned or socially widespread" suggests that even *social* hostility to such practices would be incompatible with Raz's liberalism.

Raz's principles, then, in seeking to expand the freedom of gays and lesbians, clearly contract the freedom of other citizens. It is not clear how Raz would like to see such constraints enforced, but his remarks on courts in another section of the paper should at least raise some concerns that judges might be given discretion to enforce them.[43]

Raz may legitimately argue that there is nothing wrong with perfectionistic liberals like himself refusing to tolerate certain kinds of intolerant actions. But what he cannot validly argue, it seems to me, is that "the case I am making does not depend on the fact that homophobia is an unfounded prejudice."[44] In fact, that is precisely the fact on which his argument does turn.

CONCLUSION

Raz concludes by posing what he calls a "catch-22" situation for moral paternalistic coercion:

If I enjoy full citizenship the government can use coercive paternalism against me where this is justified by right reason. However, if it pursues moral paternalism

---

[42] Traditionalists might distinguish between their attitudes toward mild but public, physical displays of affection on the part of (1) heterosexuals, and (2) homosexuals on the grounds that the former represent steps toward fuller sexual acts that are immoral or moral depending on their circumstances, while the latter represent steps toward fuller sexual acts always and everywhere immoral.

[43] I pointed out, in an earlier article on Raz, his omission of a concern for limits on *courts* in his discussion of the doctrine of liberty (as if courts were always protectors of liberties, though they are capable of being a threat to liberties). I have no doubt that Professor Raz would recognize that the doctrine of liberty requires limits on courts, as well as the other departments of government, but I do not think it is unfair to say that his omission of this point reflected a certain habit of mind of contemporary liberals. Some American judges would like to use Raz's arguments for non-discrimination in ways that deny traditional individuals and groups important aspects of liberty. See "Being Worthy of Trust: A Response to Joseph Raz" in *Natural Law, Liberalism, and Morality*, pp. 132–33, and Justice Antonin Scalia's opinion in *Romer v. Evans* 517 U.S. 620 (1996).

[44] Raz, "Liberty and Trust," p. 126.

against me it will, by definition, be preventing me from following my way of life, and it denies the validity of propositions I hold true and which underpin my way of life. If it does so, however, it denies me full citizenship. In short, the eschewing of moral paternalism is required to secure people full citizenship, and quite apart from the fact that it is the duty of government to grant its subject full citizenship, it cannot resort to moral paternalism for by doing so it undercuts its right to do so, for it loses the trust of those against whom coercion is used.[45]

But this argument is finally unpersuasive.

First, Raz has never given a sound reason why moral paternalism ought to be treated differently from other kinds of paternalism, such as seatbelt laws or motorcycle helmet laws, which "prevent me from following my way of life" no less than moral paternalism. The acceptance of non-moral coercive paternalism shows that there is nothing *intrinsically* wrong with preventing people from following their ways of life or with denying the validity of propositions they hold true or which even underpin their way of life.

Second, Raz has not been clear as to what constitutes full citizenship, and the example of non-moral coercive paternalism (e.g., seatbelt laws) shows that either (1) full citizenship is compatible with punishment and restrictions, or (2) granting full citizenship to all is not a necessary moral requirement of government.

Third, Raz never proves that resort to moral paternalism undercuts the relevant form of trust, since he concedes that a refusal to trust that is unreasonable does not undercut government's legitimacy; and he has not shown that those coerced by moral paternalism have reasonable grounds for considering that the government does not consider them as people who matter in their own right, whose fate is of intrinsic value. The opposition of a government to a group's beliefs and way of life, as the example of non-moral coercive paternalism (or, for that matter, even the example of non-paternalistic coercive regulation) again shows, is perfectly compatible with – indeed, may be the very way of expressing – its deep concern for the value and fate of that group, as well as the rest of society.

Precisely because Raz rightly maintains his position that feelings of depreciation (denial of equal concern and respect) must be objective – based on reasonable grounds – his attempt to delegitimize discrimination

---

[45] Ibid.,"Liberty and Trust," pp. 127–28.

on grounds of sexual orientation, without recourse to assumptions about the moral right and wrong of homosexual acts, is a failure. Moral paternalism is based, not on a depreciation of citizens, but on a desire to assist them in living morally valuable lives. As such, perfectionistic liberals should recognize its value, and retreat from their unwarranted embracing of the harm principle.

6

"Offensive Liberalism"

Macedo and "Liberal" Education

Diversity and Distrust[1] is part of Stephen Macedo's ongoing project of describing and defending a robust "transformative" liberalism. One of its chief purposes is to demonstrate the harmony between John Rawls's political liberalism (free of commitment to any "comprehensive" philosophical or theological views) and a liberalism with a strong commitment to shape its citizens' moral character, that is, to shape them into (political) liberals. In other words, liberalism can be both "neutral," with respect to substantive comprehensive philosophical and theological views, and also deeply committed to encouraging the formation of civic virtues essential to this "political liberalism." *Diversity and Distrust* is the part of the project that defends public education as an essential element in that transformative undertaking and that makes an argument for limiting parental rights to control education, especially the rights of those parents who do not fully embrace liberalism, such as fundamentalists – all of this, without committing itself to any particular comprehensive views.

In this chapter, I argue that Macedo's book fails to accomplish its objective. It is true that it shows the harmony between Rawls's political liberalism and his own transformative liberalism, but it does so only by offering a fine example of how Rawlsian political liberalism is really a comprehensive liberalism. And in the final analysis, it shows how this "offensive liberalism" is a significant threat to freedom.[2]

---

[1] Stephen Macedo, *Diversity and Distrust: Civic Education in a Multicultural Democracy* (Cambridge, MA: Harvard University Press, 2000).

[2] Nor is Macedo's book the only example of such offensive liberalism. On educational issues, Macedo is only one of a significant number of contemporary liberals who make

DIVERSITY AND DISTRUST

Diversity and Distrust, Macedo says in his preface, is about "liberalism's transformative ambitions."[3] Liberals have too often uncritically valued diversity and difference, "but the core claim of this book is that diversity needs to be kept in its place," limited by a "liberal educative project that shapes diversity for civic purposes."[4] "Liberal democratic public institutions count on shaping wider social norms and expectations so that people are gently encouraged to behave in ways that are broadly supportive of our shared civic project."[5] That is, liberalism wants (in a tough-minded but gentle manner) to make us and our children, if not liberals, at least not a threat to liberalism. Illiberal religions – for example, fundamentalist and pre–Vatican II Catholicism – are the main threat to liberal societies, and so the "success of our civic project relies upon a transformative project that includes the remaking of our moral and religious communities."[6] The chief arena in which this battle is fought is public education.

In Part I of the book, Macedo reviews the history of American public education and defends the "basic contours of the Court's jurisprudence" since World War II against charges of hostility to religion, arguing candidly that "maintaining an educational establishment that teaches our children that important public issues can be deliberated upon without considering religious questions is itself part of the education for liberal democratic citizenship properly understood."[7] But Macedo also criticizes John Dewey's "civic totalism," arguing that liberalism itself must accommodate some religious and philosophical pluralism.[8]

Part II of *Diversity and Distrust* takes up the objections of some contemporary Protestant fundamentalists to public schooling. Macedo examines *Mozert v. Hawkins*, in which Tennessee fundamentalists sought exemption from a public school reading program, claiming that it advanced religious views hostile to their own (secular humanism), by

---

strong claims for liberalism to direct the education of children, in the name of autonomy, even in ways that very substantially curtail or override parental rights in education. See, for example, Amy Gutmann, *Democratic Education* (Princeton, NJ: Princeton University Press, 1987), Eamon Callann, *Creating Citizens: Political Education and Liberal Democracy* (Oxford: Clarendon Press, 1997), and Meira Levinson, *The Demands of Liberal Education* (Oxford: Oxford University Press, 1999).

[3] Macedo, *Diversity and Distrust*, p. xi.
[4] p. 3.
[5] Ibid., p. x.
[6] Ibid.
[7] Ibid., p. 121–22.
[8] Ibid., p. 139.

exposing their children to diverse religious beliefs. Macedo concedes "that the mandatory reading program interferes with the *Mozert* parents' ability to teach their children their particular religious views," but defends the decision to deny them exemptions.[9]

In a key chapter, Macedo takes up the question of how we can justify our common civic project. He quickly dismisses arguments that rely on the definition of some objective human good or on a comprehensive liberalism based on "the value of individual moral autonomy and the importance of critically reflecting on all of one's inherited beliefs – political, religious, and otherwise."[10] In a modern world characterized by a diversity of religious and philosophical views, the only way to avoid being stuck with Hobbesian skepticism is to put aside debatable religious and philosophical positions and "attempt to justify the most basic matters of justice on grounds widely acceptable to reasonable people."[11] This approach turns out to be Rawlsian political liberalism and public reason.

Public reason is neutral because it is justified independent of comprehensive religious and philosophical views. Macedo acknowledges that it is not necessarily neutral in its effects, including the effects of advancing some religions at the expense of others. Totalistic faiths (like that of the fundamentalists and Catholicism), will be at a disadvantage, not because liberalism says that they are wrong as a matter of religious truth, but because they are wrong as a matter of political morality. Mutual respect requires us to give our fellow citizens reasons that they can share with us, that is, not reasons based on our comprehensive views, but "public reasons." It is possible, however, to "consider pleas of marginal groups for accommodation and exemptions" when we can do so "at a reasonable cost to civic aims and values."[12] But, Macedo points out, "[w]e need to remember how such people would behave if they had political power."[13]

Applying this analysis to the *Mozert* case, Macedo argues that there is no reason to provide "religious fundamentalists with a right to shield their children from the fact of reasonable pluralism.... Each of us can reasonably be asked to surrender some control over our own children for the sake of reasonable common efforts to ensure that all future citizens

---

[9] Ibid., p. 162.
[10] Ibid., p. 166.
[11] Ibid., p. 168.
[12] Ibid., pp. 189, 195.
[13] Ibid., p. 197.

learn the minimal prerequisites of citizenship."[14] Moreover, "awareness of alternative ways of life is a prerequisite not only of citizenship, . . . but also of being able to make the most basic life choices."[15] This intransigence is justified, therefore, because "the political basics are at stake here: toleration and knowledge of our society's diversity."[16] Fundamentalists must be satisfied with the right to challenge the reading program on the grounds that it was unbalanced and heavily biased against their religion, which would be a legitimate objection.

In Part III, Macedo takes up questions of school reform. He emphasizes the civic purposes of public schooling: inculcating "liberal virtues of toleration, openness, self-criticism, and mutual respect," which are "values that overarch more particular communities."[17] Parents do have a right to subject children to efforts to inculcate their visions of good character, but

> [w]hat is crucial from a liberal standpoint is that no one educational authority should totally dominate: that children acquire a measure of distance on all claims to truth in order to be able to think critically about our inclusive political ideals and detect conflicts between those inclusive ideals and their more particular moral and religious convictions.[18]

School choice (which is most defensible in troubled urban school systems) is not the general answer to current problems of public education, which are best met by making public schools smaller, lesser centralized, and less bureaucratized. There is no need to turn away from the common school ideal, although it is possible that some voucher programs would be useful, as long as they are "accompanied by public conditions and regulations" that "have the effect of excluding pervasively sectarian institutions."[19]

Macedo concludes by arguing that "[r]ecent versions of liberalism have tended to put so much emphasis on the definition and defense of the most basic rights and principles of justice that they have neglected the wider set of somewhat less basic principles and institutions that are nevertheless crucial to the health of a liberal democratic society."[20] We need to "adopt

---

[14] Ibid., p. 202.
[15] Ibid.
[16] Ibid., p. 203
[17] Ibid., pp. 233–34.
[18] Ibid., p. 238.
[19] Ibid., pp. 270, 271.
[20] Ibid., p. 278.

a more judgmental liberalism, one that is prepared to make and defend
moral judgments about the way that people use their rights."[21]

DISTRUSTING *DIVERSITY AND DISTRUST*

Diversity and Distrust is an important statement of contemporary liberalism, especially because of its recognition of the importance of citizen
character. Like any other form of government, liberalism cannot be indifferent to the ideas and moral values of its citizens, and it must make efforts
to secure the kind of civic qualities on which the well-being of the nation
is dependent. Macedo is admirably candid about the character–shaping
needs and intentions of a vital liberalism.

Macedo also makes substantial efforts to state his opponents' cases
fairly, and he is willing to acknowledge facts that other liberals would
gloss over. For example, he is very straightforward in admitting the considerable degree of nativism and anti-Catholicism that played roles in
the establishment of the American system of common schools. He also
provides a somewhat balanced evaluation of current public schools, recognizing not only their strengths, but their weaknesses as well.

In the end, however, *Diversity and Distrust* fails to make a persuasive
case for the "tough-minded" liberalism he advocates. His recognition of
the importance of character is undercut by the narrowness of his views
about its content. His attempts, following Rawls, to distinguish between
a "political" and a "comprehensive" liberalism are unsuccessful. And his
brand of liberalism exemplifies the danger of liberal tyranny.

Liberal Regimes and Character

Modern liberals often ignore the importance of character for maintaining
a healthy liberalism. This flows from their understanding of the nature
of liberalism. Liberalism emerged as a reaction to the religious wars that
accompanied the Protestant Reformation, and it sought to secure peace
and security for nations and citizens by narrowing the range of legitimate
government concerns and especially by putting religious questions off
limits.

Contemporary liberals – most notably John Rawls – have expanded
this strategy by putting moral as well as religious questions off limits.

---

[21] Ibid.

Government is not to act on the basis of any "comprehensive" philosophical or religious beliefs. It should not premise its action on the superiority of any particular way of life. Rawls's *A Theory of Justice* and his later *Political Liberalism* spawned a generation of liberal works that touted "neutrality" as an essential requirement of liberalism.[22]

But neutrality seems to dictate that government ought not to concern itself with the character of the citizenry. Government's responsibility was limited to protecting fundamental rights and to guaranteeing the essential requirements of equality, setting the conditions for people to make their own choices about what kind of people they want to be.

Beginning with his *Liberal Virtues*, Macedo has argued that a liberal regime cannot be indifferent to the character of its citizens.[23] *Diversity and Distrust* carries that theme forward, insisting that a "political liberalism" can have only a qualified neutrality.[24] It cannot be neutral on the question of liberalism itself or its essential prerequisites, for example, tolerance and mutual respect for fellow citizens who have profoundly different comprehensive views.

Macedo is right that a healthy liberal government should foster a certain form of tolerance and mutual respect (although I will argue below that it is a form different from the one advocated by Macedo), but I want to criticize the narrowness of Macedo's concern for "liberal virtue."

The argument that regimes require certain qualities in their citizens is as old as political science. Aristotle makes that argument in his *Politics*, contending that democratic governments should try to educate their citizens as democrats.[25] But there is another part of Aristotle as well, one that

---

[22] John Rawls, *A Theory of Justice* (Cambridge, MA: Belknap Press/Harvard University Press, 1971) and *Political Liberalism* (New York: Columbia University Press, 1993). These works also had a significant influence on legal thought, such as Ronald Dworkin's *Taking Rights Seriously* (Cambridge, MA: Harvard University Press, 1977) and Bruce Ackerman's *Social Justice and the Liberal State* (New Haven, CT: Yale University Press, 1980).

[23] Stephen Macedo, *Liberal Virtues* (Oxford: Clarendon Press, 1990).

[24] Rawls himself makes this explicit in *Political Liberalism*, pp. 191–94.

[25] "But of all the things which I have mentioned that which most contributes to the permanence of constitutions is the adaptation of education to the form of government.... The best laws, though sanctioned by every citizen of the state, will be of no avail unless the young are trained by habit and education in the spirit of the constitution, if the laws are democratical, democratically, or oligarchically, if the laws are oligarchical." Aristotle, *Politics*, Book V, 9, 1310a12–18 in *The Basic Works of Aristotle*, Richard McKeon, Ed. (New York: Random House, 1941), p. 1251.

is not reflected in *Diversity and Distrust*, namely, the need to moderate the regime:

Neither should we forget the mean, which at the present day is lost sight of in perverted forms of government; for many practices which appear to be democratical are the ruin of democracies, and many which appear to be oligarchical are the ruin of oligarchies. Those who think that all virtue is to be found in their own party principles push matters to extremes; they do not consider that disproportion destroys a state...[26]

Governments in the real world are always imperfect, and pushing their principles to an extreme does not support, but rather endangers them.

Macedo is right to recognize the need for liberal governments to educate their citizens in liberal principles. What he fails to acknowledge is the importance of *moderating* those principles as well. Indeed, the whole Rawlsian project (of which Macedo's work is a variant), it seems to me, is an effort to purify modern liberal democracy of any "foreign" (i.e., non-liberal democratic) elements, to construct a perfectly consistent form of liberalism. In doing so, it pushes democratic and liberal principles to an extreme, and endangers liberal democracy. So, for example, the principle of citizens "living as they like" has been substantially embodied in contemporary political theory (e.g., Rawls and Macedo), liberal legal theory (e.g., Ronald Dworkin and David A. J. Richards[27]), and constitutional doctrines of "privacy" (e.g., the Supreme Court's abortion jurisprudence.[28]) A student of Aristotle, on the other hand, might consider laws promoting "public morality" – which restrict personal liberty in some ways – a useful "balance" in a democratic regime.[29]

---

[26] *Politics*, Book V, 9, 1309b18–23, 31–35 (McKeon, p. 1251). This applies not only to "practices," but also to education. The passage on education in the *Politics* continues: "Now, to have been educated in the spirit of the constitution is not to perform the actions in which oligarchs or democrats delight, but those by which the existence of an oligarchy of a democracy is made possible.... And in democracies of the more extreme type there has arisen a false idea of freedom which is contradictory to the true interests of the state.... In such democracies every one lives as he pleases, or in the words of Euripides, 'according to his fancy.' But this is all wrong: men should not think it slavery to live according to the rule of the constitution, for it is their salvation." *Politics*, Book V, 9, 1310a19–22, 25–27, 32–36 (McKeon, p. 1251).

[27] Ronald Dworkin, *Taking Rights Seriously* (*supra*, n. 2) and *Freedom's Law* (Cambridge, MA: Harvard University Press, 1996); David A. J. Richards, *Toleration and the Constitution* (New York: Oxford University Press, 1986).

[28] *Roe v. Wade* 410 U.S. 113 (1973) and *Planned Parenthood of Southeastern Pennsylvania v. Casey* 505 U.S. 833 (1992).

[29] See, for example, Harry Clor, *Obscenity and Public Morality* (Chicago, IL: University of Chicago, 1969), and *Public Morality and Liberal Society* (South Bend, IN: University of

Macedo (following Rawls) talks about liberalism as if there were only two general kinds, namely, Rawls's (and his own) "political liberalism," and "comprehensive liberalism"(e.g., "Kantian autonomy or Millian individuality").[30] But the range of forms of liberalism may be understood more broadly to include communitarian and perfectionist liberals.[31] These different forms of liberalism may be placed on a spectrum from most to least liberal, their place being determined by how far they push the core principles of liberalism, especially liberty and equality. But the most liberal theory is not necessarily the best liberal theory. From an Aristotelian perspective the best liberalism would be a qualified or moderate liberalism, just as Aristotle seems to suggest that the best democracy is a somewhat less democratic democracy.[32]

Macedo's recognition and forceful articulation of the need for liberalism to cultivate a certain citizen character loses sight of the need to leaven "liberal citizen traits" with character traits, such as moderation and self-control, that are more typical of other forms of government.

Futility of "Public Reason"

Diversity and Distrust rests squarely on Rawls's concept of "public reason," and is therefore undercut by the deficiencies of that concept. As I have argued above, the concept of public reason is either so broad that it includes natural law arguments (vitiating its use to justify a political liberalism excluding comprehensive views) or so narrow – especially in the Rawlsian sense of public reason – that it provides no useful guidance for political life.[33]

Macedo calls for liberal regimes to shape the character of their citizens, encouraging them to be liberals (e.g., to be tolerant, respectful of other persons). However, this does not violate the requirements for public reason, he says, because the "point is not to promote a comprehensive philosophical doctrine of autonomy or individuality, but to make sure that

---

Notre Dame Press, 1996) and his contribution to *How Democratic Is America?* Robert Goldwin (Chicago, IL: Rand McNally, 1971).

[30] Macedo, *Diversity and Distrust*, p. 169.

[31] Joseph Raz, *The Morality of Freedom* (Oxford: Clarendon Press, 1986); William Galston, *Liberal Purposes: Goods, Virtues, and Diversity in the Liberal State* (New York: Cambridge University Press, 1991).

[32] *Politics*, Book IV, 4 and Book VI, 4 (McKeon, pp. 1212–13, 1268–70).

[33] See chapter two, also published in a slightly different form, with Robert George, as "Natural Law and Liberal Public Reason," *American Journal of Jurisprudence* 42 (1997): 31.

no authority imposes an intellectual tyranny on children, which would thwart their right to freedom."[34]

In practice, it is doubtful that the distinction between political and comprehensive liberalism can be maintained. Macedo himself honestly says that "[n]o doubt some of the distinctions that separate a civic liberalism from a comprehensive liberalism are fairly subtle."[35] He then proves how subtle they are by making the following statements: (1) "A basic aim of civic education should be to impart to all children the ability to reflect critically on their personal and public commitments for the sake of honoring our shared principles of liberal justice and equal rights for all," and (2) "Public schoolteachers and authors of material for public schools should avoid advancing the notion that children need to think about their religious beliefs critically for the sake of better understanding religious truth."[36] So all children should learn to think critically about their personal (including religious) commitments and beliefs for political purposes, but they should not be told that they need to do so for religious purposes. One is tempted to ask, "at what age can children be expected to grasp this subtle distinction successfully?" For that matter, it is tempting to ask whether for anyone, adults or children, the practical differences would amount to much.

Macedo notes that "it is tempting to say that the only real difference between civic and comprehensive liberalisms is that proponents of the latter are simply more candid in admitting that liberal institutions are based on an ideal of life as a whole, and that 'civil' toleration [religious toleration on political grounds] inevitably promotes 'religious' toleration [toleration as the correct religious position]." He rejects this contention on the ground that "political liberalism stands for a measure of restraint that would be unnatural for one committed to a vision of the good life as a whole informed by autonomy or individuality."[37] Yet he acknowledges that "[i]n practice these distinctions can be difficult to apply. It may well be that a public school program that teaches civil tolerance will have the effect of indirectly promoting religious tolerance."[38] What this suggests is that Macedo's arguments establish, not that "political liberalism" is essentially different from comprehensive liberalism, but that it is simply a milder version of comprehensive liberalism, one that accomplishes the

---

[34] Macedo, *Diversity and Distrust*, p. 238.
[35] Ibid., p. 239.
[36] Ibid.
[37] Macedo, *Diversity and Distrust*, p. 175.
[38] Macedo, *Diversity and Distrust*, p. 176.

same purposes, but more indirectly. (One wonders what Macedo would think of public actions that were facially neutral but that had indirect effects promoting *non-liberal* comprehensive views.)

The reasonable expectation we should have then, is that a civic education shaping citizens according to *political* liberalism will tend to produce more *comprehensively* liberal citizens. One hint of this can be found in Macedo's discussion of school reform, where he notes in passing that "families are no longer what they were. The proportion of stable two-parent families has declined considerably."[39] He also points out that there has been "a cultural shift with respect to our expectations for children: away from academic achievement and toward consumerism."[40] While the reasons for these trends are complex, it is reasonable to ask whether liberalism has played a role in these substantive changes in liberal democratic societies.

In a regime that stresses free choice, will there be a predictable pattern of substantive choices, suggesting that the regime may be more directive than it appears to be? The answer to this question will turn on one's theory of human psychology, and especially the relative power of reason and passions in most human beings. In general, liberal theorists tend toward one of two possible positions, both of which are somewhat optimistic: either (1) reason is the dominant force in human beings, and so, in choosing for themselves, they will generally exercise choice in a more or less rational manner, or at least in an increasingly rational manner over time, given human corrigibility,[41] or (2) (more commonly) human passions are the more powerful element of human psychology, but there is no reason to believe that choice according to passions will be harmful.[42]

A more classical view (say, Aristotelian or Thomistic) would consider human passions so powerful that, in the absence of social norms controlling them, they would likely dominate many human beings' choices, often diverting them from acting for good reasons. Thus, the classical view would find it unsurprising that a liberal regime of choice would tend to have certain substantive outcomes. For example, the proportion of stable two-parent families might decline considerably and the forces of consumerism might become very powerful.

---

[39] Macedo, *Diversity and Distrust*, p. 255.

[40] Macedo, *Diversity and Distrust*, p. 256.

[41] This is the progressive view of human beings that seems dominant in Mill's *On Liberty*, Elizabeth Rapaport, Ed. (Indianapolis, IN: Hackett, 1978).

[42] This is a view often underlying libertarian defenses of free speech rights to pornography. On this point, see Clor, *Obscenity and Public Morality* (*supra*, n.10), Chapter 3.

Consider the educative implications of political liberalism's attitude toward religion. Macedo characterizes political liberalism as a position "*above* our many *narrower* sectarianisms"; our common political morality, he says, "*overarches* our particularisms"; and we must attend to "tensions between particular moral and religious communities and our *larger* civic ambitions."[43] Liberalism, whether consciously or unconsciously, tends to establish the political horizon as the broadest one, within which other, more particular horizons are found. But Judaism, Christianity, and Islam, among other religions, have histories lasting centuries or millennia, and they are spread across the globe. On what ground can they reasonably be considered "narrower" or "smaller," more "particular" perspectives within the supposedly overarching, grand horizon of "political liberalism," a 35-year-old, late twentieth century perspective concentrated primarily in the Anglo-American academy? That political liberalism might be right, and the universalistic religions wrong, is a possibility. That political liberalism does not implicitly embrace, and promote, certain (liberal) comprehensive views is utterly implausible.

Dispensing With Consent

Political liberalism offers itself as a political theory that is necessary to obtain a genuine, stable peace and security within a system of social cooperation, a peace based on principle rather than a mere shifting balance of forces among competing comprehensive views, each threatening to pursue hegemony when social conditions permit it. Our liberties and fundamental rights are thereby thought to be secured more effectively by political liberalism. But political liberalism may, in fact, foster its own kind of tyranny.

What is the source of political liberalism's authority? Rawls and Macedo do not seem to propose that "we, the people" formally adopt political liberalism as the foundation for our form of government. It seems more probable – although it is not clear – that in some Dworkinian sense, they are proposing political liberalism as an "interpretation" of our current political arrangements. They can thus piggyback on the consent Americans gave to the Constitution.

It might be argued that Rawls and Macedo simply are proposing political liberalism, without necessarily maintaining that it carries political authority. I do not think that position is persuasive, however. Macedo,

---

[43] Macedo, *Diversity and Distrust*, pp. 222, 262, and 278 (emphasis added).

for example, takes up as a central question, "how should judges have decided the case of *Mozert v. Hawkins County Board of Education?*" His book – his elaboration of a "tough-minded" liberalism that sees no reason to permit fundamentalists to exempt their children from public school teaching that undermines their religious beliefs – is the answer to that question.

Macedo says that American judges were right to deny accommodation to the *Mozert* parents on the grounds that they were asserting "a totalistic belief system that led them to refuse to acknowledge the political authority of reasons that could be shared with their fellow citizens."[44] Of course, it is Rawls and Macedo (and perhaps, though not likely, the appeals court judges) who denied that the fundamentalists' reasons "could be shared with their fellow citizens." The fundamentalists would undoubtedly have been very willing to share their reasons with their fellow citizens, but Macedo and Rawls have declared those reasons off limits. There is no compelling evidence that most other Americans would side with Macedo and Rawls in that difference of opinion.

Moreover, Macedo explicitly considers the question of what legal standard the Supreme Court should employ to decide cases involving claims for religious exemptions from public laws, and, based on his arguments regarding political liberalism, he proposes "a more flexible intermediate standard" for such cases[45] – a standard flexible enough to leave the judges with plenty of discretion to decide cases according to . . . well, according to whatever they consider the best version of our political principles. Political liberalism is not intended to be simply a theory. It is intended to be a standard for political action in American democracy.

It is not surprising that this is revealed especially in sections dealing with judicial power, since it is much more likely that advocates of political liberalism could achieve their goals by inducing judges to accept such an approach than it would be for them to persuade the political branches. The latter are not likely to find the arguments persuasive. Would their constituents? Would the American people consent to political liberalism? Any answer to that question is pure speculation, but it is hard for me to believe that a majority, much less a supermajority, of Americans could be induced to vote for a proposition that required them, in some serious sense, to put their deepest comprehensive moral beliefs "off-limits" in political decision making.

---

44 Macedo, *Diversity and Distrust*, p. 196.
45 Macedo, *Diversity and Distrust*, p. 201.

Accordingly, a much more promising strategy for political liberals (following the pathway blazed by Ronald Dworkin[46]) would be to persuade judges that political liberalism is already somehow implicit in our political arrangements, as the theory that "makes sense out of" what we already say and do.

On the kinds of questions involved in *Mozert*, judges would find ready allies among the intelligentsia and those whose views they largely shape: journalists and the media in general, artists and entertainers, academics, teachers in the public sector, and unions – in short, "the new class."[47] This alliance, invoking the principle of "judicial independence," is usually able (especially by its power to frame public questions) to wield the requisite political power to frustrate the very limited political checks on judges.

Macedo's book, then, falls within the broad outlines of the modern efforts – successful on so many occasions – of political liberals to obtain through courts the goals they are unable to secure through the ordinary political process, that is to say, the goals that they are unable to obtain democratically.

Offensive Liberalism

At times, *Diversity and Distrust* sounds as if it were focused on defending liberalism against enemies that are attacking it. For example, Macedo argues that "most Americans do not experience a profound tension or split between their religious and political convictions *because they are not inclined to impose their religious beliefs on others through politics.*"[48] This conjures up an image of fundamentalists engaging in a political offensive that somehow uses the political process to spread their own religious beliefs throughout the populace.

Should fundamentalist mobs break into other churches to obstruct their worship, or if fundamentalists attempt to force other citizens to pray, they would rightly be subject to the force of just liberal laws that protect our religious liberties. Even to invoke such visions, however, is to realize that these are not the issues in our society or in *Diversity and Distrust*. The key issue here, it turns out, is the scope of religious believers' rights to inculcate their own religious beliefs in their own children. And the battle that is the

---

[46] Dworkin, *Taking Rights Seriously* (*supra* n. 22), especially Chapters 4–5; see also his *Law's Empire* (Cambridge, MA: Belknap Press/Harvard University Press, 1986).

[47] On the new class, see John C. McAdams, "Testing the Theory of the New Class," *The Sociological Quarterly*, 28 (1) (March 1987): 23.

[48] Macedo, *Diversity and Distrust*, p. 227 (emphasis added).

focus of *Diversity and Distrust* is occasioned by Macedo's insistence on limiting those rights, on the basis of a right, and perhaps a duty, of liberal government to expose children to competing worldviews. We are dealing here, not with a liberalism on the defensive against attacks, but with an offensive, crusading liberalism.

Liberalism and the Need for Tolerance

The first ground for this liberal power is liberalism's requirement of tolerant citizens, that is, citizens who, for purposes of our shared political life, are capable of putting their own comprehensive views to the side and working with others on the basis of reasons we can share. But, Macedo argues, how can we hope for a tolerant citizenry, if citizens do not *know* other people who have different views and *learn* to have respect for them and cooperate with them? Only by experiencing the fact of differences and mingling with others who embody those differences are we likely to attain a genuinely tolerant society. Without that tolerance, liberal government is always fragile. And the most effective way to obtain that essential prerequisite of liberal government is the public school system.

The enemies of liberalism, then, are those who are not tolerant *and also* those who refuse to permit the necessary training for tolerance or who prevent the public school system from achieving its goal of teaching tolerance. For example: Vicki Frost, one of the fundamentalist parents who wanted to opt their children out of a public school reading program that exposed them to contrary religious beliefs in an "uncommitted, even-handed" way.[49] "This very exposure to diversity, they claimed, interfered with the free exercise of their religious beliefs by in effect denigrating the truth of their particular religious views."[50] Macedo candidly concedes that the mandatory reading program interferes with the *Mozert* parents' ability to teach their children their particular religious views: the

effects of a reading program that evenhandedly exposes children to religious and moral diversity may not be apparent from the perspective of those whose religious views have adjusted to the fundamental principles of our political order, but they are abundantly clear to people who hold certain religious views.[51]

Nonetheless, the parents' desire to shield their children from contrary religious views conflicts, according to Macedo, with the need to teach

---

[49] Macedo, *Diversity and Distrust*, p. 158.
[50] Ibid.
[51] Macedo, *Diversity and Distrust*, p. 162.

children "about the religious differences that peacefully coexist among their fellow citizens."[52] Religious fundamentalists have no "right to shield their children from the fact of reasonable pluralism."[53]

Is it empirically true that "exposure to diversity" – learning about other people's ideas – is essential in order to foster the tolerance that liberalism requires in its citizenry? Remember, the tolerance required is not a belief that all ideas are equally true or valuable, or even a belief that all people have the *moral* right to believe what they wish. It is a belief that other people have the *legal* or *political* right to believe and practice as they wish. If that is the political idea of toleration, on what grounds can it be maintained that exposure of children to religious ideas contrary to their families' deepest moral and religious beliefs is necessary? One can certainly imagine a case in which broad exposure to different ideas might be *useful* to foster tolerance. That it would be *necessary* seems implausible.

It is also hard even to conceive that contemporary liberal governments would be in any way significantly endangered by parents limiting their children's exposure to diversity. We live in a culture whose means of communication make it almost impossible to avoid exposure to a variety of ideas. It is only in very rare cases that parents even make the attempt to prevent exposure to all other ideas – the case of the "hyper-Amish," perhaps, in which parents would cut their children off from the outside world entirely (no TV, movies, magazines, newspapers, books, and – above all – friends and acquaintances).

The fact of the matter is that the fundamentalist children in Tennessee were in no danger of having no exposure to other ideas. Macedo points out that the parents had no objection to their going to a public school, which – entirely apart from curricular content – would guarantee that the children would have exposure to lots of ideas quite opposed to their families' religious beliefs – from the television shows talked about on the playground no less than from the newspaper articles discussed in history class. One wonders whether there is any evidence that the fundamentalists in *Mozert* were any less *politically* tolerant of others than non-fundamentalists – unless liberals were to tendentiously impose their own substantive liberal views of what tolerance means, such as abortion and homosexual rights and no voluntary public school prayer. Were nineteenth century American Catholics, including those thoroughly imbued with the "illiberal" Catholic teaching described by Macedo, in practice

---

[52] Macedo, *Diversity and Distrust*, p. 201.
[53] Macedo, *Diversity and Distrust*, p. 202.

less *politically* tolerant of their fellow citizens' rights? Macedo makes no case for a genuine threat to political tolerance from those he characterizes as holding views incompatible with liberalism. Only vague, unproven fears that fundamentalists are or might become less politically tolerant lie behind liberals' curtailing of parental rights to control the content of their children's education.

Liberalism and Freedom to Make Life's Basic Choices

There is a second ground for liberal insistence on teaching children about different religious views: "[t]he justification for some measure of public authority lies in the fact that children are not simply creatures of their parents, but are independent persons with their own lives to lead." This does not mean "that the public insists on acting as a third adoptive parent, but rather that governments and the democratic community recognize the moral independence of each individual and insist on due regard for that independence, even from parents."[54]

Public schools cannot teach or inculcate any religious views, but they can, and should, expose children to a variety of religious views. "[A]wareness of alternative ways of life is a prerequisite not only of citizenship . . . but also of being able to make the most basic life choices."[55] The goal of liberalism is to protect people's rights to *choose* – but how can people choose if they do not know the possible objects of choice? So liberalism should offer children knowledge of various offerings on their menu of life choices.

Moreover, Macedo argues, the evidence suggests that the civic virtues needed by modern democracies are nurtured "where individuals are enmeshed in a variety of cross-cutting, only partially overlapping patterns of association. These complex patterns of membership nurture broad forms of trust and cooperation not only among those in one's particular group, but among citizens as a whole." So, for example, the "homogeneity and tribalistic insularity of the Amish community is at odds with the pluralistic patterns of membership that contribute to liberal freedom and democratic civil society."[56]

The argument here seems to be that liberalism has to break down, indirectly at least, the tendency to have a single, coherent source of

---

[54] Macedo, *Diversity and Distrust*, p. 243.
[55] Macedo, *Diversity and Distrust*, p. 202.
[56] Macedo, *Diversity and Distrust*, p. 221.

self-identity. People should be encouraged to have multidimensional identities that contribute to identification with fellow citizens and therefore support liberal social cooperation and civic harmony.

Macedo develops this argument more fully in his discussion of school reform and civic values: the "multiplicity of our memberships and affiliations is itself an important element of civic education, for that multiplicity deters the tribalistic and unified identities that may go along with the deepest forms of communal affiliation but at the expense of breeding hostility to outsiders." So it is good that it "will be hard in a social structure like America's – pluralistic rather than tribalistic, characterized by cross-cutting rather than consistently reinforcing memberships – to settle comfortably and permanently on final answers to many of life's questions." According to this view, a "measure of alienation from any and all associations and commitments goes with modern freedom, and some will find this unnerving." In fact, Macedo concludes, "[i]t would truly be unfortunate if many people had psychological needs that could only be satisfied in all-encompassing associations. Then we would have to radically rethink the value of the liberal civic order explored here."[57]

Macedo is right, I think, that if we believe there *are* final answers to life's questions – if we are unwilling to concur in the contemporary liberal dogma that there are no final answers – we would indeed have to question *Macedo's* liberal civic order. Macedo describes these people in terms that suggest they are somewhat neurotic (their "peculiar psychological makeup means that they need deeper forms of membership than those that tend to be fostered by liberal civic life),"[58] but he is confident that "[m]ost people are not like that" and so we can tolerate having "havens outside the mainstream for those with peculiar needs."[59] But God help them if they come out of their havens, into the public schools, and object to their children being educated according to liberal pedagogy!

By this point, it seems pretty clear that the educational program demanded by Macedo's political liberalism is simply one form of comprehensive liberalism. The more Macedo expands the virtues that need to be inculcated in citizens in liberalism's transformative project, the more clearly those virtue are seen to be the virtues of comprehensive liberal philosophical positions. Macedo's claim that these qualities are chosen, not for their philosophical truth, but for their political value, is

---

[57] Macedo, *Diversity and Distrust*, p. 251.
[58] Macedo, *Diversity and Distrust*, p. 251, quoting Nancy Rosenblum.
[59] Ibid.

unpersuasive. Once the process goes as far as Macedo takes it, the only fair way to characterize the result is not, as he would have it, that political liberalism requires virtues that *happen to* correspond to the virtues promoted by comprehensive philosophical liberalism, but rather that political liberalism needs to promote philosophical liberalism, which simply breaks down the alleged distinction between the two.

Parental Rights

Macedo acknowledges a certain range of parental rights, and also says, rightly so, that they must be limited. Should parents want to immolate their children to propitiate their gods, for example, it would be perfectly reasonable for public authority to step in and prevent them from doing so. But establishing the principle that there are some limits on parental authority does not take us very far. What are those limits? How far do they extend?

Macedo's position on the power of government to overrule parental objections to the exposure of children to contrary religious views rests on unstated and undefended assumptions – a whole theory of child and adolescent psychological and moral development, in fact. For example, as to the issue of providing children with the menu of life's basic choices, is it truly necessary to qualify parental rights? Could we permit parents to control children's menus until age 18 and then permit their now-adult children to survey the larger menu as they choose at that time?

The assumption behind Macedo's position appears to be that it is necessary to provide the broader menu earlier. One ground for this might be that exposure to other ways of life at age 18 is too late: parental control up to that time would so dictate one set of answers to life's questions that the child would be incapacitated from "really" viewing the menu after age 18. But the goal implicit in this argument – that children be prepared to consider all life choices "objectively" at age 18 – is simply utopian. Nothing that government could do would achieve this, since we all carry with us (before and after age 18) the effects of many influences on us, parental and otherwise.

A more likely ground for intervention to limit parental rights to direct education might be that control by parents through age 18 would curtail the subsequent menu, as a *practical* matter, since certain forms of preparation before age 18 are necessary in order to pursue certain menu items. For example, Justice Douglas pointed out in his *Wisconsin v. Yoder* dissent that Amish opposition to high school education for their children might make it impossible for a child to pursue a dream of being "a pianist or an astronaut or an oceanographer."[60]

But this argument would prove too much, justifying very deep intrusions into family life. Parents are constantly making decisions that practically curtail future life choices for their children. If I refuse to pay for gymnastics lessons for my daughter on the grounds that the money would be better spent on a music class for her, that is likely to rule out any childhood dream that she will become a gymnast. If I live in an urban area, that will make it quite difficult for one of my children to become a farmer. If I choose to be a teacher rather than a lawyer, with the consequent financial implications, my childrens' practical opportunities will be curtailed in various ways. Can government intervene to counter all these choices, as well as their practical implications?

We rightly permit parents to make many decisions that have important practical implications curtailing the future choices their children can make, while limiting that power in extreme cases (e.g., by punishing child abuse, prohibiting child labor, or overriding parental objections to blood transfusions). But establishing as a *general principle* that the state may intervene in the family and curtail parental rights by offering children a menu of alternative lifestyles, with a view to maximizing their future range of choices, would be a principle radically undermining the rights of parents to direct the upbringing of their children.

Laying Out the Options Neutrally?

Even assuming that it is desirable to maximize children's options, is there a way to present life options to children, consistent with liberal neutrality? Political liberals maintain that they wish to curtail parental educational rights, not to favor one particular comprehensive view (e.g., comprehensive liberalism), but merely to facilitate citizens' genuine freedom of choice among lifestyles. Accordingly, the effort of liberals to expand the menu of options for children honors the appropriate requirements of liberal neutrality.

But does it? Let us look at one example relevant to current educational programs: sex education. At what age should children be presented with sexual options, and how full a range of those options should be presented? Political liberalism would limit the options in certain ways, of course: rape would be ruled out, as a violation of others' rights.

[60] 406 U.S. 205, at 244 (1972).

What about the full range of other options, running from sexual activity integrated (only) within indissoluble heterosexual marriage through a whole range of sexual lifestyles, to less or unconventional ones, including unrestricted promiscuity, homosexuality (in more and less monogamous forms), polygamy, and bestiality? Should these be presented as sexual "options" to adults, at age 18? Should they be offered to children at age 16? 14? 12? When are children "mature enough" to have these options described and make decisions about them? Do they all mature at the same time? If not (as is obviously the case), who can make the decision as to when maturity has been attained (and on what "neutral" grounds)?

More generally, are there times during adolescent development when young people are particularly susceptible to appeals to moral norms contrary to those of their parents? Can presentation of options be skewed by the lesser or greater degree of rebelliousness (justified and unjustified) felt by most adolescents at certain times?

If younger children tend to adhere to parental views simply on the basis of their close personal identity with their parents, and if the normal course of moral development is for children to "appropriate" these views – or other views – for themselves at some age, moving from reliance on authority to self-reflective morality, what is the best time and best way to expose them to different moral views? Is there any one "best" time, or will it be determined in part by other, variable factors? For example, will adolescents' openness to their parents' more developed explanations of sexual moral norms that have earlier been accepted simply on the basis of parental authority – and their susceptibility to contrary views communicated directly and indirectly by magazines, television and movies, friends, and teachers – be affected by whether there are current tensions between them and parents over a multitude of other matters, including curfews, driving habits, family chores, and drinking or smoking? Timing in pedagogy is crucial, and the widely varying forms and pace of adolescent development make general rules about pedagogical decisions problematic.

Liberal theories of education tend to have the intellectualistic cast of John Stuart Mill's *On Liberty*, which has often been described as looking at life as a sort of graduate seminar. Children are implicitly viewed as carefully examining a "menu" of options, gradually sorting through the various arguments for this or that way of life, and trying to decide which one to adopt. There is strikingly little attention to the role of the passions and emotions and their interaction with highly contingent events (what particularly is going on in this child's life at this time), and how they affect such decision making.

Answers to these questions turn on very controversial theories of child and adolescent psychological and moral development – as well as broader theories of human nature, especially the role of reason and passions – which are likely to have important substantive implications about choices young people make. No one set of answers can be justified on the basis of a merely political liberalism. Comprehensive views, consciously or unconsciously, will shape profoundly important pedagogical decisions.

Neutrality in *Mozert*?

The above arguments assume that the reading program at issue in *Mozert* genuinely had the purpose of offering choices to children, rather than suggesting answers. Macedo focuses on the parents' objections to mere exposure to a diversity of viewpoints, because that is the interesting theoretical question he wants to pursue. But Macedo himself honestly admits that there are questions about the program. The parents "might have objected, say, that the purported 'diversity' of views in the readers lacks respectful depictions of religious ways of life. They might have charged the readers with combining glowing portrayals of secularist, this-worldly ideals of life and disparaging portraits of more conservative forms of religious belief."[61] Macedo points out in a footnote that "of 47 stories referring to, or growing out of, Religions (including Islam, Buddhism, American Indian religion and nature worship), only three were Christian, and none Protestant."[62]

But the problems are even deeper than those acknowledged by Macedo. Macedo thinks that liberalism has met its obligation of neutrality on comprehensive views in *Mozert* if students are free to speak up about their religious views and if "there is no compulsion to affirm or deny a religious belief."[63] "By simply leaving aside the religious questions as such, Lively rightly leaves the school door open to reasonable fundamentalists – that is, to those willing to acknowledge *for civic purposes* the authority of public reasonableness."[64] Macedo rejects the proposition that "the only real difference between civic and comprehensive liberalisms is that proponents of the latter are simply more candid in admitting that liberal institutions are

---

[61] Macedo, *Diversity and Distrust*, p. 203.
[62] Macedo, *Diversity and Distrust*, p. 314, n. 12.
[63] Macedo, *Diversity and Distrust*, p. 175, quoting Appeals Court Judge Lively.
[64] Ibid. (italics in original).

based on an ideal of life as a whole, and that 'civil' toleration inevitably promotes 'religious' toleration." The crux is not candor, he says, but the fact that "political liberalism stands for a measure of restraint that would be unnatural for one committed to a vision of the good life as a whole informed by autonomy or individuality." Political liberalism avoids "taking a stand, as a political matter, on the question of religious truth."[65]

It turns out that the real difference between civic and comprehensive liberalism can be described this way: civic liberalism has the *effect* of advancing comprehensive liberalism, but it does not choose this deliberately on religious grounds. That is, civic liberalism advances comprehensive liberalism *indirectly*. (I consider it doubtful that one could go so far as to describe this approach as advancing liberalism "unintentionally," given the congruence that "happens to" exist between the liberal views that are advanced and the supposedly incidental comprehensive liberal views held by most theorists of political liberalism.)

Macedo cites one of the poems in the readers the *Mozert* parents complained about, "The Blind Men and the Elephant." This poem portrays blind men feeling an elephant, who "arrive at laughably various judgments about what the whole must be like." The poem concludes:

> And so these men of Indostan
> Disputed loud and long,
> Each in his own opinion
> Exceeding stiff and strong,
> Though each was partly in the right
> And all were in the wrong!
>
> Moral
> So oft in theologic war,
> The disputants, I ween,
> Rail on in utter ignorance
> Of what each other mean,
> And prate about an Elephant
> Not one of them has seen![66]

Macedo's comment on this poem is that it could be taught as advancing either a political or religious form of toleration. Either (1) it could be "an allegory about the burdens of judgment and the difficulty of arriving

---

[65] Ibid.
[66] Macedo, *Diversity and Distrust*, pp. 176–77.

at publicly justifiable religious truths," or (2) "it could be understood to assert as a religious matter that anyone who thinks they have religious truth is really in ignorance," that is, a religiously based lesson in skepticism.[67]

But Macedo simply cannot reasonably read the poem in the former, ambiguous way, holding out the hope that it is merely an allegory about the burdens of judgment (unless one were willing to concede that the Rawlsian burdens of judgment argument is itself a form of religious skepticism, which Macedo would have to deny). It is *clearly* an assertion of a form of religious skepticism. (This observation is not undercut by its internal contradiction, so common to skeptical views: namely, that a criticism of various religious views on the ground that each is only a partial view of the whole is itself an assertion of knowledge about the whole, that is, a distinct claim to religious truth.) When Macedo goes on to argue that the *Mozert* parents "confuse" political arguments for religious toleration with religiously based arguments for skepticism or indifference regarding religion, the confusion is his. The parents are right that there is a slant in this particular case, and it seems likely that there is often a slant against religious fundamentalism in public education.[68]

Macedo goes on to give the only argument that can "save" this poem for political liberalism: the poem is not presented in the reader as true – it is simply "presented 'for what it is worth.'"[69] But Macedo rightly notes that "fundamentalist parents disposed to accept a political liberal settlement might well look with suspicion on the poem and the readers as a whole. One wonders how many depictions of fundamentalism the readers presented 'for whatever they are worth.'" Yes, one does. Recall the observation, noted above: "of 47 stories referring to, or growing out of, Religions (including Islam, Buddhism, American Indian religion and nature worship), only 3 were Christian, and none Protestant."[70]

What, then, is the basis for refusing the *Mozert* parents' claim to exemption from the reading class? It is that "the court decided that where explicitly religious views were expressed, as in the poem, the effect was only to present a possible point of view, not to teach that view as religious truth.

---

[67] Macedo, *Diversity and Distrust*, p. 177.

[68] It is tempting to say that this will be true of all minority views. But the fact is that very small minorities will probably get a much fairer hearing in public schools than will fundamentalists, since the latter are viewed by many people in education as a threat to freedom, while the former, not being a threat, can be viewed more benignly.

[69] Macedo, *Diversity and Distrust*, p. 177.

[70] Macedo, *Diversity and Distrust*, p. 314, n. 12.

Where a positive view on toleration was taught in the readers, it was one of civil rather than religious toleration."[71]

But this argument is too narrow. The court's contention, if it is to characterize the situation more fully, must be extended beyond "explicitly religious views" presented in the readers. It applies much more broadly to *the nature of the reading program as a whole*. The presentation in the readers (and in any school based on political liberalism) of a wide range of religious and nonreligious worldviews or perspectives must be taken as presenting only possible points of view, not any specific truth (religious or nonreligious). The deep problem with political liberalism is that that claim is unpersuasive.

Political Liberalism and a "Sociology of Knowledge"

Put to the side the question of whether the presentation of a wide range of conflicting answers to a question implies anything about the answer to that question *as a matter of logical necessity*. When we ask "what public schools teach children," we are not asking about only what may be squeezed out of statements according to strict logical analysis. We are asking how public schools actually shape the minds, the ideas, the attitudes of our children. (This might be viewed as a kind of "sociology of knowledge" approach.)

For example, if a very attractive, popular second grade teacher came into her public school classroom each day, and – without saying a word to the students – silently crossed herself and prayed intensely for half a minute, and then began the class, I have no doubt that certain civil libertarians would object strongly that the teacher was "teaching" the children religion, that is, influencing them to view religion (in this case, the particular religion of Christianity) positively. I think they would be correct in characterizing her activity that way. The key here, though, would not be anything that was said, but the relationship of admiration and respect that the children have for the teacher, and their resultant inclination to admire and perhaps emulate what she does.

We should approach the question of the effects of teaching a "menu" of life choices in the public schools with that same sensitivity to indirect effects. The first thing to be said is that no such menu is ever complete. It is simply not possible to lay out all possible life choices. A selection must be made. The principles behind that selection are a key, though

---

[71] Macedo, *Diversity and Distrust*, p. 177.

indirect, factor in what the children are being taught. While there is no strict logical necessity – and, in fact, logically it is entirely unwarranted – to draw the conclusion that choices on a particular menu are considered by those who make the selection to be more choiceworthy than choices off that menu, nonetheless it seems highly likely, perhaps even inevitable, that many children will implicitly draw that conclusion.

For example, the exclusion of homosexual relationships from the category of "family choices" until relatively recently in our history surely did reflect and reinforce the widespread belief that homosexual relationships were not normal or even appropriate. The inclusion of homosexual relationships in the category of family choices in some schools recently surely reflects and reinforces the belief that homosexual relationships are one legitimate form of family life. The very inclusion of a choice on the menu gives it a legitimacy it would otherwise not have, which is why, for example, adult incest and polygamy are still not on public school "family choice menus."

The menu of choices presented in school relative to the origins of man is likely to be limited. Macedo himself (following the Court) quickly dismisses the Louisiana "equal-time-for-creation-science" law at issue in *Edwards v. Aguillard*,[72] as a "thinly veiled attempt to introduce religious views of man's origin into public schooling."[73] That is, where secular science and fundamentalists' religious beliefs come into conflict, the public schools will teach fundamentalist children scientific propositions that, in effect, say: "your families' religious beliefs are wrong." Efforts by fundamentalists to harmonize science with their faith, in the form of "creation science," will not even be permitted to be heard (unless the students wish to debate their teachers). It takes no particular sympathy with creation science itself to be concerned about the implications of the principle that current scientific theories or prevailing secular beliefs should trump religious free exercise concerns. Children's menus should be broad, it appears, but not so broad as to include scientific theories put forward with a view to harmonizing science with fundamentalists' deepest beliefs.[74]

[72] 482 U.S. 578 (1987).
[73] Macedo, *Diversity and Distrust*, p. 160.
[74] To be clear, I should add that my own way to resolve the problem would not be something like the Louisiana law. The only effective way to guarantee parental free exercise rights in the education area is to make public funding available to all parents to educate their children at schools of their choice, as long as those schools satisfy the legitimate state interests by meeting reasonable educational minimum requirements. Those reasonable educational minimum requirements, at some age, might even include a requirement of

CONCLUSION

Macedo is honestly concerned that there be limits on liberalism. Among other things, this means that liberalism should not totally exclude the possibility of religious exemptions from secular laws, and so Macedo is willing to permit judges to grant exemptions. But judges should refuse demands for exemptions unless accommodation promotes our public values, grounded on good public reasons. Examples of inappropriate accommodations include *Wisconsin v. Yoder*,[75] which undermined the potential life choices of Amish children, and *Mozert*, since fundamentalists are even worse than Amish: they "are not sectarians living apart, but are a group that is increasingly politicized and hostile to many liberal values and practices."[76]

And so, Macedo says, "[w]e will need some fortitude in the face of those fundamentalists of all stripes who refuse ever to acknowledge the political authority of reasons, principles, and a point of view above our many narrower sectarianisms."[77] What an image: Ivy League academics reaching into their reserves of moral courage, to overcome the "temptation" to give fundamentalists exemptions from education that concededly undermines their children's faith!

We should, Macedo argues earlier in the book, "tolerate the intolerant, as long as they do not genuinely threaten the survival of free institutions, but we need not bend over backward to make life easy for them."[78] Macedo does not give persuasive reasons to show how *Yoder* and *Mozert* were cases in which the Amish and fundamentalists were "threaten[ing] the survival of free institutions," nor is it clear how the

familiarity with the theory of evolution – but genuine political neutrality should not withhold from fundamentalist parents the opportunity both to teach their children the theory of evolution and to teach them that this theory is wrong. One suggestion that only complicates matters is that the public schools have an advantage in preventing intellectual tyranny over children, because "professionalism among teachers may help the schools stand for a measure of critical independence from both civic and parental convictions" (Macedo, *Diversity and Distrust*, p. 238, citing Amy Gutmann). But this simply raises the question of how to attain critical independence from the prevailing views of the professionals, who may themselves be guilty of uncritical acceptance of fashions in their particular professions, or in their disciplines, or in education programs, or in society at large. On elite opinions, and their frequent sharp disjunction from general opinion, see Robert Lerner, Althea Nagai, and Stanley Rothman, *American Elites* (New Haven, CT: Yale University Press, 1996).

75 *Wisconsin v. Yoder* 406 U.S. 205 (1972).
76 Macedo, *Diversity and Distrust*, p. 209.
77 Macedo, *Diversity and Distrust*, p. 222.
78 Macedo, *Diversity and Distrust*, p. 147.

Amish or fundamentalists could fairly be characterized as "intolerant," if we mean by that term "intolerant of the legal rights of others." But it is certainly clear that he would not bend over backward to make life easy for them. What this suggests is that liberal intolerance goes well beyond the case of "threats to the survival of free institutions." It extends as well to cases of threats to the fostering of the virtues of comprehensive liberalism, especially control of education by parents who are not open-minded and liberal enough to permit their children's faith to be exposed to challenges at the time and in the form decided upon by public educational authorities.[79]

Macedo chides other liberals for failing to be sufficiently forthcoming about the ways in which a liberal democracy must try to shape the character of its citizens. I think that it is fair to chide him, not for lacking candor, but for failing to see that his liberal regime is clearly a form of comprehensive liberalism and that its efforts to shape character violate even a constrained form of liberal neutrality. His more modest form of liberalism – although more accommodating than the Deweyan liberalism he criticizes – is, in the long run, just as antithetical to views that are not *comprehensively* (not just politically) liberal, especially traditional religious beliefs, which Macedo wants to treat as a kind of psychological abnormality: "[i]t would truly be unfortunate if many people had psychological needs [which he also calls "peculiar"] that could only be

---

[79] I have confined myself in the text to discussing Macedo's arguments about public education. But the possible scope of liberal educational tyranny is not confined to public schooling. Macedo himself appears to grudgingly accept *Pierce v. Society of Sisters* (upholding the right of parents to send their children to nonpublic schools), but he does so only under certain conditions: "I have conceded the right to opt out of public schooling (which the Court affirmed in *Pierce*), but that right should be understood to be conditioned by a public authority to regulate private schools to ensure that civic values are satisfied and the child's right to freedom is preserved" (p. 202). He explicitly says that "in most states private schools and home schooling are only minimally regulated" (p. 202) and he concludes that "private schools have no right to resist reasonable measures to ensure that all children learn about the many ways of life that coexist in our polity" (p. 203). Private schools do not provide a guarantee of an "exit" provision from state inculcation of liberal principles. They too, in principle, may be compelled to teach "tolerance" and even to teach about ways of life contrary to their deepest religious and moral views. It is unsurprising, then, that Macedo maintains that "[w]ere the survival of free institutions really to depend on it, and were it efficacious to do so, a law making *public* school attendance mandatory would not be inconsistent with basic liberal views" (p. 147, emphasis in original). What is most striking about this statement is not so much the magnitude of the condition (mandatory schooling only if it were *really* necessary), but the fact that Macedo can imagine that mandatory public schooling would ever be necessary to defend "basic liberal values."

satisfied in all-encompassing associations."[80] Religion is tolerable only if it is understood as one of the many voluntary associations to which we belong, and not as "all-encompassing."

Macedo is correct in saying that, if we reject such a view, "we would have to radically rethink the value of the liberal civic order explored here."[81] We *should* reject such a view and Macedo's understanding of the liberal civic order. This does not entail a rejection of liberalism itself, which can be understood in other ways that truly respect the important and fundamental liberties that would be curtailed in Macedo's liberal democracy.[82] Our efforts will be best spent, not in erecting the liberalism described in *Diversity and Distrust*, but in finding a more reasonable way to accommodate the perennial tensions between our pluralism and our fundamental personal and communal commitments. That more reasonable way is natural law liberalism.

---

[80] Macedo, *Diversity and Distrust*, p. 251.

[81] Ibid.

[82] Robert George outlines an approach that includes a deep commitment to civil liberties – and hence is fairly understood as a form of liberalism – in his *Making Men Moral* (Oxford: Clarendon Press, 1993), especially in Chapter 7, "Toward a Pluralistic Perfectionist Theory of Civil Liberties."

PART II

LIBERALISM AND NATURAL LAW

7

Understanding Liberalism

A Broader Vision

The discussion in the first part of this book leads to the conclusion that, in a variety of ways, contemporary liberal theory provides an inadequate foundation for a public philosophy. The question in Part II is whether our dissatisfaction with contemporary liberalism should lead us to abandon liberalism entirely. I want to reject that proposal because there is so much in liberalism that is desirable and essential to an adequate public philosophy. While liberalism, like all forms of government, has its weaknesses, on the whole, properly understood, we should value its substantial contribution to our political well-being. The question is how to understand it properly. My argument is that it is best understood in the form of what I will call natural law liberalism.

In this chapter, I want to examine what liberalism is and to identify its core principles. In the next chapter, I will describe natural law and its various forms, indicating the particular form that I consider the best foundation for a public philosophy, and demonstrate that there are substantial resources for valuing liberty in the classical natural law tradition. In the following chapter, I will discuss the relationship between liberalism and natural law – so often one of hostility – and try to show why, if each is properly understood, they should be fundamentally harmonious.

UNDERSTANDINGS OF LIBERALISM

The term "liberal" today, as it always has, describes both a political philosophy and a political program. For the typical American, it can imply particular political stances, or at least strong inclinations, on abortion and homosexual rights, on economic regulation, social welfare programs, gun control, censorship of pornography, and Church–State separation. Why this particular constellation of policy views or orientations deserves the term "liberal" is not immediately clear, however, in light of the fact that, in the past, persons universally described as liberals had quite different views on some of these issues. During the nineteenth century, to take one instance, liberals would have had attitudes toward economic regulation virtually the opposite of those considered liberal today.

The best explanation for the use of the term at any given time comes from looking at liberalism as a tradition of political thought extending over centuries, as well as from examining the historical process by which liberals passed on to their successor-liberals a generally consistent set of political views. However, in this process, each generation modified the received liberal wisdom in certain ways, as they confronted new circumstances and issues, or worked through older, unresolved problems of liberal theory.[1] In such a process, the movement of thought from one generation to another might be limited, but over the course of a number of generations, the changes could be, and have been, quite substantial.

In general, liberalism refers to a family of political philosophies whose origins date to the seventeenth century. It has been a broad movement in politics and society, whose primary purpose has been the expansion of freedom through enlightenment. Liberals have sought to achieve their goals by displacing older hereditary and established hierarchies and authorities (political, social, and religious) – regarded as forms of despotism – with limited government based on equality before the law and broad personal freedoms, especially freedom of religion and thought and discussion.

But, as we have seen in Part I, the term "liberalism" is often used to refer to the specific, dominant late twentieth century expression of liberal political philosophy, represented most importantly in the thought of John Rawls.[2] This version of liberalism, which claims to be the proper working out of the liberal political tradition, broadly speaking, maintains that government should be neutral with respect to the question of the human good, embracing a notion of justice that prescinds from the truth of "comprehensive" philosophical, theological, or moral views. This approach has been characterized by one of its critics, Michael Sandel, as "the procedural

---

[1] This description does not assume that the changes were necessarily improvements – they might have been changes for the better or for the worse.
[2] John Rawls, *A Theory of Justice* (Cambridge, MA: Harvard University Press, 1970) and *Political Liberalism* (New York: Columbia University Press, 1993).

republic," that is, a nation that provides a broad framework or procedure for individuals to pursue their own goals, without attempting to influence the substance of those pursuits (except insofar as they interfere with the similar rights of others to pursue their own goals).[3] It can also be referred to as "antiperfectionist" liberalism, because it denies that political life should aim to perfect its citizens, according to some standard of human excellence. Although this term is useful, it is important to note that many contemporary antiperfectionist liberals do recognize that ultimately liberalism must be understood, and defended, as contributing to moral improvement in important ways.[4]

What is the relationship between these two meanings of liberalism, between the broad tradition of liberal political theory and its dominant contemporary form? There are three main answers. One possible relationship is that contemporary liberal political theory is the logical fulfillment of the aspirations of the broad liberal tradition, that it has thought through quandaries of earlier liberal political theory and achieved a more coherent political theory that is also properly adapted to the circumstances of our time. This has involved winnowing out some elements of earlier expressions of liberalism that were unconsidered remnants of pre-liberal thought now understood to be inconsistent with liberalism. (This position can be subdivided into those who reject contemporary liberalism – and therefore the principles from which it is said to have ineluctably flowed as well – and those who embrace contemporary liberalism, and who therefore view earlier forms of liberalism somewhat critically, as incomplete liberalism, but also somewhat benignly, as the first steps toward a fuller form of it.)

A second position on the relationship between liberalism old and new is that contemporary liberalism is merely one possible working out of broad liberal principles. It is not logically and necessarily implied by the most important principles of earlier forms of liberalism, but it is a defensible or plausible development of them. (And, again, people with this view can divide as to whether the development is a good one.)

---

3 Michael Sandel, *Democracy's Discontent* (Cambridge, MA: Harvard University Press, 1996).
4 See, for example, my discussion of Ronald Dworkin, in *Liberalism at the Crossroads*, Wolfe and Hittinger (Lanham, MD: Rowman and Littlefield, 1994), pp. 23–41, especially pp. 31–39. (See also Chapter 2, endnote 2, above.) While Rawls's neutralist "political liberalism" is the most influential form of contemporary liberalism, it should be remembered that there are other forms of explicitly non-neutralist liberalism ("comprehensive liberalisms"), such as those of Brian Barry and Jeremy Waldron, and also "perfectionist liberalisms," such as those of Joseph Raz and William Galston.

A third position would be that contemporary liberalism is a departure from, or even a betrayal of, the broad liberal tradition, because its efforts to sort through elements of earlier liberal thought and to discard parts that are inconsistent with what it holds to be the central logical thrust of the tradition are actually destructive of a proper coherence or balance represented by that earlier liberalism. Those who hold this position can, of course, vary on the question of which earlier strand of liberalism (or combination of parts of them) is considered a more adequate expression of liberalism.

Most of contemporary political thought can be viewed as representing variants of one of these three different positions – which is to say that contemporary political thought and discussion can be understood as competition among various forms of liberalism, all within the broad context established by the liberal tradition broadly understood. The "liberalism–communitarianism" debate, according to this view, is not really a debate between liberals and non-liberals, but a debate within liberalism. Likewise with the "liberalism–republicanism" debate, and so too even with the "liberalism–postmodernism" debate.[5] The thesis of this book is that the same argument can be made regarding liberalism and contemporary natural law theory.

A BRIEF HISTORY OF LIBERALISM

We must begin a history of liberalism[6] with a description of what it is *not*. That is, what was the form of political thought *against* which liberalism was born and developed?

One form of pre- and anti-liberal thought was the theory of the "divine right" of kings. Rulers derived their power from some supernatural or divine authority, irrespective of whether the ruled consented to this authority. In the *First Treatise of Government*, Locke argued that this theory was

---

[5] Peter Berkowitz makes this point in his "Liberalism, Postmodernism, and Public Philosophy" in *Public Morality, Civic Virtue, and the Problem of Modern Liberalism*, T. William Boxx and Gary M. Quinlivan, Eds. (Grand Rapids, MI: William B. Eerdmans, 2000), pp. 158–60.

[6] For another brief history of liberalism, see John Gray, *Liberalism*, 2nd ed. (St. Paul, MN: University of Minnesota Press, 1995), Part One. More detailed articles on many of the thinkers described here may be found in *History of Political Philosophy*, 3rd ed., Strauss and Cropsey, Eds. (University of Chicago, 1987). I make no pretense that the thumbnail sketch of liberalism presented in this chapter is comprehensive. For all its brevity, however, it serves the purpose of setting the stage for my subsequent efforts to identify the core principles of liberalism.

a form of paternalism, a development of rule held by the hereditary patriarch of a kinship group, and thus "natural" in the same way that parental rule over children is natural. The object of his attack in this essay was the divine right claims of the Stuart dynasty in England.

Liberalism also from its inception was a response against a prevailing idea that the scope of legitimate government power extended to virtually all human affairs, and in particular to religion. While no one in medieval times – after the inception of Christianity – argued that government power was unlimited, there was no sharp demarcation between public and private that put whole areas of human concerns simply "off-limits" to government. Liberalism was born with an insistence that certain questions were in principle beyond the scope of government. Most importantly, the political community was not the arbiter or enforcer of religious truth, and religious persecution was one of the chief evils which liberal political philosophy challenged.

The precursor of liberalism was Thomas Hobbes. His starting point, portraying man in "a state of nature," was the fundamental equality of all human beings, who share the same first "law of nature," namely, the desire for self-preservation. As men in the state of nature pursue this goal, what results is a "war of all against all," in which life is famously "solitary, poor, nasty, brutish, and short." With a view to pursuing more effectually their self-preservation, men eventually leave the state of nature, forming a social contract, and thereby establish civil society on the basis of consent. The scope of legitimate civil power is limited, in principle, to the protection of the right of self-preservation. But Hobbes thought that the only effective way to attain this goal was by fear: the establishment of an absolute power that could compel men to respect each others' fundamental rights.[7]

The magnitude of this absolute power makes it difficult to describe Hobbes simply as a liberal. But the starting points he provided – equality in a state of nature, with the desire for self-preservation constituting the first law of nature, and government being established by a social contract for limited purposes – were the foundation for a later, more fully developed liberalism.

John Locke, writing at the end of the seventeenth century, is widely regarded as the central figure of classical liberalism. His starting points were similar to Hobbes, in that he described a state of nature in which all men are equal, above all in their desire for self-preservation, and exercise their own executive power to enforce their preservation. This state of

[7] Thomas Hobbes, *Leviathan*, Oakeshott, Ed. (New York: Collier, 1962).

nature eventually gives way to a social contract establishing civil society, with its limited purpose of protecting the rights of man. But there are important differences in Locke. For example, Locke presented the desire for self-preservation as being instilled in man by God, giving an ostensibly theistic foundation to the law of nature (in contrast to Hobbes's frank materialism). He also developed a strong connection between the initial, fundamental right to life and other rights that are necessarily implied in it, especially liberty and property.

Most importantly, Locke argued that Hobbes's absolute power was as great a threat to life, liberty, and property as the anarchy of the state of nature was. Rather than setting up an absolute power, it is incumbent on men to establish a civil society in which government is limited and the limits are effective. The foundation for legitimate government power is consent, and civil power is limited not only in its purpose – protecting the rights of man – but by its structure. The legislative power, appropriately circumscribed, is the most fundamental power, but Locke also articulated the principle of separation of powers, distinguishing executive and "federative" powers as well (the judicial power being a part of executive power, and the federative power involving not the execution of laws but the defense of the commonwealth against threats to its preservation from foreign and domestic violence). This separation of powers helps to limit the power of rulers and thereby serves to protect rights.[8]

Locke, like Spinoza before him in the seventeenth century, also dedicated a great deal of attention to religious toleration. Locke employed a mixture of different kinds of arguments to defend toleration. Some of them were specifically scriptural and theological arguments. Other arguments focused on the nature of legitimate government power, whose concerns are, in principle, limited to temporal matters, and do not extend to care of man's eternal salvation. Religious opinions are a private matter, therefore, and religious persecution is unjustifiable.

Montesquieu, writing in the mid-eighteenth century, followed Locke in many ways, though he was less doctrinaire in some respects, not limiting legitimate governments to those based on consent, but taking into consideration the great variations of nations in their history, circumstances, and culture. His *Spirit of the Laws* began with a typology of governments that divided them into forms of monarchy, despotism, and republic, and his description of the republic was strikingly classical, with its emphasis on virtue as its moving principle. But this typology was undercut

---

[8] John Locke, *The Second Treatise of Government*, in *Two Treatises of Government*, Laslett, Ed. (Mentor, 1960).

in subsequent sections of the work, which contained a long and admiring chapter on the English constitution. Montesquieu developed liberal political thought by adding an emphasis on the importance of the sense of personal security, without which men are not truly free. This emphasis on personal security helps to explain his shift from Locke in describing the separation of powers (followed by America's founders), separating out and giving greater prominence to the judicial power (subsuming Locke's federative power into the executive power).

The eighteenth century Scottish Enlightenment – including David Hume, Thomas Reid, Adam Smith – made significant contributions to the development of liberal thought. Adam Smith, in particular, departing from the prevalent mercantilism, developed the economic theory of liberalism, arguing for expanded personal economic freedom and initiative, operating within a framework that channeled the pursuit of self-interest, as if guided by an invisible hand, toward the public good.

Meanwhile, on the European continent, the French *philosophes* led the Enlightenment project of undermining the religious orthodoxy so closely identified with the privileges of aristocracy in the *ancien regime*. Precisely because of the political strength of the Catholic Church in France, French liberalism took a more strongly anticlerical cast than British liberalism, as exemplified in the writings of Voltaire (a political absolutist, but a strong advocate of intellectual freedom and an opponent of clerical despotism). In figures such as Diderot and Condorcet, Enlightenment thought was suffused with an extraordinary belief in progress through the efforts of human reason.[9]

One of the influential critics of Lockean-style liberalism and of progress, Jean-Jacques Rousseau, did contribute to its unfolding in certain ways. Beginning from a more idyllic state of nature, in which men were equal, but weak and relatively unthreatening to each other, men were irreversibly thrust into civil society, with its inequalities and oppression, by the assertion of individual property rights. Once in civil society, individuals could achieve their freedom only through their participation in the formation of and their affirmation of the "general will." But, in addition to a strong (and potentially oppressive) participatory republicanism, developed in *The Social Contract*, Rousseau also had a romantic individualistic side, which found expression in other works, especially his *Confessions*.

Immanuel Kant played a key role in the development of liberalism by giving autonomy a central role in his philosophy. Individuals should act

[9] See Gray, pp. 18–19.

free of external compulsion, so that their acts were truly "the execution of their choices," but also free of internal compulsions such as "uncontrolled desires, passions, or prejudices." This would leave their actions to be "controlled by reason, understood as conformity to universalizable principles"[10] and including the command to always treat humanity (one's own and others') as an end, not a means. Obedience to these imperatives was the formal criterion for morality, and justice, based on reciprocity, was understood in terms of rights and duties (rather than classical virtue). The role of the state was to protect "every man's liberty to perform every external act that he pleases so long as he does not encroach on the same liberty in others." Yet man's liberty was not "freedom to do whatever he likes even within the limits of similar freedom of others, but was rather his freedom from obeying any external laws to which he might not have consented" – his consent being understood (following Rousseau) as implicit in the sovereign general will of a republican government, whose aim was to protect the rights of man (rather than to secure through moral education the substantive well–being and happiness of its citizens).[11]

The American Revolution represented the first opportunity to establish a new government along strongly liberal lines, beginning with the Declaration of Independence, with its self-evident principles, largely drawn from Locke, and crystalizing in the Constitution that reflected the "new science of politics" to achieve the goal of free popular government. The greatest exposition of its leading principles, *The Federalist* (authored by Alexander Hamilton, James Madison, and John Jay), contributed to liberal thought in a number of interesting ways: by developing the idea of separation of powers further (especially the institutional mechanisms necessary to make it effective), by defending the compromise that created a republic with a strong national government for certain purposes and with states that retained important powers of their own, by adding to the earlier American innovation of written constitutions the principle of enforcement through judicial review, and especially by defending the benefits of an extended republic whose diversity would help to prevent the formation of tyrannical majorities.

The central, shattering historic event of the modern era was the French Revolution, which uprooted and cast aside the ancient continental

---

[10] This description is from John Kekes in his *Against Liberalism* (Ithaca, NY: Cornell University Press, 1997), p. 3.

[11] See Pierre Hassner, "Immanuel Kant," in *History of Political Philosophy*, Strauss and Cropsey, Eds., pp. 603–604, 605.

European political, social, and religious hierarchies and attempted to establish a new republic based on the rights of man. The Revolution moved from an earlier moderate phase of constitutional monarchy, through radical republican utopian aspirations and bloody repression, to a Napoleonic empire whose armies carried the ideals of liberty, equality, and fraternity from one end of the continent to the other. Despite the reaction that set in after 1815, the Revolution had undone the old world in a way that made a return to it impossible.

During the first part of the nineteenth century, liberal ideals were articulated in France by Benjamin Constant, in his *Ancient and Modern Liberty*, which contrasted the ancient freedom of republican participation with the modern freedom of personal liberty. Among the leading French liberals was Alexis de Tocqueville, whose *Democracy in America* was not only a remarkably perceptive book about America, but also a keen analysis of the interior forces moving modern democracies, especially the passion for equality. Tocqueville, a liberal democrat himself, was aware that democratic tendencies could be self-destructive as well as beneficial, and he highlighted especially the potential danger of democratic despotism. Unlike many other liberals, Tocqueville, while defending the separation of Church and State, denied that there was a necessary hostility between religion and democracy. He argued, to the contrary, that religion was an essential support for democracy, because it helped to provide a necessary fixed moral framework for the flux of democratic political life and served as an antidote to self-destructive democratic tendencies such as individualism and materialism.

Nineteenth-century continental Europe saw an ongoing clash between the representatives of declining monarchies and aristocracies and religious authorities and the emergent forces – often themselves at odds – of republicanism, nationalism, bourgeois liberalism, socialism, and anticlericalism. The forces of liberalism were not as successful on the continent as in England and America: in some places less absolute monarchies survived (in the Austro-Hungarian Empire and in a newly united Italy), in others new forms of authoritarianism emerged (Bismarck's unified Germany), and in others, republicans and monarchists continued to battle, with often-varying fortunes (as in France and Spain). Moreover, among political thinkers, the influence of anti-liberal writers, such as Marx and Nietzsche, was striking.

In England, liberalism took a turn in the early nineteenth century with the utilitarianism of Jeremy Bentham and John Mill. Social utility, understood as the maximization of pleasure and the minimization of pain, was held to be the standard of political action. These thinkers exemplified the strong reformist element in liberalism, as, for example, in Bentham's proposals for reform of the English penal system.

Meanwhile the Liberal Party, under the leadership of Cobden and Bright, exercised considerable political power, successfully advocating a shift to free trade policy. (This party was the referent for the first widespread usage in English of the term "liberal.") Under William Gladstone, the Liberal Party often dominated British government in the middle and latter part of the century, standing for "freedom, free trade, progress, and the Seventh Commandment" as well as "reform" and "peace"[12]

John Stuart Mill, perhaps more than anyone since John Locke and Adam Smith, came to embody liberal ideals, especially in his early and middle years. Mill made powerful arguments for freedom of thought and discussion, and for the "harm principle," according to which government and society ought to interfere with individuals' freedom only in cases where their acts affect other people in a direct and tangible way. However, he shared Tocqueville's concern about the despotic power of democratic opinion, and emphasized (drawing on German romanticism) the need for individuality. He was also a trailblazer of liberalism in his discussion of *The Subjection of Women*. In his later years, he exemplified an important strand of developing liberal thought, in his abandonment of orthodox liberal ideas on economic freedom and his growing socialist sympathies.

The split of late-nineteenth-century liberalism on the economic question is exemplified in the writings of Herbert Spencer and T. H. Green. Spencer pressed the emphasis on economic freedom to considerable extremes, adding a sort of Darwinian gloss on the reasoning for it. Green represented the view that economic freedom might entail not merely the protecting of property rights as they currently stood, but also active government measures to equalize the standing of the propertied and unpropertied.

In his classic *Liberalism*[13] L. T. Hobhouse, just before World War I, was able to identify the following as the elements of liberalism: civil liberty (rule of law, equal liberty under law), fiscal liberty (no taxation without representation), personal liberty (including liberty of thought, discussion, and religion), social liberty (equality of opportunity, as against class and

---

[12] George Dangerfield, *The Strange Death of Liberal England* (New York: Capricorn Books, 1935), p. 7. (Dangerfield adds sardonically that "peace" meant "wars to be fought at a distance and, if possible, in the name of God.")

[13] L.T. Hobhouse, *Liberalism* (Henry Holt and Co., 1911).

gender privileges in education and occupations), economic liberty (free trade rather than protectionism, but with some measure of legitimate industrial regulation, including limits on the power of economic associations such as trade unions and corporations), domestic liberty (wives being free and responsible, marriage resting on a purely contractual basis, with duties imposed on parents – by the state as Over-Parent – relative to the care of children), local and racial and national liberty (including autonomy of nations and racial equality), international liberty (noninterference, hostility to the use of force and armaments and the military spirit), and political liberty and popular sovereignty (with the executive and legislature being responsible to the whole community, but with some limits on the franchise).

But, ironically, this classic definition of liberalism appeared on the eve of World War I, during which the Liberal Party, rent by various tensions, especially those regarding economic liberty, self-destructed, giving way to the emerging Labour Party as the main opponent of the Conservative Party in English politics.

The division within liberalism on economic questions was also making itself felt in America, where the late-nineteenth-century laissez-faire individualism of the so-called "Gilded Age" saw enormous fortunes made, and, again, often defended on Darwinian grounds. During this period, the judiciary developed expansive new concepts of substantive due process, which were often employed to defend property rights.

Pitted against these tendencies was a developing Progressive movement. Some Progressives focused on reform of the structure of government. For example, the early Woodrow Wilson sought to diminish the checks and balances of federalism and separation of powers that inhibited a more active national government, and reformers at the state and local level pressed for democratization of party nomination procedures and for the direct democratic power of initiative and referendum.

But the main thrust of Progressivism dealt especially with the purposes of government, above all, its relationship to property and wealth and the goal of establishing greater economic equality. Reformers such as Upton Sinclair attacked the perceived injustices and inequities of capitalism. Political and social critics such as Charles Beard and Vernon Parrington criticized the Constitution as undemocratic and the founders as self-interested property owners. Progressive writers aspired, not to capitalism, but to a more economically egalitarian society, such as the fictional socialist utopia of Edward Bellamy's *Looking Backward*, or the national democracy of Herbert Croly's *The Promise of American Life*. Among the most influential of social thinkers, John Dewey outlined in highly general and formalistic terms a progressive, pragmatic, secular public philosophy.

At a time when other Western democracies were drawn toward fascist and socialist alternatives, Franklin Roosevelt's New Deal public philosophy drew on the Progressive impulse, significantly reforming the economic system and increasing the role of government in the regulation of business, the protection of workers' rights, and the provision of a broad array of social welfare services. Roosevelt judges, who retreated from judicial intervention in economic affairs, initiated a less broadly visible, but significant transformation of free speech and religious rights.

The Cold War following World War II saw America emerge as the leading opponent of the totalitarian Marxist–Leninist state of Stalin and his successors. As the great liberal democratic power in the world, America helped to establish liberal democracies in the defeated Axis powers, and (after the fall of Eastern Europe and China) supported Western Europe (and Japan) in its resistance to external and internal forces allied with the Soviet Union.

At the same time, the United States began to confront its own internal problems of racism, established *de jure* in the South, and *de facto* throughout the rest of the nation. The civil rights revolution proceeded from desegregation of the military, through the *Brown* school desegregation decision, protests and civil disobedience under the leadership of Martin Luther King, Jr., passage of the Civil Rights Act of 1964 and Voting Rights Act of 1965, to increasingly controversial school desegregation and bussing controversies.

During the early 1960s, John F. Kennedy embodied hopes for a liberal renewal of society, and after his death his civil rights and social welfare programs were carried on and expanded dramatically through Lyndon Johnson's Great Society and War on Poverty. Meanwhile, the Warren Court expanded the role of the courts in bringing about liberal social reform, beginning with the 1954 *Brown* decision and moving on during the 1960s to expansive decisions in the areas of criminal defendants' rights, reapportionment, Church and State (especially school prayer), free speech and obscenity, and privacy.

Even as liberalism seemed triumphant, however, the focus of national life was shifting, and the conflict of the late 1960s ushered in a new era, aptly described as a time of "culture wars." Over the course of the next several decades American liberalism found itself under assault from two directions. Left-wing critics, appealing to the ideals of the civil rights movement, domestic opposition to the Vietnam War, concern about economic inequalities, and the "sexual revolution," condemned the United States in the name of radical, participatory democracy and personal autonomy. At the same time, new critiques emerged on the right. "Neo-conservativism" was born among liberals disillusioned with 1960s liberalism on two points: first, the failure of contemporary liberals to defend liberal democracy against its enemies (communism abroad, and radicals at home), and second, the failure of contemporary liberals to see the utopian character, and hence the failure, of many of their domestic programs (e.g., the war on poverty, and ways of responding to increasing crime). In addition, the religious right emerged during the 1970s, especially in reaction to what it perceived as an attack on traditional religious and moral values led by the Supreme Court, with its decisions secularizing public schools and establishing abortion rights.

During the same period, however, in the academy a neo-Kantian liberalism was powerfully presented in the work of John Rawls's enormously influential *A Theory of Justice* (1971), significantly revised in articles culminating in *Political Liberalism* (1993). Rawls developed a new variation of social contract theory to provide a foundation for the two key elements of late-twentieth-century liberalism: the commitments to protect and expand personal autonomy and to pursue greater economic equality. Rawls's influence extended well beyond academic political philosophy, serving as the intellectual foundation for legal thinkers such as Ronald Dworkin and Bruce Ackerman.

But this revivified liberalism met vigorous opposition from various forces, especially those in the academy associated with multiculturalism and communitarianism, as well as a renewed intellectual conservatism, whose limited numbers in academia were given a stronger voice by frequent conservative political successes in the last part of the twentieth century. Even the retaking of the presidency by Democrats during the 1990s failed to signal broad liberal success, given the loss of Congress in 1994 to the Republicans, erratic public support for the liberal political agenda, and the accommodation of the Clinton administration to certain conservative impulses, such as welfare reform.

In the early years of the new millennium national political life was deeply influenced by the terrorist attack on the World Trade Center and the Pentagon in 2001. These events had the considerable effect of stimulating traditional American patriotism and reinforcing broad government powers in the national security area. They also reinforced strongly the sense that American and Western ideals were not unchallenged in the world, and made the essential features of Western liberalism (in the broad sense) stand out sharply, in contrast to Islamic fundamentalism.

What can we draw from this thumbnail sketch of the history of liberalism to help us identify the core of liberalism? In the following section, I want to avoid defining liberalism simply in terms of the most important liberal political philosophers – because there is so much variation among them, on many issues, from Locke to Rawls. At the same time, we face the same problem if we define liberalism primarily in terms of a political program, since the programs identified as liberal have changed significantly over time. So, instead, I will try to identify what I consider the most important, "core political principles" and the most important "tendencies" of liberalism, understood as a broad intellectual and social movement.

CORE PRINCIPLES OF LIBERALISM

Liberalism is not a single, seamless political philosophy. Rather, it is a tradition with considerable variation. Still, to call it a tradition, we must be able to identify a solid core. Liberal political philosophers will not all have embraced each element in this core, but most of them – especially as the tradition develops over time – will have accepted most of those elements, or will have contributed in a significant way to the development of at least some of them.

What is the core of liberalism? I will try to describe it as five principles and five "tendencies."

The first principle of liberalism is the foundation of human dignity rooted in equality. If human beings are not born equal in all regards, they are at least equal in certain fundamental natural rights, among which are "life, liberty, and the pursuit of happiness." No just political order can simply discount or ignore the well-being of certain members of the political community, reducing them to mere means to the well-being of others. This rules out slavery, serfdom, and rigid social castes. (There have been, of course, theoretical defenses of these social forms that contend they do conduce to the well-being of the "lower orders" on whom they are inflicted, but the general practice of these institutions shows that these theoretical defenses are specious.)

Second, political rule requires consent. No one group or class of people is born with a right to rule others. Autocracy, aristocracy, and theocracy are forms of despotism that deprive people of their requisite participation in the process of rule. How broad that participation should be is controversial, even within the liberal tradition, but the consistent liberal impulse has certainly been to expand it. Consent in liberal theory began as consent to the form of government, which (in principle) might not be democratic. But in general – and increasingly over time – liberals have called for increasing, actual popular participation within the form of government. This rules out any form of absolute government and points in the direction of thorough-going democracy.

Third, the purpose of government is the protection of rights. These rights begin with certain fundamental natural rights (life, liberty, pursuit of happiness), but then they are elaborated as a series of legal rights. Among these rights, five categories stand out: (1) political rights (especially voting), (2) religious freedom and toleration (typically including prohibition of an established religion), (3) freedom of thought and discussion, (4) property rights, and (5) impartial legal procedures and equality before the law. These rights are not absolute – they can and must be limited in certain ways – but, appropriately limited, their protection is the primary purpose of political life.

Fourth, to accomplish its purpose, government must be strong, but limited. As Madison argued, we must establish a government that can control the governed (so that rights will be secure) and that can itself be controlled (so that it will not threaten rights). The government must have adequate powers to defend itself, at home and abroad, and it must have adequate power to enforce its laws, for the achievement of legitimate public purposes. The most effective ways to limit government, without depriving it of its necessary powers, are principles such as representative democracy (especially accountability of rulers through elections), separation of powers, and an independent judiciary.

Fifth, men should be governed by law. The rule of law – government according to general standards that apply to all citizens – is the best way to approximate the aspect of justice that demands that those in like circumstances should be treated alike, and the best guarantee that no undue partiality will be shown some people or classes at the expense of the legitimate concerns of others.[14]

---

[14] John Kekes, in the first chapter of his insightful *Against Liberalism* (Cornell University Press, 1997) lists five basic values of liberalism, namely, pluralism, freedom, rights, equality, and distributive justice, and he then goes on to identify what he calls "the true core of liberalism, inner citadel for whose protection all the liberal battles are waged: autonomy" (p. 15). The differences between his list and mine are suggested by the emphasis on autonomy, which indicates that Kekes is orienting his description of liberalism more toward contemporary varieties of it. He states, for example, that his interpretation of liberalism

TENDENCIES OF LIBERALISM

To these five principles – equal human dignity, consent of the governed, individual rights, effective limited government, and the rule of law, – might be added other "tendencies," which are perhaps too vague to be called principles, but which tend strongly to inform or animate most liberal thought.[15]

First, the liberal tradition tends to be a rationalist tradition, a tradition of reason and "enlightenment." Inherited truths are submitted to critical analysis, and freedom of inquiry vis-à-vis political and ecclesiastical authorities is highly valued. Modern science assumes a central place in intellectual life and often becomes a model for philosophy. The emphasis on reason and human equality makes education, as the foundation for equality of opportunity, a prominent liberal ideal.

Second, the liberal tradition tends to be reformist, examining the past and present with a critical eye, proposing changes to improve the condition of men, and experimenting with new social forms and policies. Traditional hierarchies (typically based on blood and inheritance) and inequalities based on the chance of birth, and legally and socially enforced limits on individual efforts, need to be criticized and displaced. The traditions of reason and reform unite in a strong tendency of liberalism to pursue what Francis Bacon called "the relief of man's estate," the general cultivation of human health, material well-being, and comfort.

Third, the liberal tradition tends toward individualism. It is concerned that an improper focus on the glory and well-being of the "community as a whole" will redound primarily to the benefit of the few, the powerful and the well-off, at the expense of the many, the weak, and the poor (or the less well-off). Because it is rooted in equality, it tends to exalt the individual, whose choices should be curtailed only to the extent that they interfere with others' rights or with requirements essential to maintain the community necessary to protect the rights of all.

Fourth, liberalism tends to promote either rationalist religion (emphasizing the more limited truths of natural theology rather than the wider

---

is one of a number of possible interpretations, and that it "is meant to be broad enough to include most versions of contemporary liberalism" (p. 2). The focus on autonomy may also explain why political participation is not singled out more specifically in his list.

[15] I am tempted (but for its awkwardness) to use the English word "springs," as Montesquieu uses the term "ressort" in *The Spirit of the Laws*, to describe these "animating principles" of liberalism.

range of beliefs characteristic of revealed religions) or secularism. It tends to be skeptical of claims of revelation, or at least of their relevance to political life. This was due historically, in no small measure, to an accidental but nearly universal (and therefore not *obviously* accidental) feature of early modern Europe: the social and political intermingling and alliance of State and Church hierarchies.

Fifth, the liberal tradition tends to be universalistic. Appealing to rational principles that apply to all men, it tends to be cosmopolitan and anti-imperialist, though it has its interventionist and non-interventionist strands.

Disputes among liberals will often concern exactly how far these principles and tendencies are to be pushed. Liberals generally allow for the fact that they are not always absolute. Most obviously, in some cases rights may conflict with each other, or they may be incompatible with certain fundamental requirements of political and social life. Therefore, religious, property, and speech rights are all essential, but they can be limited in certain ways for the public good. This common-sense recognition makes it more difficult to determine what the "true" liberal position is, since there will be significant differences among liberals themselves on the scope of liberal principles.

Nonetheless, there is a solid, identifiable core of liberalism, which is seen most easily by comparing it with very different forms of government, such as Roman republicanism, medieval feudalism, seventeenth century French monarchy, Ottoman despotism, traditional Latin American feudal oligarchy, twentieth century totalitarianism (Nazi, Communist, Chinese), or contemporary Islamic fundamentalism. In the sometimes bitter disputes of politics (disputes that may admittedly concern absolutely fundamental principles), people in the United States (and in the West generally) can sometimes forget how much they have in common.

That is one reason why it is worthwhile to fight the tendency to identify "liberalism," despite its rich and varied tradition, simply with certain strands of liberalism that are dominant in the Anglo-American academy today. This applies both to the political liberalism of John Rawls and to the avowed comprehensive liberalism of many of his critics. In doing so, we would lose sight of the deeper underlying commonalities among the various forms of contemporary political thought solidly rooted in the liberal tradition, which extend far beyond the leading forms of contemporary liberalism. Those other forms include, I want to argue, not only communitarianism, with its obvious affinities for liberalism (obvious, because major communitarians, such as Michael Sandel, are readily identified as moderate political liberals), but also forms of thought usually not at all identified with liberalism – above all, natural law theory.

DEFINING LIBERALISM TOO BROADLY?

It is easy to anticipate one criticism that this approach to defining liberalism will generate. Critics who are sympathetic to contemporary liberalism will argue that my description defines liberalism too broadly, trying to include within its scope many thinkers who are actually *critics* of true liberalism. In their view, contemporary liberalism is the rightful embodiment of and standard-bearer of liberalism, the result of thoughtful sifting of earlier statements of liberalism that has weeded out elements that are inconsistent with the historical thrust of liberalism toward greater equality and liberty. From this perspective, my description of liberalism either leaves out essential elements of liberalism or dilutes them unacceptably. For example, rather than saying, as I do, that liberalism is generally oriented toward the protection of rights, contemporary liberals will insist on a much more full-blooded version of rights, including especially a strong form of Mill's harm principle.

This same criticism of my description of liberalism is likely to come from contemporary thinkers who are highly critical of liberalism. In their case, the right of contemporary liberalism to carry the standard of liberalism – its claim to be the logical or proper outcome of the inherent logic of liberalism – is endorsed, precisely as a way of criticizing liberalism as a whole. If contemporary liberalism has radicalized the thrust of liberalism toward equality and liberty, they say, that is because there are deeper epistemological and philosophical tendencies of the liberal tradition that lead necessarily in that direction. They differ from contemporary liberals primarily in their negative evaluation of that movement.

My argument is squarely based on the view that it is possible to identify the core of historical liberalism, as a movement toward greater political and intellectual freedom and equality, and to distinguish it from the more specific and more radical contemporary forms of liberalism. Most importantly, I contend that the "greater political and intellectual freedom and equality" at which liberalism has aimed is compatible with a natural law intellectual framework, rooted in truth and morality. That is because freedom and equality cannot be the only purposes of government. Freedom is freedom for something and equality is equality in certain respects.

This is not a new idea. It is essentially the familiar strand of the liberal tradition articulated most impressively by Alexis de Tocqueville.

Tocqueville characterizes a healthy liberal society as one in which the flux and freedom of the political world is made possible by a certain intellectual and moral framework:

Thus in the moral world everything is classified, systematized, foreseen, and decided beforehand; in the political world everything is agitated, disputed, and uncertain. In the one is a passive though a voluntary obedience; in the other, an independence scornful of experience, and jealous of all authority. These two tendencies, apparently so discrepant, are far from conflicting; they advance together and support each other.

Religion perceives that civil liberty affords a noble exercise to the faculties of man and that the political world is a field prepared by the Creator for the efforts of mind. Free and powerful in its own sphere, satisfied with the place reserved for it, religion never more surely establishes its empire than when it reigns in the hearts of men unsupported by aught besides its native strength.

Liberty regards religion as its companion in all its battles and its triumphs, as the cradle of its infancy and the divine source of its claims. It considers religion as the safeguard of morality, and morality as the best security of law and the surest pledge of the duration of freedom.[16]

Tocqueville here invokes "the spirit of religion," which might suggest that his characterization of liberalism is quite different from my formulation, which emphasizes natural law rather than religion. I do not think that there is a great difference, however, if one examines what Tocqueville considers to be the core of religion. First, religion is a form of hope:

The short space of threescore years can never content the imagination of man; nor can the imperfect joys of this world satisfy his heart. Man alone, of all created beings, displays a natural contempt of existence and yet a boundless desire to exist; he scorns life, but he dreads annihilation. These different feelings incessantly urge his soul to the contemplation of a future state, and religion directs his musings thither. Religion, then, is simply another form of hope, and it is no less natural to the human heart than hope itself. Men cannot abandon their religious faith without a kind of aberration of intellect and a sort of violent distortion of their true nature; they are invincibly brought back to more pious sentiments. Unbelief is an accident, and faith is the only permanent state of mankind. If we may consider religious institutions merely in a human point of view, they may be said to derive an inexhaustible element of strength from man himself, since they belong to one of the constituent principles of human nature.

When Tocqueville refers to religion, he appears to be thinking not so much of revealed religion as of natural religion. In commenting on the power of majority opinion, he says that "if we examine it very closely, it will be perceived that religion itself holds sway there [in the United States] much

---

[16] *Democracy in America*, Vol. 1, chap. ii (Phillips Bradley, Ed., p. 43–44).

less as a doctrine of revelation than as a commonly received opinion."[17] This is the religion of the Declaration of Independence, which is a more natural and rational religion, though at the same time it is more than mere Deism – as the Declaration's citations of "divine Providence" and "the Supreme Judge of the world" demonstrate. It is, one might say, the religion of the first tablet of the Ten Commandments, when the Decalogue is viewed from the perspective of the natural moral law.

Second, Tocqueville sees religion – specifically, Christian denominations in the United States – as sharing a common morality:

> The sects that exist in the United States are innumerable. They all differ in respect to the worship which is due to the Creator; but they all agree in respect to the duties which are due from man to man. Each sect adores the Deity in its own peculiar manner, but all sects preach the same moral law in the name of God.... Moreover, all the sects of the United States are comprised within the great unity of Christianity, and Christian morality is everywhere the same.[18]

The "Christian morality" which is shared by all is largely what we would identify as natural law morality today.

Tocqueville's "spirit of religion," then, is close to what may be called "the spirit of natural law." His liberalism seeks to place the drive for equality and liberty in a certain intellectual and moral framework that helps to direct that impulse, and to protect it from taking forms that would undermine the well-being of society and its citizens.

The goal of identifying and defending a *moderate* liberalism – but one that does not thereby cease to be liberal – has an eminently respectable precedent then. Nor is Tocqueville alone in this regard. Many of the earlier or classical forms of liberalism recognized the importance of public morality (including religion) as an essential part of the foundation for liberal government, in ways that contemporary liberals would spurn. Locke's exclusion of atheists from toleration and the general recognition among liberal writers of the need for public regulation of sexual morality (in support of the family) are among the most important examples. It is not difficult, then, to maintain that contemporary forms of liberalism have no monopoly on the label.[19]

---

[17] *Democracy in America*, Vol. II, chap. ii (Phillips Bradley, Ed., pp. 10–11).

[18] *Democracy in America*, Vol. I, chap. xvii (Phillips Bradley, Ed., p. 303).

[19] A contemporary example of Tocqueville's moderate liberalism is the work of contemporary political theorist Pierre Manent, author of *Tocqueville and the Nature of Democracy* (Lanham, Md.: Rowman and Littlefield, 1996), *The City of Man* (Princeton: Princeton University Press, 1998), *Modern Liberty and Its Discontents*, Daniel J. Mahoney and Paul Seaton, Eds. (Lanham, MD: Rowman and Littlefield, 1998).

The more difficult question, I think, is whether a liberalism firmly grounded in traditional natural law – the natural law that seems to have been at the heart of the order early liberals reacted against – is possible. To that question I turn to in the remaining chapters of Part II.

8

Understanding Natural Law

"Natural law" is a term that has been used with even more varied and incompatible meanings than the term "liberalism." Moreover, persuading people to examine it and take it seriously can be particularly difficult because, in some of its classic forms, natural law is often considered to be discredited by its historical associations with the defense of slavery and religious persecution. In this volume, however, I am trying to argue for a particular form of natural law that is not fairly subject to criticism for supporting slavery or religious persecution.

In this chapter's effort to describe natural law, I will begin with an historical overview of natural law, giving somewhat greater attention to the natural law thought of Thomas Aquinas, whom I take to be the greatest representative of the tradition, and then identify four different ways in which the term can be used. I will then describe a new form of Thomistic natural law theory developed in recent years, and offer some observations on it, and go on to describe a core of natural law teaching on which I think various contemporary schools of natural law can agree. The last part of the chapter will be an examination of some of the resources in natural law theory for an appreciation of the importance of the central liberal principle of liberty.

A BRIEF HISTORY OF NATURAL LAW

When Aquinas elaborated a natural law theory, he was not beginning from scratch or operating in a vacuum. He was the heir to centuries of reflection on nature and morality, which came to him through various strands of thought. Indeed, it may be said that classic (Thomistic) natural law theory is part of a "family" of doctrines or concepts or ethical and political theories that share certain fundamental features. Among the most important are the natural right tradition of Plato and Aristotle,[1] the Stoic tradition (e.g., as described in certain works of Cicero[2]), Roman law,[3] and Augustine.[4] Aquinas drew on all these sources in forming his natural law teaching.

Natural Right

Greek political philosophy did not, for the most part, use the term "natural law." Yet Plato and Aristotle (following Socrates) are still sometimes regarded as the originators of natural law doctrine. Why? These political philosophers were the opponents of the Sophists, who argued that law was based on convention, and to this notion they opposed the idea of "nature" as the source of right and the standard by which human law was to be measured.

Socrates is credited by Aristotle as the founder of the "natural right" tradition. As portrayed in the Platonic dialogues and in Xenophon, he employs the dialectical method to "serve as a gadfly to the conventional opinion of the Athenians," writes Paul Sigmund:

by persistent questioning directed at the refinement and definition of concepts in order to arrive at a better understanding of the objects of actions which they represented. This definition was to be arrived at by analyzing the function or structure of the objects or actions represented by the concept being examined, and it was on this central insight that Plato built his later theories.[5]

Plato makes justice the central concern of his *Republic*, in which he uses dialectic to refute the sophistical positions embraced by Thrasymachus

---

[1] See, in particular, Aristotle's *Rhetoric* Book I, sections 10 and 13 (McKeown, pp. 1359, 1370).

[2] See especially Cicero's *Republic* and *Laws* (Loeb Classical Library, Vol. XVI, ed. Keyes, 1928). The extent to which Cicero's views are accurately stated by any of the particular participants in these dialogues is a subject of scholarly debate. See, for example, Ernest Fortin, "Augustine, Aquinas, and the Problem of Natural Law," *Mediaevalia*, Vol. 4 (1978), pp. 183–86.

[3] Particularly important contributions from Roman law are found in Gaius, Ulpian, and Justinian. See Paul E. Sigmund, *Natural Law in Political Thought* (Washington, D.C.: University Press of America, 1971), chap. 2.

[4] Augustine developed his doctrine, not of natural law, but of the eternal and human laws, in *On Free Choice of the Will*, trans. Benjamin and Hackstaff (Library of Liberal Arts, Bobbs–Merrill Company, 1964).

[5] Sigmund, *Natural Law*, p. 6.

and presented by Glaucon, and then unfolds an understanding of justice in the city and justice in the soul. While "direct appeals to nature as a source of norms do not appear frequently in the *Republic* ... the basic argument of the *Republic* amounts to an assertion that there is an order in nature and human nature which is universal, objective, and harmonious [and] conformity to this order brings harmony, virtue, and happiness." Sigmund concludes by explaining the ambivalence of Plato toward an ideal of natural law:

> To the extent, then, that Plato believed that there were universal principles inherent in nature which imposed a moral obligation on all men, he was enunciating a natural-law theory. Insofar as he viewed any given law as an inadequate representation of the eternal principles of justice, he was asserting a theory of natural (i.e., ideal) justice rather than one of natural law.

Aristotle develops the notion of nature in the *Physics* (II, 1):

> All the things mentioned ["animals and their parts, and the plants and the simple bodies (earth, fire, air, water)"] present a feature in which they differ from things which are *not* constituted by nature. Each of them has within itself a principle of motion and of stationariness (in respect of place, or of growth and decrease, or by way of alteration) ... *nature is a source or cause of being moved and of being at rest in that to which it belongs primarily*, in virtue of itself and not in virtue of a concomitant attribute.[6]

Nature is intelligible, orderly: things have intrinsic ends, and their full development consists in achieving a completion or perfection with respect to these ends.

Man's end consists especially in reason, as Aristotle argued in the *Nicomachean Ethics*. Human acts are right and wrong by nature, insofar as they correspond to ways of achieving, or failing to achieve, the development of the rational capacities with which man is endowed by his nature.

Aristotle does not generally speak of "natural law" – it is not mentioned in his most important ethical work, the *Nicomachean Ethics*, for example – although he does mention it briefly in the *Rhetoric*.[7] The context of these references (as Ernest Fortin points out[8]) is a discussion

---

[6] Richard McKeon, *The Basic Works of Aristotle*, p. 236 (italics in original).

[7] "By special law I mean that written law which regulates the life of a particular community; by general law, all those unwritten principles which are supposed to be acknowledged everywhere." (I, 10) "For there really is, as every one to some extent divines, a natural justice and injustice that is binding on all men, even on those who have no association or covenant with each other. It is this that Sophocles' Antigone clearly means when she says that the burial of Plyneices was a just act in spite of the prohibition: she means it was just by nature." (I, 13)

[8] Ernest Fortin, "Augustine, Aquinas, and the Problem of Natural Law," p. 182.

of forensic oratory, in which the rhetorician is effectively a lawyer dealing with wrongdoing, and therefore the formulation of natural "law" may be a variation appropriate to that context. (Note, too, that the invocation of the story of Antigone suggests a more specific context, in which the rhetorician must make an argument in the face of an explicit, contrary positive law.)

Aristotle more generally speaks of what is "right by nature." The natural right teaching of the *Nichomachean Ethics* tends to unfold, not by a strict demonstrative argument, but by a sorting out of common opinions. The emphasis is on virtue as the mean between excess and defect, with special attention to the virtuous activity of magnanimity, justice, friendship, and contemplation. So it may be said that Aristotle reflects the ambivalence about "natural law" (as opposed to natural right) that is characteristic of Plato.

In addition, Aristotle's view on the universality and changeability of natural right is not clear. When discussing natural justice in Book V of the *Nichomachean Ethics*, Aristotle divides political justice into parts: natural justice, "that which everywhere has the same force and does not exist by people's thinking this or that," and legal justice, "that which is originally indifferent, but when it has been laid down is not indifferent" (e.g., specifying the amount necessary to ransom a prisoner). Some people, he says, observing change in the things recognized as just, think that all justice is changeable.

> This, however, is not true in this unqualified way, but is true in a sense; or rather, with the gods it is perhaps not true at all, while with us there is something that is just even by nature, yet all of it is changeable; but still some is by nature, some not by nature. It is evident which sort of thing, among things capable of being otherwise, is by nature; and which is not but is legal and conventional, assuming that both are equally changeable.[9]

(It is hard to resist the temptation to think that Aristotle is speaking tongue-in-cheek when he says that anything about this matter, as he describes it, is "evident.") This passage, unsurprisingly, has given rise to conflicting interpretations,[10] since in the same breath it seems to say that natural justice is both unchangeable and changeable.

Whatever the ambiguities or ambivalence of some of its teachings, however, classical Greek political philosophy established nature (in contrast

---

[9] *The Basic Works of Aristotle*, p.1014.
[10] Compare, for example, Leo Strauss in *Natural Right and History*, chapter 4 "Classic Natural Right," with John Finnis, *Moral Absolutes* (Washington, DC: Catholic University of America Press, 1991), pp. 31–41.

to convention) firmly as the standard of right and the foundation for law, providing an essential element of future natural law theory. This makes it possible to recognize that natural right, in both its Socratic–Platonic and Aristotelian forms, and natural law are distinct, but at the same time to regard them, as did Leo Strauss in *Natural Right and History*, as "three types of classic natural right teachings, or three different manners in which the classics understood natural right."

The Stoic Tradition

It is difficult to say much with certitude about the Stoic tradition (especially its origins), because relatively little writing by the early Stoics has survived, and much of what we have has come down to us in fragments, or in reports by other writers (especially Cicero).[11] But some of the key Stoic concepts seem to have included a universal law, which was a law, not of the polis, but of the cosmopolis; this law was logos or "right reason which pervades all things and is identical with Zeus, lord and ruler of all that is"[12]; it assigned to each kind of being its right way, so that certain things may be said to be right by nature.

According to Zeno, the founder of Stoicism,

the goal of human striving was life according to nature. This was the same as the virtuous life. The reason was that any individual nature is a part of the nature of the whole cosmos, and so life according to nature means life according to right reason; and living according to right reason is living virtuously. In such virtue does eudaimonia or human happiness consist.[13]

The teaching of later Stoics (e.g., Panaetius) included the important ideas that "all men possess the common capacity to participate in divine reason, and the whole human race shares a fundamental equality and universal brotherhood."[14]

There is considerable debate over the relationship of Cicero to Stoic thought, but much of what we know about Stoicism comes from characters in his dialogues who articulate Stoic doctrines, including a natural

---

[11] For some serious doubts about whether the early Stoics even had a natural law teaching, and the possibility that Cicero himself may be the first to give it content (even if he did not fully embrace it), see Ernest Fortin, "Augustine, Thomas Aquinas, and the Problem of Natural Law," pp. 182–83.

[12] Sigmund, *Natural Law*, p. 21, citing Diogenes Laertius from another source.

[13] Joseph Owens, *A History of Ancient Western Philosophy* (New York: Appleton–Century–Crofts, Inc, 1959), p. 390.

[14] Sigmund, *Natural Law*, p. 21.

law.[15] Laelius, one of the participants in the dialogue *De Re Publica*, gives a statement of this teaching:

True law is right reason in agreement with nature; it is of universal application, unchanging and everlasting; it summons to duty by its commands, and averts from wrongdoing by its prohibitions... It is a sin to try to alter this law, nor is it allowable to attempt to repeal any part of it, and it is impossible to abolish it entirely... And there will not be different laws at Rome and at Athens, or different laws now and in the future, but one eternal and unchangeable law will be valid for all nations and all times, and there will be one master and ruler, that is, God, over us all, for he is the author of this law, its promulgator, and its enforcing judge.[16]

This notion of natural law shows that it includes the idea that things are right by nature, as classical natural rights thinkers held, but that it includes other ideas as well, which contribute to the unfolding of natural law theory, especially the notion of a lawgiver (God), and a more clear-cut assertion of the universality and unchangeability of the natural law.

Roman Law

Cicero described a "the law of nations" that was a sort of "common law" of mankind, and the existence of such a law contributed to the notion of a "natural" law across nations:

For there is no principle enunciated by the philosophers – at least none that is just and honorable – that has not been discovered and established by those who have drawn up codes of law for States. For whence comes our sense of duty? From whom do we obtain the principles of religion? Whence comes the law of nations, or even that law of ours which is called "civil"?[17]

This "consensus of all nations [*gentium*] is to be considered the law of nature."[18] Later figures of Roman law took up the idea of natural law and developed it in different ways.

These differences can be seen in two of the most important writers, Gaius and Ulpian, whose work is incorporated into Justinian's *Corpus of*

---

[15] For a discussion of the debate over Cicero, see Walter Nicgorski "Cicero and the Rebirth of Political Philosophy" in the *Political Science Reviewer* Vol. 8 (1978), p. 63. Nicgorski is somewhat more inclined than other recent thinkers (e.g., Leo Strauss) to think that Cicero – while explicitly adhering to the Academic school – was sympathetic to the Stoic natural law doctrine portrayed in his *De Re Publica*.

[16] Cicero, *De Re Publica*, Book III, chapter xxii, Loeb edition (Harvard University Press, 1970), p. 211.

[17] Ibid., Book I, chapter ii, p. 15.

[18] Cicero, *Tusculan Disputations*, Book I, ch. 13, No. 37; cited in Sigmund, *Natural Law*, p. 24.

Civil Law. Gaius, who wrote in the second century, carried on Cicero's identification of the law of nations and natural law:

All nations which are governed by statutes and customs make use partly of law which is peculiar to the respective nations, and partly of such as is common to all mankind. Whatever law any nation has established for itself is peculiar to the particular state [*civitas*], and is called civil law, as being the peculiar law of the state, but law which natural reason has laid down for mankind in general is maintained equally by all men, and is called *jus gentium*, as being the law which all nations use.[19]

Ulpian, writing a century later, gave a very different definition of natural law:

Natural law is that which all animals have been taught by nature; this law is not peculiar to the human species, it is common to all animals which are produced on land or sea, and to fowls of the air as well. From it comes the union of man and woman called by us matrimony, and therewith the procreation and rearing of children...*Jus gentium* is the law used by the various tribes of mankind, and there is no difficulty in seeing that it falls short of natural law, as the latter is common to all animated beings, whereas the former is only common to human beings in respect of their mutual relations;...[20]

(We will see that Thomas Aquinas integrates these different understandings of natural law into a larger whole.) Drawing on later Stoic teaching, Ulpian also maintained that "by natural law all were born free" and "slavery came in through the *jus gentium*," ideas that harmonized with teachings of the early Church Fathers.

Augustine

The Stoic notion of a universal law ordained by God that governs all things, reinforced by Roman law concepts of a law of nature and an early state of nature in which men were free and equal, was easily adapted for their purposes by Christian thinkers, especially some of the Fathers of the Church, who likewise, based on Scripture, believed in both a state before the Fall (*The Book of Genesis*) and a law written on the hearts of men by God (St. Paul's *Letter to the Romans*).

St. Augustine, perhaps more than any of the other Fathers of the Church, confronted the question of the relationship between faith and political life, in *The City of God*. The cultural context in which he

---

[19] Contained in Sigmund, *Natural Law*, pp. 33–34.
[20] Contained in Sigmund, *Natural Law*, pp. 32–33.

developed his thought was one in which Christians confronted philosophy and proclaimed Christianity the true philosophy. The sharp distinction between faith and reason – which we take so much for granted today – was not so sharp among early Christian thinkers: philosophy was the love and pursuit of wisdom, and wisdom was to be found, above all, through faith in Christ. (So Augustine, in *On Free Choice of the Will*, can tell his young interlocutor, Evodius, "lean upon piety and follow the paths of reason."[21])

Whereas Augustine does not speak of a natural law in *On Free Choice of the Will* (the first part of which includes some of his most philosophical writing), he does discuss the eternal law and the temporal law. Augustine says that temporal law is changeable (e.g., the proper form of government for a given people at a given time), but that there is a "law called the highest reason [*summa ratio*], which ought always to be obeyed" and which is "immutable and eternal"; and "there is nothing just and lawful" in temporal law "which men have not derived from eternal law." And "to put in a few words, as best I can, the notion of eternal law that has been impressed upon our minds: it is that law by which it is just that everything be ordered in the highest degree."[22] If, in his notion of eternal law, Augustine does not distinguish sharply between natural and divine law, it is important to recognize that this account of eternal law identifies it closely with reason, and, in this way, contributes to the development of natural law thought.

Thomistic Natural Law

The greatest representative of the classic natural law tradition is Thomas Aquinas, whose teaching is developed in the Treatise on Law in the *Summa Theologiae*, and which draws on Aristotle, the Stoics, Roman law, and Augustine, as well as Scripture (both the Old and New Testaments). Thomistic *natural* law is, paradoxically, a teaching developed in a theological rather than a philosophical work. The *Treatise on Law* (I–II, QQ.90–108) is set in the discussion of man's moral life, and is the first of two parts (together with the following section on grace) regarding "extrinsic principles" of human action. It follows an earlier general discussion of intrinsic principles (powers of the soul, and good and bad

---

[21] Augustine, *On Free Choice of the Will* (Indianapolis: Bobbs–Merrill Company, 1964), p. 13.
[22] Augustine, *On Free Choice of the Will*, pp. 14–15.

habits – virtues and vices), and precedes a discussion of virtues in particular (the theological virtues and the cardinal virtues).

Thomas's definition of law in general is that it is an ordinance of reason
for the common good, made by him who has care of the common good,
and promulgated.[23] The most comprehensive law is God's eternal law, and
other forms of law include natural law, human law, and divine positive
law.[24]

Thomas describes the natural law as the rational creature's

> share of the Eternal Reason, whereby it has a natural inclination to its proper act
> and end; and this participation of the eternal law in the rational creature is called
> the natural law...the light of natural reason whereby we discern what is good
> and what is evil, which is the function of the natural law, is nothing else than an
> imprint on us of the Divine light. It is therefore evident that natural law is nothing
> else than the rational creature's participation of the eternal law.[25]

The precepts of the natural law are the first principles of the practical
reason (paralleling the first principle of speculative reason, the principle
of non-contradiction).

> The first principle in the practical reason is one founded on the notion of good,
> viz. that good is that which all things seek after. Hence this is the first precept
> of law, that good is to be done and pursued, and evil is to be avoided. All other
> precepts of the natural law are based upon this; so that whatever the practical
> reason naturally apprehends as man's good (or evil) belongs to the precepts of the
> natural law as something to be done or avoided.[26]

But since good has the nature of an end

> all those things to which man has a natural inclination, are naturally apprehended
> by reason as being good, and consequently as objects of pursuit...Wherefore
> according to the order of natural inclinations, is the order of the precepts of the
> natural law.[27]

There are various inclinations in man. First, in accordance with the
nature of all substances, we seek the preservation of our own being,
according to its nature, so that "whatever is a means of preserving human

---

[23] Aquinas, *Summa Theologiae*, I–II, Q. 90, art. 4.
[24] Aquinas, *Summa Theologiae*, I–II, Q. 91.
[25] Aquinas, *Summa Theologiae*, I–II, Q. 91, art. 2.
[26] Aquinas, *Summa Theologiae*, I–II, Q. 94, art. 2. For a classic analysis of the first principle
of practical reason, see Germain Grisez, "The First Principle of Practical Reason: A
Commentary on the Summa Theologiae, 1–2, Question 94, Article 2" in the *Natural
Law Forum* Vol. 10 (1965), p. 165.
[27] Idem. On this point, see also Ralph McInerny, *Ethica Thomistica*, rev. ed. (Washington,
DC: Catholic University of America Press, 1997), pp. 40–46.

life, and of warding off its obstacles, belongs to the natural law." Second (drawing on Ulpian), according to the nature we share with animals, things "which nature has taught to all animals, such as sexual intercourse, education of offspring and so forth" belong to the natural law. Third, according to man's own nature, man has "an inclination to the good, according to the nature of his reason" which includes a natural inclination "to know the truth about God and to live in society," so that the natural law includes whatever pertains to this inclination (e.g., shunning ignorance, avoiding offending those among whom one has to live).[28]

All virtuous acts *as such* belong to the natural law, since virtue is nothing other than acting according to reason. But specific virtuous acts may or may not be prescribed by the natural law, since nature inclines to some of them at first, while others are the result, not of immediate inclination, but of the "inquiry of reason" which shows them "to be conducive to well-living."[29]

As "regards the general principles of practical reason, truth or rectitude is the same for all, and is equally known by all." As "to the proper conclusions of the practical reason, neither is the truth or the rectitude the same for all, nor, where it is the same, is it equally known by all." So, for example, it is right for all to act according to reason, and from this principle it follows that "goods entrusted to another should be restored to their owner." But this is true only "for the majority of cases" – there may be cases where it is not true, as when someone would reclaim property for the purpose of engaging in treasonous acts. (And the more the application of a principle descends into matters of detail, the greater the likelihood of such exceptions.)

So "the natural law, as to general principles, is the same for all, both as to rectitude and as to knowledge. But as to certain matters of detail, which are conclusions, as it were, of those general principles, it is the same for all in the majority of cases, both as to rectitude and as to knowledge, and yet in some few cases it may fail, both as to rectitude...and as to knowledge" (through being perverted, for example, by passion or evil habit).[30]

The first, most general principles of the natural law are known to all and cannot be blotted out of the heart of man, although their application to a particular action may be, on account of concupiscence (disordered

---

[28] Idem.
[29] Aquinas, *Summa Theologiae*, I–II, Q. 94, art. 3.
[30] Aquinas, *Summa Theologiae*, I–II, Q. 94, art. 4.

inclinations) or some other passion. But the secondary and more detailed principles of the natural law "which are, as it were, conclusions following closely from first principles" can be blotted out of the heart, by evil persuasions or vicious customs and corrupt habits.[31]

Aquinas drew the general outlines of natural law theory, but his primarily theological purposes limited the degree to which they were more fully developed. However, he began a tradition that included subsequent thinkers, many of whom were commentators on his work, and most of whom shared his theological framework, but who applied his broad outlines to questions he never considered himself. This work – little known in the Anglo-American academy – contains much that is still thought-provoking and valuable today.[32]

But I will not trace the history of Thomistic natural law theory through the subsequent centuries. At this point, I just want to note that after several centuries of distinguished commentators (culminating in the sixteenth century Spanish commentators and early Jesuits such as Suarez), the natural law tradition ceased to exert much influence on the broad development of Western political and ethical theory, and especially Anglo-American thought. This absence of influence or even interest (due in great part to the Reformation rejection of Catholicism) continued down through the twentieth century, when, as the fruit of a late nineteenth century revival of Thomistic studies (stimulated by Leo XIII's *Aeterni Patris*), scholars such as Etienne Gilson, Jacques Maritain, and Yves Simon emerged and had some appreciable influence in academic circles, and occasionally outside it.[33]

Modern Natural Rights

Meantime, a new and very different form of "natural law" emerged and did exercise profound influence on Western thought: the modern natural

---

[31] Aquinas, *Summa Theologiae*, I–II, Q. 94, art. 6. I confine myself to this brief discussion of natural law in the earlier parts of the *Treatise on Law*. It should be noted, however, that much of what Thomas has to say about the natural law can be found in his comments on the moral precepts of the Old Law (which he treats as a statement of natural law precepts) in the latter part of the *Treatise on Law* (especially Q. 100).

[32] The tradition that followed Aquinas is on impressive display, for example, in James Gordley's *The Philosophical Origins of Modern Contract Doctrine* (Oxford: Clarendon Press, 1991).

[33] One manifestation of this influence can be seen in the "Universal Declaration of Human Rights." See Mary Ann Glendon, *A World Made New: Eleanor Roosevelt and the Universal Declaration of Human Rights* (Random House, 2001).

rights theory of emergent liberalism, described in the preceding chapter.[34] This natural rights tradition employed the language of "the law of nature," and Locke's presentation of it had the appearance of continuity, with his explicit invocations of natural theology and his citations of the "judicious Hooker," an Anglican divine generally considered to be in the old natural law tradition.[35] But even a cursory examination of the content of natural rights political philosophy shows a fundamental change: from the natural law's orientation toward the positive fulfillment of the capacities of human nature – toward the *summum bonum* of virtue – there has been a move to an orientation toward a *summum malum*, the loss of self-preservation, with questions regarding man's ultimate fulfillment (e.g., virtue for its own sake, apart from its political utility) being largely relegated to a very private sphere.[36]

In Thomas's terms, Locke's natural law attends to the first level of human inclinations, which human beings share with other substances, namely, the inclination to self-preservation. Perhaps Locke's natural law includes the second level as well, what "nature has taught to all animals, such as sexual intercourse, education of offspring and so forth," insofar as this involves what is necessary to collective self-preservation of the human species. But what of the highest of the three levels of human inclinations: the "inclination to the good, according to the nature of his reason," which includes a natural inclination "to know the truth about God and to live in society" (so that the natural law includes whatever pertains to this inclination, e.g., shunning ignorance, avoiding offending those among one whom has to live)? Here, it seems, Locke would deny, or at least seriously truncate, Aquinas's natural law. While men may still have a sort of generic desire for knowledge and even for virtue, Locke's political philosophy denies the naturalness of political life and makes only certain limited aspects of the knowledge of God relevant to a truncated common good.

[34] The subject of the subtle changes in the natural law tradition that prepared the way for modern natural rights is a fascinating one. For a particularly interesting account of the change, see Michael Zuckert, *Natural Rights and the New Republicanism* (Princeton University Press, 1994).

[35] Thomas Hibbs has pointed out to me that Daniel Westberg raises serious questions about this assumption about Hooker. See Westberg "Thomistic Law and the Moral Theory of Richard Hooker" *American Catholic Philosophical Quarterly* Vol. 68 (1994), pp. 203–214.

[36] This theme of the shift from natural right and natural law, on one hand, to natural rights, on the other, was one of the fundamental themes in the scholarship of Leo Strauss; see, for example, *Natural Right and History* (University of Chicago, 1953).

LEVELS OF NATURAL LAW

Taking this brief history of natural law as a starting point, I want to try to identify four different forms or levels of "natural law" thought. They range from the very broad – highly abstract and formal – to the relatively concrete and specific, and can be differentiated by the range of thinkers that are comprehended within the category.

Natural Law as Objective Value

The first and most abstract notion that can be called "natural law" is that human beings are a certain *kind* of being, and the features of that being should direct our understanding of how human beings should live. This approach implies the existence of some sort of objective moral law knowable through reason. It is implicit in what is perhaps the most basic intuition giving rise to natural law, namely, the sense that there must be some general standard in light of which it is possible to judge human laws or conventions. The classic instance of this idea is found in Sophocles' *Antigone*, in which a sister disobeys a law by burying her brother, and claims a warrant in higher law for so doing.

At the same time, the understanding of natural law at this level of generality is very formalistic. Almost any thinker would fall in this category, except for those who resist the temptation to think that there are *any* norms or standards independent of human will that govern human action.

This understanding of natural law is well described by Russell Hittinger in his broad-ranging and insightful article, "Liberalism and the American Natural Law Tradition."[37] Hittinger points out that some contemporary uses of "natural law" identify it with the position that "values are woven into the fabric of the world" and thus, "value judgments and the moral prescriptions derived from them are not regarded as merely subjective statements of approval or disapproval; nor is the binding quality of the judgment about objective goods simply a function of the standards which we invent."[38] In this view, virtually "any account of morality – whether personal, moral, or political – that grounds at least some reasons for action in objective values, or at the very least, anthropological values" qualifies as natural law. "Natural law, then turns out to be any understanding of the relationship between law and morals which is neither positivistic nor

---

[37] Russell Hittinger, "Liberalism and the American Natural Law Tradition" 25, *Wake Forest Law Review*, 429 (1990).
[38] Ibid., p. 466.

nihilistic" and "formulated at this level of generality, natural law theory of one sort or another represents the great tradition of the West."[39]

Hittinger cites a classic discussion of "higher law" by Edward Corwin, an influential constitutional scholar in the first half of the twentieth century:

> There are, it is predicated, certain principles of right and justice which are entitled to prevail of their own intrinsic excellence, altogether regardless of the attitude of those who wield the physical resources of the community. Such principles were made by no human hands; indeed, if they did not antedate deity itself, they still express its nature as to bind and control it. They are external to all Will as such and interpenetrate all Reason as such. They are eternal and immutable. In relation to such principles, human laws are, when entitled to obedience save as to matters indifferent, merely a record or transcript, and their enactment an act not of will or power but one of discovery and declaration.[40]

Hittinger goes on to point out that this definition of natural law includes many thinkers who would never have used the term of their own work and who are ambivalent, or hostile, to the "epistemological ideal of attunement to an evident order of being"[41]: for example, Kant and his descendants, including John Rawls and Alan Gewirth, and contemporary legal thinkers such as H.L.A. Hart, Lon Fuller, Lawrence Tribe, Ronald Dworkin, David A.J. Richards, and various Supreme Court justices.

This definition of natural law is interesting in its recognition of a common feature that such a wide variety of opposing thinkers hold in common – the principle of objective value – but its very breadth also limits its usefulness.

Natural Law Rooted in Human Nature

A second form of natural law, and still at a very high level of generality, is what natural law, natural right, and natural rights thinkers have in common: the idea that there is a stable human nature that at least sets limits to how men should act in order to maximize the conditions for achieving a satisfactory existence.

Paul Sigmund's *Natural Law in Political Thought* offers an account which identifies some common elements in these various thinkers. Despite the apparent variety of content attributed to natural law, he says,

---

[39] Ibid., pp. 466–67.
[40] Ibid., p. 467.
[41] Ibid., p. 479, quoting Richards.

there seems to be a central assertion expressed or implied in most theories of natural law. This is the belief that there exists in nature and/or human nature a rational order which can provide intelligible value-statements independently of human will, that are universal in application, unchangeable in their ultimate content, and morally obligatory on mankind.

Besides deriving different substantive principles from natural law, the theorists that we will examine attribute a variety of meanings to nature, which is their source. They have equated the natural with the rational; the divine; the distinctively human; the normally operating; the frequently recurring; the primitive; the elements not subject to human artifice or control; the self-evident; and the nonhistorical. It is therefore necessary in analyzing these theories, to determine in which sense natural law is being used in a given case.

... in all its diverse forms, the theory of natural law represents a common affirmation about the possibility of arriving at objective standards, and a common procedure for doing so – looking for a purposive order in nature and man.[42]

Given the diversity of conceptions of "nature" in this account, very different philosophies may count as "natural law," which explains why it can include Plato and Aristotle, Roman law, Thomas Aquinas, Hobbes and Locke, and even Rousseau and Burke, Hume, Bentham and Mill, and Kant.

While Sigmund mentions "reason" as only one possible understanding or aspect of "nature," I think that virtually all the thinkers that he puts in the category of natural law place some emphasis on some understanding of reason. At the same time, "reason" is a very protean concept, which can have very diverse meanings. In particular, there is a fundamental difference between "instrumental rationality," which takes human ends as somehow given and then focuses on the means to achieve them, and the broader, classical sense of reason as a capacity to grasp or perceive human ends as well as the capacity to devise means to achieve them.

Considering classical (natural right and Thomistic natural law) and modern (natural rights) political philosophy as falling within the category of natural law requires a broad definition of the essential features of natural law – only a shade narrower than the first definition above. The first concept of natural law focused on the idea of objective value, while the second concept adds that this objective value is rooted, somehow, in human nature, which also suggests that the value is permanent and universal. (It therefore excludes not only the positivistic and nihilistic approaches Hittinger considered excluded in the first concept, but also the notions of objective value that are rooted in essentially malleable notions

---

[42] Sigmund, *Natural Law,* pp. viii–ix.

of human nature, and especially modern or post-modern approaches that view human beings as characterized above all by the capacity for self-definition, and hence as not bound by any fixed nature.) Objective value rooted in nature need not entail a full or well-developed theory of the human good: it could simply be an identification of certain substantive evils to be avoided, as it is in natural rights theories that make self-preservation the fundamental desideratum.

But, as in the case of the first concept of natural law, the use of the term to encompass such a wide range of fundamentally differing philosophies limits its utility.

Natural Law and a Natural Order of Ends

A third notion of natural law, which has much more substantive content, is what natural law and natural right thinkers have in common: an idea of a natural order, with various kinds of beings whose fulfillment or realization consists in developing and perfecting immanent capacities. This order is discovered, not created, by human beings. Human beings achieve a good life by living in accord with the natural order, and specifically by developing the capacities inherent in and distinctive of human nature. (While pleasure is recognized as good, it is always a derivative or secondary good attached to some more basic human good – good as a means, not an end – and it can be the source of disorder when it becomes an end in itself, as it often does for many human beings.) A flourishing human life is one of intellectual virtue (e.g., wisdom, developed in the philosophic life of dialectic and contemplation) and moral virtue (e.g., the cardinal virtues of prudence, justice, fortitude, and temperance). Preeminent among the moral virtues is practical wisdom, whereby men, guided by a general perception of human goods and by right desire, choose the practical good, the right way of acting here and now. The common good (the good of the self-sufficient community – the polis, a broader political community, or even a universal Church) has a special eminence.

Both natural right and classical natural law are based on epistemological realism: human knowledge is not merely of appearances, much less a mere mental construction, but goes to natures or essences. These approaches do, of course, recognize the plethora of obstacles to accurate human perception of reality, including the limits of the human intellect per se (e.g., its dependence on sense and imagination, which makes knowledge of immaterial realities more difficult), cultural blinders, the weaknesses of given intellects, and the distortion of perception by disorder in the will (e.g., the tendency of human beings to "see" what they *want* to see). But, despite all these obstacles, natural right and natural law maintain that the human mind is capable of grasping reality itself.

Natural right and natural law share a similar philosophical *anthropology*. This understanding of human nature includes first, an internal ordering of the human faculties: reason–spirit–desire in the earlier, natural right tradition, or intellect–will–passions, in the Thomistic tradition, with reason or intellect exercising a directive function in well-developed human beings. Second, it views human beings as an integrated mind–body, so that it is neither reductionist (reducing mind to body as, for example, materialists do) nor dualist (separating them, and thereby viewing body and mind as "the ghost in the machine").

Natural law is not, as it is sometimes misperceived, simply an identification of "typical patterns of behavior in nature," and especially in human life. Nor is it a theory based primarily on biological impulses or drives. "Nature" in natural right and classical natural law is understood as the full development of the inherent capacities of a being. The nature of a being is what it is when it is fully developed. In non-human beings, "their respective inclinations to their proper acts and ends" are simply "imprinted in their being," so to speak, and these ends are achieved without deliberation or choice (although some beings are defective and do not achieve their full natural development, due to internal defects or external obstacles). Man, a rational creature, on the other hand, having a "natural inclination to its proper act and end," must undertake deliberation and choice to achieve his ends – this sort of creature "partakes of a share of providence, by being provident both for itself and others."[43]

If the gap between the first two concepts of natural law is fairly small, the differences between those two concepts and this one are very substantial. The common substantive content of natural law theories – the emphasis on natural teleology, virtue, and practical wisdom – on this understanding of natural law is much broader. This is not surprising, given that Aquinas's thought is, after all, characterized as "Christian Aristotelianism." The commentaries on Aristotle form an important part of his corpus of writing, and Aristotle is, for him, "the Philosopher." Still, there remain important differences. Some of these differences are the result of revelation (for example, the typology of law that includes divine positive law) and others are perhaps differences that can be argued about even

---

[43] Aquinas, *Summa Theologiae*, I–II, Q. 91, art. 2 (p. 997).

within Aristotle's own framework of reason (e.g., the difference between Aristotle's Prime Mover and Aquinas's Creator).

Classical Thomistic Natural Law

The fourth and most determinate sense of natural law, strictly or properly speaking, is classical Thomistic natural law: human beings flourish and achieve such happiness as is possible in this life by living good lives, following a law inscribed in their being: above all, lives of virtue or excellence, and especially intellectual virtue. They choose particular ways of living well, guided by the self-evident basic principles of natural law, which they grasp through practical reason and by right desire (largely the fruit of proper habituation).

This ethical order is rooted in an ontological order, an order of being, although this natural law is not known or understood by deducing moral norms from a theoretical understanding of that order – rather, it is grasped in the first instance by acts of the practical reason recognizing certain self-evident principles. In the theological context in which Aquinas wrote, that order was the eternal law, which includes divine positive law, which is derived from revelation, and natural law, which is man's rational participation in this eternal law. According to Aquinas, however, the broader context of the natural law is not only what is known through divine revelation, but also includes knowledge through natural reason of God the Creator's existence, power, and providence – a "natural theology." Therefore, the term "natural law" is more properly used of Thomistic natural law, rather than classical natural right (which rarely speaks of natural law), because it is understood to come from a "lawgiver," and it is in this sense that I primarily use the term.

CONTEMPORARY NATURAL LAW DEBATES: THE "NEW NATURAL LAW THEORY"

Among the most significant contemporary representatives of the natural law tradition are the advocates of what has come to be called the "new natural law theory." Germain Grisez was the originator of this theory, and John Finnis and Robert George are its most prominent representatives among contemporary political and legal theorists. Because of its success in attracting some recognition in secular academic circles, I think it is worthwhile describing briefly. To do so, I will draw on the writings of political scientist Robert George, the preeminent exponent of classical natural law among contemporary American political scientists, for a summary of this recent form of natural law theory, and then raise some questions about it. In the end, however, I want to stress that, for purposes of articulating a public philosophy, what it has in common with traditional natural law theory is more important than the differences.

The New Natural Law Theory

George begins[44] by observing that human beings normally act for *reasons*, although sometimes their actions are irrational (e.g., based on emotions rather than reason). Those reasons include basic human goods, which are intrinsic goods (goods-in-themselves requiring no further justification) and instrumental goods (which are good because of their ultimate relationship to some basic good). Much of the time, human choices are choices between two actions for which there are reasons, with neither choice having reasons which "defeat" the other choice. But even actions based on reasons may be practically unreasonable, as for instance when an action is based on a reason (e.g., the praiseworthy desire to discover a cure for AIDS) but the action is contrary to a moral norm (e.g., performing deadly tests on a nonconsenting AIDS victim, which is contrary to the moral norm against murder).

Basic goods are first-order reasons for action, and these goods embrace life (including health and vitality), knowledge, play, aesthetic experience, sociality (friendship broadly conceived), practical reasonableness, and religion (ordering one's life in accord with the ultimate source of meaning and value). The first four are substantive goods, while the last three are reflexive (meaning that the latter necessarily involve human choice in their definition). These basic goods are self-evident in themselves (although they are not necessarily recognized by all) and indemonstrable, "grasped in non-inferential acts of understanding by the mind working inductively on the data of inclination and experience."[45] These goods are also "incommensurable," i.e., no measure of one or several goods can be said to "outweigh" another.

The very multiplicity of first-order reasons presupposes second-order reasons that direct choice, by excluding options. Moral norms provide

---

[44] This entire section is a summary of George's account of natural law in the introduction to *Making Men Moral* (Clarendon Press, 1993), drawn from my review of that book in the *Political Science Reviewer*, Volume XXV (1996), pp.354–404.

[45] George, *Making Men Moral*, p. 13.

such second-order reasons. Integral or complete human well-being and fulfillment – "the complete human fulfillment of all persons and communities in the basic human goods" – is (in this life, at least) "an ideal," which cannot actually be chosen. It does, however, direct choice, since it provides the fundamental principle of morality that "in voluntarily acting for human goods and avoiding what is opposed to them, one ought to choose and otherwise will those and only those possibilities whose willing is compatible with a will toward integral human fulfillment."[46] This fundamental principle must be specified by considering different ways in which feelings fetter reason and deflect a person from fully reasonable choosing, a consideration which produces moral principles ("requirements of practical reasoning") "intermediate" between the first principle of morality and specific moral norms (e.g., norms against rape and theft). Examples include "the Golden Rule" and "the so-called Pauline Principle" (which forbids the doing of evil that good may come).

All of this assumes a model of human action in which people not only choose extrinsic ends to satisfy their desires but choose for the sake of ends intrinsic to themselves as persons. Choices (whether of an intrinsic good, or of a means, or of voluntarily accepting incidental side effects of acting for an intrinsic good or a means) are self-constituting: they shape a person's character by integrating the moral good or evil of his choices into his will.

Observations on the New Natural Law Theory

The relationship between this new natural law theory and more traditional Thomism is hotly debated. One is less surprised about this controversy when one discovers that Grisez and Finnis have expressed some reluctance about even using the term "natural law" in reference to their approach.

I want to begin with two observations. First, I consider Grisez's moral theory, at the very least, to be a significant contemporary formulation of natural law, which cannot be dismissed out of hand. Some of its traditionalist critics tend to write it off as either slightly baptized Kantianism or contemporary analytic philosophy, and that reaction seems to me to be unwarranted.

Second, on the other hand, my understanding of the new natural law theory leaves me with some important reservations. One important question separating the "new" natural law theory from more traditional

---

[46] *Making Men Moral*, p. 16.

formulations of natural law is the relationship of theoretical and practical reason. Do practical judgments about what human beings should do entail theoretical knowledge of human nature?

Grisez and his collaborators, including George, argue that no practical propositions (what man "ought" to do) can be drawn from theoretical propositions (what he "is"). Practical reason starts from its own self-evident principles: the first principle of practical reason ("good is to be done and pursued and evil avoided"), the primary precepts of the natural law (the basic goods), and the first principle of morality ("choose only what can be willed consistent with willing the full or integral human good"). Further and more specific moral principles are derived from these, by way of the various requirements of practical reason (or "modes of responsibility"), such as the Golden Rule and the Pauline Principle (evil may not be done that good may come of it).

Ralph McInerny and other critics of the new natural law theory argue that the notion of "good" entails that it be "perfective" of the being for which it is a good, and that this requires knowledge of the kind of being it is – that is, it involves theoretical knowledge of some sort. This knowledge may be, and often is, "implicit" – not articulated by the person making the judgment – but it is still theoretical knowledge in some important sense. Moreover, as moral analysis moves toward more specific moral judgments, action in accordance with reason, understood as including consideration of the *kind* of being we are, seems to be key. I remain unconvinced that knowledge of human nature, in this sense, is unnecessary in arriving at a knowledge of moral norms.[47]

McInerny argues, following Aristotle, that there is an "ultimate end" of human beings, which – while not limiting good action to only one kind – does provide some kind of hierarchy of human ends. For Aristotle, that end is contemplation. For Aquinas, it is "beatitude," fully achievable only in God, but attainable in a more imperfect way on earth.

---

[47] For example, I find the analysis of contraception and why it is wrong by Grisez and his collaborators – that it involves a "contralife" will – unpersuasive. Putting this in traditional terms, the new natural law theory sees contraception as a violation of the Fifth Commandment, "Do not kill," rather than (the more traditional natural law view) the Sixth Commandment, "Do not commit adultery" (acting in ways inconsistent with the intrinsic ends of the conjugal act). Moreover, their analysis makes contraception impossible to distinguish from natural family planning, in my opinion, despite their efforts to show the contrary, and it gives insufficient emphasis to the *nature* of the sexual act, ordered to procreation and marital unity, as Janet Smith argues in *Humanae Vitae: A Generation Later* (Washington, D.C.: The Catholic University of America Press, 1991).

In contrast, Grisez, Finnis, and George deny that there is a hierarchy of human ends. There is an ultimate end (realizing the basic goods of all persons), in the limited sense of "an ideal." But one cannot say that one basic good is "better than," and should take precedence to, another basic good. "None of these [basic goods] is so absolutely prior that it prevails in every morally good choice."[48]

But why should one be permitted to talk of a hierarchy among goods only when one good would always prevail in every morally good choice? Of course, different goods will prevail in different situations – whether to pursue the good of speculative knowledge by a study of Aristotle is a question that will surely (and legitimately) be answered differently by a scholar and a janitor. But recognizing the legitimacy of various goods is still compatible with ranking activities as higher to lower – philosophic knowledge being intrinsically nobler than the cleanliness that contributes to health and beauty, for example – without the lower in any way being denied its essential goodness.[49]

Another reservation about the new natural law theory is reflected in Ernest Fortin's review of John Finnis' *Natural Law and Natural Rights*. Fortin argued that the new natural law theory can "claim the merit of ascertaining with quasi-mathematical rigor and determinateness the specific norms by which human choices are to be guided," thus overcoming "one of the conspicuous deficiencies or would-be deficiencies of the Thomistic teaching, which leaves it at saying that all such norms are derived from the common principles of the natural law without stipulating any rule or method by which the process of derivation might be carried out."[50] But perhaps the Thomistic teaching's relative lack of such quasi-mathematical rigor was a better reflection of the nature of the subject matter (as the "would-be" of Fortin's quotation suggests). That may partly explain why the virtues loom much larger in Aquinas' thought, and why the practical reasonableness of the new natural law theory seems somewhat truncated, relative to classical prudence.[51]

---

[48] Grisez et al. "Practical Principles, Moral Truth, and Ultimate Ends" in the *American Journal of Jurisprudence* (1987), p. 139.

[49] Note too that it is possible to argue that various instantiations of one basic good can be higher than *and* lower than instantiations of another good. Deeper philosophic knowledge may outweigh greater health (part of the good of life) in one case, while life itself outweighs more extensive knowledge of butterflies.

[50] Ernest Fortin, "The New Rights Theory and the Natural Law" *The Review of Politics*, p. 593.

[51] Ibid., p. 597.

Finally, I will add that the absence of "synderesis" – the habit by which human beings hold natural law principles – in the new natural law theorists may contribute to their somewhat less "imperative" conception of the first principle of practical reason. I find in "conscience" (understood here, by extension, more as a quasi-faculty than – its more strict definition – as a judgment) a powerful support for the notion that natural law is indeed *law* in a stronger sense than mere prescription. The empirical human reality of guilt when we have not done what we *should* have – for all the fact that it can be suppressed in many cases – seems to me a strong witness to the imperative character of the first principle of practical reason. (And this can be maintained independently of a divine will theory, although the existence of a God who commands would obviously strongly reinforce this natural sense of obligation.)

CORE AGREEMENT ON NATURAL LAW

Whatever one's final determination about the complete adequacy of the new natural law theory, I want to place greater emphasis on the fact that it is possible to identify a core of common agreement between it and the more traditional natural law doctrine, and that this core can and should serve as the foundation for a public philosophy (the elements of which I shall detail in a subsequent section).

What are the essential elements of this "common" natural law theory? Let me suggest the following:

1. Human beings naturally know that they ought to pursue good and avoid evil.
2. This directive to pursue good and avoid evil entails, among other things, that we ought to act according to reason.
3. A corollary to the principle that we should act according to reason is that obtaining pleasure is never a *sufficient* reason for performing an action – the activity that gives pleasure must be *judged* by our reason to be good.
4. Acting according to reason means acting for the sake of certain human goods, and we naturally know certain basic human goods. This is true despite the pluralism of modern societies, which is often given as a ground – wrongly – for assuming the impossibility of establishing social agreement on certain basic human goods. (Even a pluralistic society, for example, can agree on recognizing life and knowledge as intrinsic human goods.)

5. Among the basic human goods are: life (a good that we share with other animate beings), begetting and raising of offspring (a good that we share with animals), and knowledge – especially knowledge of the most important things, the fundamental structure of reality – and living in society (goods proper to beings with reason).

6. All good human actions are justified as pursuits of some genuine human good; actions are evil either because the object of the act is evil, or the motive is evil, or it is done under the wrong circumstances.

7. The basic human goods can be elaborated, and in doing so we recognize the outlines of certain classic moral commands, such as the Golden Rule, the ends do not justify the means, and the Ten Commandments (which include worship God, honor parents, and do not murder, steal, commit adultery, or lie).

8. Because of the diversity of human goods and the ways of achieving goods (not all of which can be pursued at the same time), universal moral principles regarding particular acts are typically formulated in negative terms. (In other words, we can more often state in universal terms what human beings ought *not* to do than what they ought to do, although there are some examples of the latter, typically at higher levels of generality.)

9. As we elaborate moral principles in more detail and consider their application to concrete circumstances, they are more difficult to know and the directives for action are less likely to be universal. For example, in general, borrowed goods should be returned to their owners, but not a borrowed gun to an owner with murderous intentions. Nonetheless, there are still some exceptionless moral norms, such as do not directly kill innocent human beings, do not torture people.

10. Human laws should serve the common good.

11. Human laws derive their justice – and people have an obligation to obey them – because of their derivation from the natural law, either as directly entailed by the commands of the natural law or as particular (though not always necessary) means to achieve the common good.

12. Because the common good is profoundly affected by the character of the citizens of the community, human law – while it cannot literally "make men moral" – has an appropriate role to play in fostering virtue (an habitual orientation to choose good and avoid evil) and discouraging vice.

13. Prudence dictates, however, that human law should encourage virtue and discourage vice particularly in those matters that involve the good of the community more directly and by directives that most people in a particular society are capable of living by.

Natural law, then, is especially concerned with practical reason's apprehension of what is good for human beings, including moral norms, and the happiness or fulfillment derived from living in accordance with these norms. An important question to which we must now turn is: what is the bearing of this concern for the human good on the central ideal of liberalism, namely, freedom?

CLASSICAL NATURAL LAW AND LIBERTY

The argument of this book is that classical natural law theory provides the best framework for the public philosophy of a liberal democracy – one superior to that of contemporary liberalism. One obstacle to accepting this argument for many people today is the belief that natural law is insufficiently appreciative of the importance of liberty. This suspicion of natural law is understandable, because there is some truth to this criticism of classical natural law (for reasons discussed below, in Chapter 10). In this chapter, however, I want to try to respond to that suspicion, and to allay it somewhat, by showing that there is less truth in the view that classical natural law was hostile to important dimensions of human liberty than is sometimes supposed.

Three points stand out when we examine classic natural law on the importance of liberty: first, the non-absolutist character of political rule, second, the limits of promotion of virtue by law, and third, the limited range of natural law precepts. Before I discuss these points, however, I would like to deal with a preliminary issue bearing on the question of liberty: namely, the stance of classical natural right thinkers on slavery.

Classical Natural Right and Slavery

It is not unusual to see Aristotle dismissed as a guide for contemporary life on the grounds that he defended "natural slavery," and, to the extent that classical natural law theorists such as Thomas Aquinas relied on Aristotle, natural law can share in that opprobrium. Any defense of natural law regarding liberty, then, needs to come to grips with this issue.

Those who have wished to defend the relevance of Aristotle and natural right thought have responded to critiques regarding his discussion of slavery in various ways. Some have suggested that Aristotle deliberately gave a theoretical defense of slavery that de-legitimated almost all actual slavery.[52] Others have argued that slavery, as Aristotle understood it, was more benign than the form we think of, and that his argument is defensible.[53] Others have defended natural right by maintaining that, even if Aristotle did intend to defend an indefensible institution, this was a case of "Homer nodding," since natural right properly understood would lead us to a different conclusion, namely, the condemnation of slavery.

To get a clearer view of the matter, it is necessary to notice that slavery is not simply equivalent to the most common images of it today, namely, race–based chattel slavery, which is rightly the object of strong moral condemnation. Slavery is a broader term that encompasses involuntary servitude in general. As such, it is not true that slavery is intrinsically – always and everywhere – wrong. Most importantly, involuntary servitude of a humane sort as punishment for serious crimes may be morally justifiable. Likewise, the most common historical origin of slave status, war, could, in principle, have been the basis of just involuntary servitude, in the case of unjust aggressors captured in a just war. Once we understand that there is such a thing as just servitude, the fact that proponents of natural right defended it in some form ceases to be an automatic disqualification for its being taken seriously.

At the same time, there is considerable truth to the claim that the natural right defense of slavery gave little theoretical support to the actually existing forms of slavery. To the extent that slaves in Greece were largely captives in war, it is difficult to argue – as Aristotle himself noted[54] – that they fit the description of a slave-by-nature as "he who can be, and therefore is, another's, and he who participates in rational principle enough to apprehend, but not to have, such a principle."[55] Moreover, most victors in wars, historically, have lacked just grounds for taking slaves because the wars they have prosecuted have been unjust. And, finally, there was no moral ground for making the status of just servitude transferable to offspring.

---

[52] See William T. Bluhm, "Aristotle's Theory of Slavery," a paper delivered at the annual meeting of the American Political Science Association, 1980 (cited in Dobbs, below).

[53] See Darrell Dobbs "Natural Right and the Problem of Aristotle's Defense of Slavery" in *The Journal of Politics*, Vol. 56, No. 1 (Feburary, 1994), p. 69–94.

[54] Aristotle, *Politics*, I, vi, in *The Basic Works of Aristotle*, McKeon, Ed. (Random House, 1941), p. 1135.

[55] Aristotle, *Politics*, I, v; ibid., p. 1133.

In cases of "natural" slavery, Aristotle characterized the relationship as one in which the master has the same genuine concern for the slave as for his own body: "where the relation of master and slave between them is natural," Aristotle says, "they are friends and have a common interest."[56] Aristotle also recommends that liberty should always be held out to slaves as the reward of their services.[57] Historical slavery hardly followed this pattern.

But even if there are grounds for just servitude in some cases, and if Aristotle's defense of slavery was an implicit criticism of most existent slavery and required that justifiable slavery be humane, it still must be conceded that there was an apparent willingness to accommodate slavery in classical thought, as there was in early Christianity (and as there was a tacit acceptance of great inequality in the medieval natural law tradition). Part of the reason for this may have been a disinclination of classical thinkers to engage in an apparently quixotic attack on a deeply embedded institution, preferring instead to adopt the course of mitigating it, of rendering it more humane. Part of it, also, may have been the assumption that a great deal of actual inequality was rooted in nature, in the sense that human flourishing depended on social arrangements of inequality that permitted some – relatively few – to have the leisure and resources necessary to develop capacities (intellectual and moral virtues such as philosophic wisdom and political prudence) necessary for the common good. To be fair to people of an earlier era, there may have been some truth in this assumption, especially under the conditions of relative material scarcity in the world in which they lived – though it was an assumption easily and often manipulated to serve, not the common good, but the self-interest of certain classes and individuals. What time – and, in great measure, liberalism – showed was that a society committed to freedom and equality of opportunity was actually more effective in attaining and making more widely available the leisure and resources necessary for fuller human development – although there was no guarantee that this leisure and these resources would be put in the service of those higher goals. That movement toward greater freedom and equality of opportunity, then, was defensible and desirable precisely as a way of attaining the classical common good more effectively, distributing its benefits more widely and permitting a wider range of people to participate in it more fully.

[56] Aristotle, *Politics*, I, vi; ibid., p. 1135.
[57] Aristotle, *Politics*, VII, x; ibid., p. 1292.

Classical natural right, then, is not inextricably intertwined with a defense of inadmissible forms of servitude, with slavery as we know it. It rightly recognized the legitimacy of some forms of servitude and the illegitimacy of others (including most actually existing slavery), and it promoted a more humane form of slavery where it did exist. Most importantly, it provided a standard of excellence for human life – intellectual and moral virtue – and a commitment to a common good that included all people, in the very name of which the movement from slavery and serfdom to growing equality of opportunity could be justified, as a way of diffusing these goods more broadly.

Non-Absolutist Political Rule

It is sometimes thought that classical (Thomistic) natural law theory was allied with political absolutism and authoritarian rule, but this is a mistake. Absolutism was really a later, early modern phenomenon rather than a medieval one. This is not surprising, given that Western Christianity – despite temptations that some political and religious rulers succumbed to – generally tended to resist theocracy, the union of religious and political power, distinguishing the things that were Caesar's and those that were God's. There were separate institutions for ultimate religious authority (in the medieval world, the papacy) and ultimate political authority (kings and emperors). The continual conflict between them testified to their separation, although it must be conceded that it took a long time to achieve a more clearly defined distinction between the two spheres.[58]

Moreover, Christian political thought was hospitable to the idea of an ordered multitude of ranks and groups in society, with power widely dispersed. (This was the historical form of what eventually was articulated as the principle of subsidiarity, the idea that each function should be performed by the lowest level of community adequate to perform it.)

In his relatively few remarks about political institutions, Thomas Aquinas tended not toward absolutism, but toward an ideal of mixed government, which is the blending of elements from various forms of government, including monarchy, aristocracy, and popular rule. Some confusion may be occasioned by his identification of kingship as the best form of government, especially in his work *De Regno* (*On Kingship*), a letter written to a king who had asked for his advice. But his understanding

---

[58] On this conflict, see Edward A. Goerner, *Peter and Caesar* (Herder and Herder, 1965).

of kingship was more nuanced, as a passage from his *Summa Theologiae* shows:

> Two points are to be observed concerning the right ordering of rulers in a state or nation. One is that all should take some share in the government: for this form of constitution ensures peace among the people, commends itself to all, and is most enduring, as stated in *Polit*. ii. 6. The other point is to be observed in respect of the kinds of government, or the different ways in which the constitutions are established. . . . Accordingly, the best form of government is in a state or kingdom, wherein one is given the power to preside over all; while under him are others having governing powers: and yet a government of this kind is shared by all, both because all are eligible to govern, and because the rule[r]s are chosen by all. For this is the best form of polity, being partly kingdom, since there is one at the head of all; partly aristocracy, in so far as a number of persons are set in authority; partly democracy, i.e., government by the people, in so far as the rulers can be chosen from the people, and the people have the right to choose their rulers.[59]

So any illusion that natural law was necessarily associated with a divine right theory of rule should be dismissed.

As Yves Simon points out in his *Philosophy of Democratic Government*, later commentators on Aquinas, including Cajetan, Bellarmine, and Suarez, like all orthodox Christian thinkers, generally saw power as originating in God, but they argued that it was given by God, not directly to rulers, but to a people, who then transmitted it to their rulers, in explicit contrast to the divine right theories of kingship, such as that of King James I of England.[60]

Classical natural law theory, then, was not necessarily associated with political absolutism. There was an appreciation of the need for balance, which involved both securing the participation of, and placing limits on, all parts of society in political rule. Those limits extended to law as well.

Limits of Law

The end of law, for classic natural law thinkers, was the promotion of the common good. So Aquinas teaches, in his *Treatise on Law*, that man has an inclination to act according to reason or virtue, and, from this perspective, it may be said that all acts of virtue are prescribed by the natural law.[61] Human law is derived from the natural law, either as conclusions

---

[59] I–II, Q. 105, a. 1.
[60] See Yves Simon, *The Philosophy of Democratic Government* (University of Chicago Press, 1951), chapter III.
[61] *Summa Theologiae*, I–II, Q. 94, a. 3.

are drawn from principles, or as specific determinations of a more general principle. But, interestingly, Aquinas answers negatively the question, "Whether it belongs to the human law to repress all vices?" Why?

Aquinas says that laws imposed on men should be in keeping with their condition, for law should be (quoting Isidore) "possible both according to nature, and according to the customs of the country." This possibility is related to interior habit or disposition (some things being possible for one who has a virtuous habit that are not possible for others):

> Now human law is framed for a number of human beings, the majority of whom are not perfect in virtue. Wherefore human laws do not forbid all vices, from which the virtuous abstain, but only the more grievous vices, from which it is possible for the majority to abstain; and chiefly those that are to the hurt of others, without the prohibition of which human society could not be maintained; thus human law prohibits murder, theft, and suchlike.[62]

In one of the responses, he adds that the danger of imposing on imperfect men precepts that they cannot bear is that "the precepts are despised, and those men, from contempt, break out into evils worse still."[63]

There are several factors, then, which counsel moderation in the use of law to repress bad habits. First, there seems to be a natural inequality among men, some – relatively few – of whom are more fully virtuous, but the majority of whom are "not perfectly virtuous," i.e., they have a mixture of different virtues and vices. Even when people's behavior is good, it is not always based on a firmly rooted habit, but is often a form of Aristotle's quasi-virtue of continence.[64] Human law is framed for these many, and it should prohibit only what the many are capable of abstaining from.

This is a warning against political utopianism and authoritarianism, which can foster a belief that it is possible to achieve an ideal state in which virtually the whole society lives up to the demands of the full range of intellectual and moral virtues, if only coercive law is employed by wise rulers in the pursuit of this goal. Human beings are a mixed lot, however, with their various strengths and weaknesses, and experience suggests that there is something like a moral bell-shaped curve: that the number of people who strive mightily for the highest human virtues, and the number of

---

[62] *Summa Theologiae*, I–II, Q. 96, a. 2.
[63] Ibid., ad 2.
[64] The appetites of the virtuous person are ordered according to his virtue, while the continent person has disordered appetites, but resists following them. *Nicomachean Ethics*, Book VII, 9.

people who lead thoroughly detestable lives, are both limited, with the vast majority of mankind falling somewhere along the spectrum in between them.[65] Law can promote certain forms and levels of virtue among men generally, but only within certain limits.

One of those limits, as Robert George has pointed out, is the danger of promoting conformism.[66] Laws act on people's external behavior and are incapable of directly forming the soul. In some cases, then, the effect of laws that prohibit vice or command virtue will be to bring about nominal compliance without genuine virtue. While such compliance may have value – at least it prevents the formation of bad habits – it also may have the effect of promoting hypocrisy, cynicism, or a deformed notion of virtue as mere correspondence with norms about external acts.

Another of these limits is that, at some point, many men who are pushed too hard to live according to higher levels of virtue will rebel. The power of law is limited and it should be employed especially on those matters in which most people will obey: the more serious vices, and especially those that are most harmful to others and to society.

Second, in addition to this broad natural inequality, there are also differences that arise from the particular features of a given political community. Thomas cites the earlier Christian writer Isidore, who says that law also must be in keeping with what is possible, given "the customs of the country." If bad habits have deep roots in a culture, law is not likely to be able to uproot them. In fact, as Thomas notes, the precepts of such a law will be despised and the ordinary citizens unable to "take" such regulation will break out into worse evils. (An example of this might be the creation of a "backlash" that would make the law worse than it might have been if it had tried to do less.) Better to aim lower, perhaps to restrict or limit certain vices successfully, rather than try unsuccessfully to obliterate them, and in the process make people despise the law (both the particular law and law in general).

What this means is that there is a definite relationship between a given country's *mores* and which vices that country's law is capable of repressing. Every people and nation has its own distinctive amalgam of virtues and vices. The attempt to prohibit vices that are deeply rooted in the community, i.e., vices to which many citizens are deeply attached, is likely to be

---

[65] "Now, since it is rarely that a godlike man is found – to use the epithet of the Spartans, who when they admire any one highly call him a 'godlike man' – so too the brutish type is rarely found among men..." Aristotle, *Nichomachean Ethics*, VII, 1 (1145a27–29; McKeon, p. 1037).

[66] *Making Men Moral*, p. xx.

a failure. Moreover, the difficulty of accomplishing such a task will likely require greater harshness in the law. This is itself a cost to be concerned about, since it may (1) aggravate the resentment against the law, (2) augment the coercive power of government and the habit of accepting greater levels of coercive government action, which is always subject to potential abuse, and (3) undermine the kind of civic "friendship" on which a polity rests, the sense citizens have that they are part of a community and not merely subject to it.[67]

Limited Range of Natural Law Precepts

The final observation to make about classical natural law and liberty is that natural law precepts have a limited extension, and leave many decisions to free choice. To put it another way, there is a very large range of human liberty in the selection of ways to life, a broad pluralism, in fact. This is in no way to deny that natural law would limit certain conduct (e.g., abortion and divorce) that contemporary liberalism would protect. The pluralism of natural law theory is decidedly narrower than that of contemporary liberalism, especially on some key moral issues. But it is nonetheless very important to point out that the precepts of the natural law say little or nothing about many aspects of life, especially those that involve choosing among an almost infinite variety of means to pursue good ends.

Nothing in the natural law tells me what occupation I should engage in. There are, of course, important limits to my choice of occupation; for example, I shouldn't (1) engage in intrinsically immoral occupations, such as burglary or prostitution, or (2) engage in legitimate occupations in immoral ways, such as fraudulent business or unjust military activity, or (3) engage in occupations for which I do not have the necessary qualities or competence. But there are very many occupations, advancing many

---

[67] This does not mean that laws are incapable of regulating an activity simply because it occurs or even because it is widespread in society. How common a practice is will be only one factor in evaluating what the mores of the community are. The fact that many people *act* in a certain way does not automatically mean that such actions are part of "the community's moral principles." As Harry Clor pointed out, in *Obscenity and Public Morality* (University of Chicago Press, 1969), community moral standards are not defined by the most marginal conduct that the community is willing to "tolerate." To embrace that approach would be to guarantee a downward spiral: it would give community approval to marginal conduct that would become more accepted, giving rise to more extreme marginal conduct, and so forth.

different aspects of my personal good and the common good, from which I am entirely free to choose.

Likewise, my choice of a marriage partner is limited in some ways (e.g., it can't be another person who is already married, or an underage person, or a person of the same sex, or, most importantly, someone who won't consent to marry me), but otherwise I am left with a wide range of people to pursue. And so on, with so many aspects of life.

Barriers of rank and class curtailed a great deal of choice in pre-modern societies in which natural law played a more prominent role. The limited economic resources of those societies also curtailed both social and individual choices immensely. But for the most part these limitations did not derive from the basic precepts of the natural law itself. It would be a serious mistake to assume that all the constraints on liberty characteristic of feudal and pre-modern societies are necessarily associated with societies based on natural law. It is necessary to distinguish those constraints on liberty that were inherent in natural law thinking, and those that were characteristic of a more determinate political and social order, in the socioeconomic circumstances of its time and place.

Natural law, then, is not hostile to liberty. Even in its classical form, there has always been a certain recognition of the importance of free will in choosing the human good, the wide latitude for human choice in pursuing the good in many ways, and the limits of law in directing the pursuit of the good. At the same time, representatives of the natural law tradition were sometimes insufficiently sensitive to certain aspects of human freedom. Contemporary natural law has moved to a greater awareness of and sensitivity to the importance of liberty, and in doing so has prepared the way for a rapprochement with liberalism.

9

Liberalism and Natural Law

Having given some basic accounts of the development and core ideas of liberalism and natural law, and specifically of the topic of natural law and liberty, I now want to turn to the question of the relationship between liberalism and natural law. I will argue that they are fundamentally compatible and that the harmony between them makes possible a genuine natural law liberalism.

THE TRUTH NATURAL LAW SEES IN LIBERALISM

In what follows, I will generally argue that proponents of natural law can and should readily embrace the core principles of liberalism, although they will take particular positions in the intra-liberalism debates over the ground and scope of some of those principles. The main principles of liberalism are not just defensible from a natural law perspective, but are good. Natural law theorists can also accept much of what I have called the "tendencies" of liberalism, but here they may see a greater need to qualify or limit these tendencies in various ways. Those qualifications redound, however, to the benefit of liberalism.

Natural Law and Core Principles of Liberalism

Let us begin by asking how a natural law theorist might evaluate the core principles of liberalism.

Human Dignity Rooted in Equality

Natural law theory is strongly committed to the notion of human dignity, rooted in human equality. This dignity involves a high respect or recognition of worth, some form of inviolability, and the inherent possession of rights. This respect is not based on the accomplishments of the particular person, but on the simple fact of being human. The idea that human dignity is universal, viewed in light of the fact that there is a tremendous range of human beings, whose accomplishments range from the great to the virtually nonexistent, suggests that human dignity is based on some sort of capacity or capacities that human beings share, rather than some given level of actualization of human capacities. The idea of "capacity" or "potential" implies a capacity or potential for something–for some end or good.

Human dignity does not depend on the actualization of these capacities. The actual exercise of human capacities may be limited because of the underdevelopment of the physical means that provide essential mechanisms by which the mind acts (as in the case of children) or in extreme cases prevented entirely, due to defects in the matter (as in cases of brain damage that frustrates the effective operation of the mind), but in such cases we deal with a defect in a being who still inherently possesses the capacities.

Nor does human dignity depend on the good use of such capacities. Human beings often fail to act well, to use their distinctive human capacities in a way that achieves their intrinsic ends. The intellect can be confused by specious errors and clouded by passions. The will can likewise be diverted from good ends by pride or passions. These failures to live up to the demands of reason occur in even the best of men, and rather frequently in most of us, and they dominate the lives of evil men. But, despite these failures, each person retains a core human dignity.

Human dignity also seems to entail a kind of "inviolability." This inviolability does not mean exemption from punishment, and there may be even more complicated matters, such as self-defense and war and the death penalty but, however we resolve those issues, we must do so in a way that respects the fact that human beings ought not to be arbitrarily harmed, or reduced simply to a means to the better life of other human beings. In that sense, human beings are "ends in themselves." This contrasts sharply with the way most people regard animals – they are seen as deserving a certain respect, but can be decisively reduced to means to the betterment of human life.

Another aspect of human dignity is that human beings are deserving of conditions that make it possible to pursue their good(s), which we call rights. Human beings are (at least when they are more fully developed) "self-directing." They have a rational capacity to see their good and to devise means to pursue it – again, unlike animals and plants and inanimate objects, which, although they have a good, must be directed to it by external forces or by an internal force over which they have no control (e.g., instinct). For human beings to be able to pursue their good(s), they need to have certain prerequisites, such as subsistence (food, clothing, shelter, medical care) and education. If it is desirable for human beings to exercise the self-directive capacity with which they are endowed by nature, then, it is desirable (good) that they have these prerequisites.

What is the source of human dignity? Every human being possesses dignity due to the distinctive human capacities he or she has, especially reason and free will. In its traditional form, this was also expressed by saying that each person had an immaterial and immortal soul that accounted for these capacities. Aquinas argues that the soul is immaterial, on the grounds that the universal concepts the intellect forms cannot be the result of simply physical changes (e.g., in the brain). The soul is immortal, because it is immaterial, and has no parts, and therefore no way to undergo corruption.

Human dignity is, therefore, not a human "construct," devised by men to make life go better. It is a recognition of the distinctive features of man's very being, which set him apart from other, lower beings.

The fundamental equality of all persons in their dignity as human beings does not entail that every human being be treated the same, in a radically egalitarian way. Relevant differences justify different treatment. Some people will be admitted to medical school and others will not, and if the different treatment is relative to their capacities to do the necessary work, that is unobjectionable. This and thousands of other inequalities are defensible. But, in the final analysis, natural law theory will concur with liberals who argue that every human being deserves "equal concern and respect."

Consent

Natural law theorists can readily accept a certain notion of consent. There are serious reasons to hesitate about fully embracing a theory of consent. First, there is the highly artificial character of most theories of consent. Most nations have never undertaken to secure consent explicitly from their citizens. More importantly, few of those that have done so have been willing to regularly re-collect this consent on a regular basis, opting instead to rely on theories of tacit consent, with all the difficulties entailed by it.[1]

---

[1] For a discussion of consent noting some of these difficulties (but more favorable to the theoretical utility of the concept than I am), see Jeremy Waldron, *Liberal Rights* (Cambridge University Press, 1993), chapter 2. See also the classic exchange between Jefferson and

Liberalism and Natural Law

Moreover, if consent is understood to be the actual source of authority, we should have misgivings about it. A natural law theory of political authority considers political power to be just that – "natural" – rather than the artificial or conventional creation of human beings in some pre-social state of nature.

Nonetheless, as Yves Simon showed in his classic discussion,[2] a more limited idea of consent makes good sense, if it is understood as popular participation in the transmission of political power to those who hold political authority (and this can include the general power to determine the form of government, as well as the more specific power to determine who will hold office). In this respect, Simon is only harkening back to a tradition at least as old as Aristotle, who notes that collecting the opinions of those who experience the effects of rule (asking the person who is wearing the shoe how it feels) is quite sensible. The idea of requiring consent also draws support from its tendency to contribute to political stability (a notion supported by Tocqueville's discussion of the advantages of democracy[3]). And, finally, it has a very strong grounding in the severe objections that can be lodged against any theory that makes political power hereditary or limits the choice of rulers to a particular social class, since no such class is particularly trustworthy to hold such power, unchecked by others. (Classes defined by wealth, education, and or any other criteria cannot be trusted to be better rulers, unconstrained by the requirement of consent.) In this sense, then, natural law theorists see consent as a legitimate and valuable aspect of good government.

Centrality of Rights

Rights are central to liberalism, but barely appear in classical natural law, which focuses on what is right by nature rather than on the rights we have by nature. Yet modern representatives of the natural law tradition have

---

Madison on the prudence of requiring each generation to explicitly consent to the fundamental laws. Letter of Jefferson to Madison, September 6, 1789, and letter of Madison to Jefferson, Feburary 4, 1790.

[2] Yves Simon *The Philosophy of Democratic Government* (University of Chicago Press, 1951), chapter 3.

[3] See Alexis de Tocqueville, *Democracy in America* (New York: Alfred A. Knopf, 1945), Vol. I, chapter 14, on the advantages of democracy, where he shows that popular participation in the making of laws contributes to the sense of the people that it is *their* law and therefore worthy of obedience (even when they have lost the legislative battle to determine the content of the law).

strongly embraced rights in the twentieth century.[4] Is this embrace merely a tactical one? Or is it, on the basis of fundamental principles of natural law theory, a mistake? I think it is neither, and I think the language of those who criticize it suggests as much.

Some scholars informed by classical philosophy, such as the late Ernest Fortin and Robert Kraynak, argue that there are dangers in the adoption of rights language, because it is imprudent to employ language whose origin is in philosophical systems (e.g., Hobbesian–Lockean natural rights theory or Kantianism) that are antithetical in so many respects to classical natural law theory and which may encourage some of the defects of those systems (e.g., individualism).[5] I do not doubt that there are important questions of prudence here, which have to be taken very seriously.

But it is also notable that such arguments do not come to grips with a key question: putting aside questions of prudence for the moment, let me simply ask whether it is *true* that people have "rights." I think the answer that any proponent of classical natural law has to give is clearly "yes." If it is *wrong* for A to hit B, then B can be said to have a *right* not to be hit by A. If it is a principle of justice that A *ought to* give x to B, then B can be said to have a *right* to x from A.

Fortin's response is that this defense of rights "does not get to the heart of the matter inasmuch as it fails to address the question of the priority of duties over rights or vice versa."[6] For ancients, duty came first, and for moderns (and liberals) rights come first, so in the final analysis "we are confronted with two vastly different conceptions of morality."[7]

But this line of reasoning is not an argument against rights as much as it is an argument against a certain understanding of rights. That is why Fortin himself ultimately suggests that what is needed is not a complete rejection of rights, but rather "a stronger notion of the common good, coupled with a more subtle formulation of individual rights."[8]

---

[4] See, for example, John Finnis, *Natural Law and Natural Rights*, and Jacques Maritain, *The Rights of Man and Natural Law* (New York: C. Scribner's Sons, 1943).

[5] See, for example, Ernest Fortin, *Human Rights, Virtue, and the Common Good* ed. Benestad (Rowman and Littlefield, 1996) and Robert Kraynak *Christian Faith and Modern Democracy* (University of Notre Dame Press, 2001) . For an approach that has deep concerns about potential problems with overemphasizing rights, but that accepts them more readily in principle (an approach I share), see Mary Ann Glendon, *Rights Talk* (Free Press, 1991).

[6] Fortin, *Human Rights, Virtue, and the Common Good*, p. 21.

[7] Fortin, *Human Rights, Virtue, and the Common Good*, p. 22.

[8] Fortin, *Human Rights, Virtue, and the Common Good*, p. 308. To avoid one source of confusion, we should note that, if duties (based on what is right by nature) are prior to

Kraynak (who deals with natural law indirectly, through a discussion of the social teachings of the Catholic Church) maintains that "Christianity actually has a deep resistance to the concept of human rights," for a variety of reasons. First, duties come before rights and people cannot simply pursue happiness as they see fit. Second, one has a duty to accept transcendent truth and its authoritative expression rather than accepting the dictates of conscience wherever they lead. Third, reflection on original sin instills a keen sense of how freedom can go awry. Fourth, the common good is placed above individual rights and the emphasis on family and man's social nature conflicts with individualism and privacy. Fifth, Christian teaching on charity makes the notion of rights seem selfish. And sixth, Christians cannot accept the premise of autonomy that underlies most doctrines of rights.[9]

But none of these arguments is decisive.[10] This is shown by the fact that, ultimately, Kraynak is willing to accept rights, as long as they are properly subordinated, by understanding "the freedom of the person to serve higher ends than autonomous reason."[11] He is willing to accept Karol Wojtyla's synthesis of metaphysics, anthropology, and Aristotelian–Thomistic ethics with Scheler and Kant, because in this synthesis "freedom is not an end-in-itself, but must serve the truth about God and the truth about the dignity of man."[12] Rights are fine as long as they are placed within a proper context.

The need to recognize a larger context for rights, however – one that implies necessary limits on them – is nothing more or less than what many an intelligent liberal would say. There is, of course, a multitude of questions about the nature and scope of rights, and about their precise place in the overall teaching of political morality. Different liberals will

---

rights, that does not necessarily mean that a person's rights are conditional on his having performed duties. One person's right to life may follow on another person's duty to respect the life of others, but the genuine rights (including the right to life) of children who are too young properly to fulfil responsibilities is a clear indication that rights are not conditional on a person's own actions.

[9] Kraynak, *Christian Faith and Modern Democracy*, p. 153.
[10] The first three arguments and the sixth are fully compatible with belief in human rights, being more concerned with their proper context and limits. Regarding the fourth argument, the common good may be said to be "above" individual rights, but it may also be said to include them as essential elements. With respect to the fifth argument, rights can be selfish, but they also inculcate limits on selfishness – which is why Tocqueville argues that the idea of rights is a way of introducing virtue into the political world. (*Democracy in America*, Vol. I, chap. XIV, pp. 244–47.)
[11] Kraynak, *Christian Faith and Modern Democracy*, p. 160.
[12] Kraynak, *Christian Faith and Modern Democracy*, p. 161.

answer those questions in different ways, and some of those answers may be very inadequate, as was shown in the earlier discussion of contemporary liberalism and autonomy in Part I. But that does not preclude natural law thinkers from embracing rights in their proper perspective, properly related to duties and understood as essential conditions for human beings to seek the good and the true. This discussion of the proper framework for understanding rights is one that can be carried on *within* the contexts of both liberalism and natural law.

Strong, But Limited, Government

Because key liberal thinkers such as Locke were reacting especially against excessive claims of royal power, it is easy to focus on their concerns to limit government. It is worthwhile to remember that limits on government were only half the issue. As Madison argued in *Federalist No. 51*: "In framing a government which is to be administered by men over men, the great difficulty lies in this: you must first enable the government to control the governed; and in the next place oblige it to control itself." The former aim is as important as the latter one, because government has the essential function of protecting rights that would be tenuous in a "state of nature" that lacked government.

Natural law theory recognizes the essential role that government plays in human life. The purpose of government is to promote, to ensure as far as possible, the common good, understood in a rich and comprehensive way, including man's physical, moral, and intellectual well-being. Note, however, that this responsibility does not imply that the state must provide for these goods directly – in fact, the common good often requires that these goods be pursued and attained by individuals, families, voluntary associations, and other levels of community and government. But the political community has the responsibility to see that, as far as possible, conditions exist for achieving the various goods of individuals and communities.

Given this broad view of the common good, few people complain that natural law theorists hold too narrow a view of government power (but see the discussion below on moral limits on government). More commonly, the concern is that natural law – because it does not limit the common good to "life, liberty, and property" – does not acknowledge sufficient limits on the power of government. But it does.

Natural law theorists do not believe in an all-encompassing government or State. They affirm a clear distinction between the public and private spheres of life, and clear limits on government.

The distinction between the private and the public is one to which Christianity, in fact, made a significant contribution. It is not central to classical political philosophy. In the ancient world, for example, there was typically not a separation, but a union of religion and political life.[13] Christianity was persecuted by Roman political authorities precisely because it insisted on a fundamental private sphere into which the public could not intervene: the sphere of faith. Natural law theory likewise recognizes that competence of government is limited and that certain actions can only be performed well if they are performed freely.

Moreover, natural law theory has articulated the principle of subsidiarity, according to which higher or more general associations should intervene in the life of lower or more particular associations only when the latter are incapable of performing a task adequately.[14] One implication of this is that public authorities ought not to insert their authority into the private worlds of families, and of many voluntary associations, except when this is necessary for the common good.

Of course, the private and the public are not completely independent. They are distinct, but they have a profound impact on each other. The private world of the family is obviously deeply influenced by the "social ecology" within which it exists, as any parent knows only too well. The public world is affected by the conduct of people in their private lives (especially when attention is paid to the aggregate pattern of private actions). That is why some acts that look simply "private" may not be so, as in the case of adult consensual acts such as hiring someone for less than a minimum wage or viewing pornography.

With respect to institutional arrangements to keep the power of government in check, natural law theory has no trouble accepting liberalism's "characteristic set of political institutions," namely, representative democracy, separation of governmental powers, and an independent judiciary.[15] While institutional questions always involve a measure of prudential judgment relative to the circumstances of a given political community,

---

[13] Fustel de Coulanges, *The Ancient City* (Garden City, NY: Doubleday Anchor Books, no date), especially Book Third.

[14] See my "Subsidiarity: The 'Other' Ground for Limited Government" in *Liberalism, and Communitarianism: Essays on the Catholic Intellectual Tradition and the Moral Foundations of Democracy*, Grasso, Bradley, and Hunt, Eds. (Rowman and Littlefield, 1995), pp. 81–96.

[15] See Berkowitz, p. 157. For an example of how natural law theory would evaluate one of these institutions, see my discussion of "Natural Law and Judicial Review" in *Natural Law and Contemporary Public Policy*, David Forte, Ed. (Georgetown University Press, 1998), pp. 157–189, especially pp. 158–160.

it is fair to say that natural law theory: (1) looks with favor on political arrangements (such as representative democracy) that promote the participation and therefore the capacities of as many citizens as reasonably possible, because this development of capacities is an important part of the common good[16]; and (2) in general looks with favor on arrangements that provide checks on political power (e.g., separation of powers and a limited form of judicial review), because of its recognition of the potential power of evil as well as good in all human beings.

Because there is such widespread agreement in the West on representative democracy, separation of governmental powers, and an independent judiciary, we can sometimes take them for granted in our discussions of liberalism. Thus, we discount more than we should the extent to which commitment to those principles constitutes liberalism. The ready embracing of them by natural law theorists, then, is another important argument for the compatibility of liberalism and natural law.

As to more specific limits on government, we start with the proposition that those who exercise governing authority are human beings bound by ordinary moral norms. While it is true that certain forms of authority pertain to government, and not to ordinary citizens, so as to justify government in doing things that others cannot do – e.g., the administration of civil and criminal law, and the power of enforcement and punishment that goes with it – governments are not exempt from general rules of morality, according to natural law theory.

A government has no right, for example, to deliberately and directly kill innocent people, on the grounds that this will redound to the greatest

---

[16] In this respect, it follows Alexis de Tocqueville, who says of democracy: "I am less inclined to applaud it for what it does, than for what it causes to be done . . . It is incontestable that the people frequently conduct public business very ill; but it is impossible that the lower orders should take a part in public business without extending the circle of their ideas, and quitting the ordinary routine of their thoughts. . . . When the opponents of democracy assert that a single man performs what he undertakes better than the government of all, it appears to me that they are right. . . . Democratic liberty is far from accomplishing all its projects with the skill of an adroit despotism. It frequently abandons them before they have borne their fruits, or risks them when the consequences may be dangerous; but in the end, it produces more than any absolute government; if it does fewer things well, it does a greater number of things. Under its sway, the grandeur is not in what the public administration does, but in what is done without it or outside of it. Democracy does not give the people the most skilful government, but it produces what the ablest governments are frequently unable to create; namely, an all-pervading and restless activity, a superabundant force, and an energy which is inseparable from it, and which may, however unfavorable circumstances may be, produce wonders. These are the true advantages of democracy." *Democracy in America*, pp. 25–52. See also Simon, *Philosophy of Democratic Government*, p. 130.

good and the greatest number. For example, the deliberate targeting of enemy civilian non-combatants in war – effectively treating civilians as hostages, harming or terrorizing them as a means to put pressure on the government – however effective in shortening a war and thus saving lives overall, is immoral. Very important ends do not justify the use of any and all means, but only moral means.

The application of these norms can be complex, as in the case of indirect or collateral killing of noncombatants in warfare – which, if truly collateral, and proportionate, can be legitimate. Similarly, the demands of truth-telling have also spawned extensive, complicated, and controversial analysis among natural law theorists.

Natural law theory thus provides a solid foundation for strong, but effectively limited, government. Many liberals will take issue with particular ways in which natural law theory does not restrict government – perhaps most importantly, its rejection of Mill's "harm principle" – but that will be a discussion that takes place *within* the broad family of liberal political theories.[17]

The Rule of Law

The rule of law has deep roots in the natural right and natural law tradition, going back to Aristotle, who argued that law is free from the passion that is innate in man. Although law cannot be perfect (since it makes universal rules that may not apply in some instances[18]), it is superior to rule by decree.[19]

John Finnis notes the way in which Aquinas follows Aristotle on the rule of law:

> But in his commentary on Aristotle's *Ethics*, at the point in Book V where Aristotle briefly summarizes the merits of the rule of law, Aquinas expands and perhaps deepens the summary a little: right government does not tolerate an unregulated

---

[17] For a much more extensive discussion of the topic, see John Finnis, "Natural Law Theory and Limited Government" in *Natural Law, Liberalism, and Morality*, Robert George, Ed. (Oxford: Clarendon Press, 1996), pp. 1–27. (Finnis's account of the limits on government according to natural law theory is excellent, though I do not join him in considering the common good as only an instrumental good.)

[18] Aristotle, *Nichomachean Ethics*, V, 10 (McKeon, p. 1020); Politics III, 14: "laws speak only in general terms, and cannot provide for circumstances" (McKeon, p. 1199).

[19] Aristotle, Politics, III, 14: "Yet surely the ruler cannot dispense with the general principle which exists in law; and that is a better ruler which is free from passion than that in which it is innate. Whereas the law is passionless, passion must ever sway the heart of man." (McKeon, pp. 1199–1200). Aristotle allows for equitable correction of the defects in the law.

rule by rulers ('rule of men'), but calls for rulers to be ruled by law, precisely because law is a dictate of *reason*, while what threatens to turn government into tyranny (rule in the interest of the rulers) is their human *passions*, inclining them to attribute to themselves more of the good things, and fewer of the bad things, than is their fair share.[20]

Moreover, as Russell Hittinger points out, so strongly does Aquinas believe in the rule of law that he says that a judge who privately knows that a man is innocent – after trying to examine "the witnesses with great care, so as to find a motive for acquitting" him, and trying unsuccessfully to remit the prisoner to a higher authority – "does not sin if he pronounce sentence in accordance with the evidence, for it is not he that puts the innocent man to death, but they who stated him to be guilty."[21] "In matters touching his own person...a man must form his conscience from his own knowledge, but in matters concerning the public authority, he must form his conscience in accordance with the knowledge attainable in the public judicial procedure."[22] The force of law, for Aquinas, is very powerful.

Finnis, speaking in his own name, provides an excellent summary of "the Rule of Law" in his *Natural Law and Natural Rights*:

A legal system exemplifies the Rule of Law to the extent (it is a matter of degree in respect of each item of the list) that (i) its rules are prospective, not retroactive, and (ii) are not in any other way impossible to comply with; that (iii) its rules are promulgated, (iv) clear, and (v) coherent one with another; that (vi) its rules are sufficiently stable to allow people to be guided by their knowledge of the content of the rules; that (vii) the making of decrees and orders applicable to relatively limited situations is guided by rules that are promulgated, clear, stable, and relatively general; and that (viii) those people who have authority to make, administer, and apply the rules in an official capacity (a) are accountable for their compliance with rules applicable to their performance and (b) do actually administer the law consistently and in accordance with it tenor.[23]

These citations confirm what there is little reason to doubt – that classical natural law is strongly committed to the rule of law.

---

[20] Finnis, "Natural Law and Limited Government," pp. 1–2 (internal citation omitted). In his *Aquinas* (Oxford: Oxford University Press, 1998), Finnis discusses this point at greater length in section VIII.2 (pp. 258–66).

[21] Hittinger, *The First Grace*, p. 104 (quoting *Summa Theologiae* II–II, Q. 64, a. 6, ad 3).

[22] Ibid., p. 105 (quoting Summa Theologiae II–II, Q. 67, a. 2). Hittinger points out, however, that we are not dealing here with a law or with legal procedures that are themselves unjust, which would be a very different case.

[23] *Natural Law and Natural Rights*, pp. 270–71.

Natural law theory, then, embraces all five of the core principles of liberalism. Like other liberals, various natural law theorists will have differences of opinion (among themselves and with others) as to the best understanding and application of these principles. Those differences are not an external critique of liberalism, but rather an internal discussion within liberalism as to the best way to understand and realize liberal principles.

Natural Law and Tendencies of Liberalism

Is natural law compatible with what I have described as the "tendencies" of liberalism, those habitual ways of thinking that infuse much liberal thought and practice? I think that, for the most part, natural law is compatible with them, though – even more than is the case with liberalism's core principles – this depends on a having a certain understanding of and giving a certain direction to those tendencies.

A Tradition of Reason and Enlightenment

First, the liberal tradition tends to be a rationalist tradition, a tradition of reason and "enlightenment." Natural law concurs in attributing profound importance to reason. Law is defined as an "ordinance of reason" and natural law is said to be "the rational creature's share of the Eternal Reason." The first principle of natural law is that "good is to be done and pursued and evil avoided," and "all those things to which man has a natural inclination, are naturally apprehended by reason as being good, and consequently as objects of pursuit." In Aquinas' listing of those natural inclinations, he moves from the lowest, the desire for self-preservation (which man shares with all substances), through inclination to have and educate offspring (which man shares with animals), to the highest, which is reason, the capacity distinctive to man. Practical reasoning is what the natural law is all about.

At the same time, natural law theorists are sensitive to the actual limitations of reason. Reason is certainly limited in particular human beings, where it typically must contend, often unsuccessfully, with the passions. Even more generally, reason across a wide range of human beings takes considerable time and cooperative effort to advance in knowledge, as the history of science shows. A great deal of what passes for knowledge is mixed with varying degrees of error that must painstakingly be winnowed out.

Ironically, in a certain way, natural law theorists have more faith in reason than do modern liberals. Modern liberalism has tended to exalt the knowledge arrived at by the empirical methods of what we call "science," i.e., the natural sciences. It rightly recognized, historically, that confusion about method was sometimes an obstacle to the development of the natural sciences. There is no question that these sciences have given us a much better understanding of many aspects of reality, and that their practical fruits (e.g., in the medical field) have been of enormous benefit. Sometimes, however, proponents of empirical science go further and make the (empirically unverifiable) assertion that the only real knowledge is their own kind of scientific knowledge. Moreover, reason for modern liberals is often reduced to "instrumental rationality," reason as a means to achieve ends that are themselves beyond the scope of reason, ends that are simply posited or the objects of desires or passions.

Natural law theorists resist the truncation of reason, maintaining that "science" comprehends knowledge achieved through different methods, and, in particular, should be understood to include metaphysics and ethics as much as physics and chemistry. They hold that human ends as well as means are discernible by reason. Moreover, they are open, in principle, to the possibility of other sources of knowledge than reason itself, especially divine revelation and rational reflection thereon (in the form of theology).

Natural law, then, is very much a tradition of reason and, in fact, helps protect a fuller understanding of reason and its capacities.

A Reformist Tradition

The liberal tradition tends to be reformist, examining the past and present with a critical eye, proposing changes to improve the condition of men, and experimenting with new social forms and policies. Tocqueville captures this spirit in his description of America, when he says that

to evade the bondage of system and habit, of family maxims, class opinions, and, in some degree, of national prejudices; to accept tradition only as a means of information, and existing facts only as a lesson to be used in doing otherwise and doing better; to see the reason of things for oneself, and in oneself alone; to tend to results without being bound to means, and to strike through the form to the substance – such are the principal characteristics of what I shall call the philosophical method of the Americans.[24]

The past is prelude. Tradition is not irrelevant – it might be a useful means of information – but it does not bind the present and future.

[24] *Democracy in America*, Vol. II, First Book, chapter I (Phillips Bradley, Ed., p. 3).

Moreover, Tocqueville argues, democratic men are drawn to the idea of the "indefinite perfectibility of man":

In proportion as castes disappear and the classes of society draw together, as manners, customs, and laws vary, because of the tumultuous intercourse of men, as new facts arise, as new truths are brought to light, as ancient opinions are dissipated and others take their place, the image of an ideal but always fugitive perfection presents itself to the human mind...Thus, forever seeking, forever falling to rise again, often disappointed, but not discouraged, he tends unceasingly towards that unmeasured greatness so indistinctly visible at the end of the long track which humanity has yet to tread.[25]

Constantly moving forward, improving things – that is the spirit of liberalism.

Does natural law share this spirit? I think it does. One must distinguish between natural law itself and the social conditions in which it was once influential, that is, late medieval Europe. Tradition and custom exercised great influence in feudal society,[26] but that does not mean that natural law is resistant to change and reform and improvement. Change for its own sake makes no sense, but change for the sake of improvement certainly does. For natural law, reform is always a prudential question: to what extent do the likely benefits of reform outweigh its costs? In principle, though, reform and improvement are very desirable. Human beings and society are imperfect in many ways, and facilitating their improvement is good. The very fact that natural law has a transcendent standard (the "eternal reason" of which it is a participation) makes it less likely to sanctify the status quo, which is always imperfect relative to that standard and in need of amelioration.

At the same time, the accent on prudence makes natural law suspicious of radical, revolutionary change, except where great goods can be achieved and the costs associated with such change can be minimized. Revolutions aiming at quick, broad, and dramatic change often aim to achieve more than can reasonably be expected, and typically entail immense costs.

Natural law, then, will be receptive to reasonable criticism of current social arrangements and will favor reform to bring them more in line with the norms provided by reason. The character and scope and pace of such change are ordinarily prudential questions that natural law theory would leave in the hands of wise statesmen.

---

[25] *Democracy in America*, Vol. II, First Book, chapter VIII (Phillips Bradley, Ed., p. 34).
[26] Tocqueville also gives some reasons for this, Ibid., pp. 33–34.

Liberalism and Individualism

One oft-noted, and frequently criticized, aspect of liberalism is its promotion of individualism. On the positive side, this tendency flows from a recognition of the equal worth of each person. Liberals were rightly critical of the subordination of the individual to the glory and greatness of "the nation" (or, perhaps, more accurately, the rulers) in pre-liberal societies. As the protagonist of a Saul Bellow novel says, "it has only been in the last two centuries that the majority of people in civilized countries have claimed the privilege of being individuals. Formerly they were slave, peasant, laborer, even artisan, but not person."[27] The general recognition of the equality of each person in society, and the equal concern and respect owed him or her, is one of the great achievements of liberalism.

Natural law has always shared this recognition of the importance of the individual, as a free, self-directing person. Its notion of a common good has never been that the good of the greater number outweighs the good of the lesser number. The common good is not a sum of individual goods, but a good that includes the good of each person in the community:

> The common good of society is neither a simple collection of private goods, nor a good belonging to a whole which (as in the case of the species in relation to its individual members) draws the parts to itself, as if they were pure means to serve itself alone. The common good is the *good human* life of the multitude, of a multitude of *persons*; it is their communion in the good life; it is therefore common *to the whole and to the parts*, on whom it flows back and who must all benefit from it.[28]

The commitment of natural law to equal regard for each person is also reflected powerfully in the contemporary work of its proponents on behalf of the right to life of each person from conception to natural death.[29] In this regard, it carries on the general trend of liberalism in expanding the protection of rights, extending them to a wider range of human beings.

At the same time, natural law theory insists on reasonable limits to individual rights. It resists, especially, a commitment to a radical notion of autonomy. A certain form of autonomy, properly understood and limited, is essential, as a very important means to a good life. Without genuine freedom and choice, it is not possible to lead a moral life. Liberals are

---

[27] Saul Bellow, *Mr. Sammler's Planet* (Viking Press, 1969), p. 228.
[28] Jacques Maritain, *Scholasticism and Politics* (Garden City, N.Y.: Image Books, 1960), pp. 72–73.
[29] See, for example, Hadley Arkes, *Natural Rights and the Right to Choose* (Cambridge: Cambridge University Press, 2002).

right to think that what is important is not just what we do, but how we do it, and especially that we freely choose to do it.

What we do does matter, however, and so personal autonomy cannot be absolutized. First, and most obviously, the autonomy of one person must be compatible with that of another, and so in some cases it is good that autonomous action be suppressed, as in cases where one person seeks to curtail the legitimate autonomy of another. This is no minor qualification, as some contemporary liberal theorists tend to treat it. It demonstrates that autonomy is not an ultimate and unqualified good: it must yield to the moral imperative of respecting the rights of others (rights in the service of pursuing human goods). Autonomy itself cannot fully account for that moral imperative, because some principle other than autonomy itself must account for why one form of autonomy – one person's preference for murder, robbery, or rape – must give way to another – other people's preferences not to be murdered, robbed, or raped. (And it can't be simply "maximization" of autonomy, since that would be subject to a familiar criticism of utilitarianism: if a whole lot of people wanted to exercise their autonomy by violating the autonomy of a very few people, autonomy would be maximized by letting them do so.)

Second, virtually everyone realizes that certain autonomous actions can undercut genuine autonomy, simply as a factual matter. One can freely choose to get drunk, but in doing so one loses autonomy – self-determination – while in that state. Genuine autonomy, then, may require people to forego certain decisions that are incompatible with the maintenance of autonomy, and so the prohibition of such decisions may not be a violation of autonomy.[30]

Third, one can freely (autonomously) choose to assume certain responsibilities that thereby limit what one can subsequently do. For example, participating in the conception of a child brings into existence obligations that limit one's future autonomy in important ways.[31]

---

[30] I say "may not" rather than "will not" because sometimes prudence dictates giving people the power to make wrong decisions (including those that reduce their real autonomy), as a way to develop their decision–making capacities. My point here is only that autonomy itself is, in principle, compatible with limitations on a person's actions.

[31] It is more controversial among liberals whether one can (autonomously) contract into a relationship that permanently curtails one's autonomy, such as indissoluble marriage. Some liberals object that such an institution is incompatible with what they hold to be essential: the permanent revisability of one's commitments. See my "The Marriage of Your Choice," *First Things*, Vol. 50, pp. 37–41 (February 1995). Ironically, many of the same liberals tend to defend the right to suicide, though suicide, however autonomously chosen, destroys the autonomous actor – it is the *ultimate* unrevisable act.

Fourth, those who value autonomy must recognize the price necessary to maintain it. Autonomy is not guaranteed, but must be defended. An autonomous individual – autonomous, in part, because he lives in a society that defends his autonomy – may therefore fairly be required to make some fair contribution to maintaining that society, for example, in the form of taxes, and in the form of compulsory military service, when that is necessary to preserve the political community. To the extent that such a society (one that defends people's autonomy) also depends on a stable family unit to be able to survive and thrive, it may rightly regulate marriage and sexuality in certain ways, and thereby constrain autonomy.

So it is a limited and appropriately constrained notion of autonomy that natural law theorists embrace, and which they recognize as an essential and key element in living a good human life, because it is necessary in order to be able to choose freely to perform good actions.[32]

Liberalism, Reason, and Religion

Liberalism has tended to promote either rationalist religion (emphasizing the more limited truths of natural theology rather than the wider range of beliefs characteristic of revealed religions) or secularism. What is unclear is how much the latter tendency, especially, has reflected certain historical circumstances and how much it is intrinsic to liberalism.

Historically, much of the liberal "enlightenment" was directed against the supposed obscurantism of traditional religious forces, especially the Catholic Church. It was widely supposed that there was a deep incompatibility between Christianity and liberalism, manifested dramatically in the French Revolution's assault on religion. This is a major question in Tocqueville's *Democracy in America*, and Tocqueville goes to considerable lengths to deny that they are incompatible.

According to Tocqueville, the depth of division between the forces of emerging liberal democracy and the representatives of the Church is primarily a function of historical circumstances. Over the centuries, the Church had become "intimately united with the governments of the earth" (the social and political order of the *ancien regime*) and had therefore "been known to exercise sovereign power founded on terror and faith." This had been a mistake, however, for when religion "connects itself with a government, it must adopt maxims which are applicable only to certain nations." Thereby, "in forming an alliance with a political power, religion augments its authority over a few and forfeits the hope of reigning over

---

[32] See, for example, Robert George, *Making Men Moral*, pp. 210–17.

all." Once "mixed up in the bitter passions of this world," the "church cannot share the temporal power of the state without being the object of a portion of that animosity which the latter excites."[33]

In fact, Tocqueville argues, religion does not need to rely on political support. Its real foundation is much stronger: "religious institutions... may be said to derive an inexhaustible element of strength from man himself, since they belong to one of the constituent principles of human nature," namely, the "desire of immortality that lives in every human heart," the hope for an afterlife.[34] Separation of church and state, therefore, not only preserves political life from religious passions, but also benefits religion.

Tocqueville also has a more positive political argument for religion. In his discussion of the New England colonists, he contrasts their moral world, in which "everything is classified, systematized, foreseen, and decided beforehand," with their political world, in which "everything is agitated, disputed, and uncertain." Yet these tendencies, "far from conflicting... advance together and support each other." Religion is content to leave politics to the human mind, while liberty "considers religion as the safeguard of morality, and morality as the best security of law and surest pledge of the duration of freedom."[35] Because of the strength of religion, "while the law permits Americans to do what they please, religion prevents them from conceiving, and forbids them to commit, what is rash or unjust."[36]

Tocqueville goes so far as to say that "[d]espotism may govern without faith, but liberty cannot.... How is it possible that society should escape destruction if the moral tie is not strengthened in proportion as the political tie is relaxed?"[37] A free society needs a moral framework that religion is especially apt to provide.

Note, however, that Tocqueville's discussion of religion is typical of liberalism in that it emphasizes, not revealed religion per se, but features of a more limited natural theology. He sees religion as a natural constituent of human nature, essentially a form of the hope for immortality. In his discussion of the political benefits of religion regarding morality, he focuses, not on dogma, but the fact that "all sects preach the same moral law" and

---

[33] Tocqueville, *Democracy in America*, Vol. I, Chapter XVII (Phillips Bradley, Ed., p. 310).
[34] Ibid.
[35] Ibid., pp. 44, 45.
[36] Ibid., p. 305.
[37] Ibid., p. 307.

that "Christian morality is everywhere the same."[38] When discussing the advantages of religious dogma for individuals and society, he points out that the "first object and one of the principal advantages of religion is to furnish to each of these fundamental questions ["general ideas respecting God and human nature," which are the "common spring" of most human actions] a solution that is at once clear, precise, intelligible, and lasting, to the mass of mankind." (Even "false and very absurd" religions do this, and are thereby very beneficial in this life.) When Tocqueville discusses "religion," then, his concern is not so much specific and particular dogmas, as it is a sort of natural core of beliefs and commands that various religions (especially various sorts of Christianity) share.

From the standpoint of revealed religion itself, Tocqueville's approach to religion and politics may be viewed as a glass that is half empty or half full. I shall have more to say (in the next chapter) on the way natural law views revealed religion and the relationship between religion and politics, but at least this much can be said now: Tocqueville shows that there are considerable resources in the liberal tradition for a respectful relationship between church and state. That relationship need not be one of hostility.

Natural law is more consistent with the liberal emphasis on rational religion than many think, because it promotes the view that there is a fundamental harmony between faith and reason. Revelation is not viewed as something that simply trumps or displaces reason. The lawgiver God of classical natural law theory is the source of both reason and revelation, and so there can be no real conflict between the two, but only apparent conflict that arises from either the defects of reason (as when natural scientists go beyond the limits of their method and assert that there is no God – a question on which, as natural scientists, they have no competence) or the misapprehension of revelation (as when believers erroneously attribute a literal reading to certain biblical passages that has led to conflict with truths discovered by the natural sciences, such as heliocentrism).

What natural law theory would object to is any assertion that unaided human reason is, in principle, the only source of knowledge, that divine revelation is somehow intrinsically impossible. Natural law would object to the unreasonableness of such an assertion, and nothing in liberalism itself demands a commitment to such an unreasonable assertion.

---

[38] Ibid., p. 303. What Tocqueville has in mind, I think, when he describes Christian morality this way (somewhat narrowly), is the politically relevant, basic principles of morality: not killing, committing adultery, stealing, lying. These are moral commands of the Decalogue, which are identified with the precepts of natural law by Aquinas.

Moreover, classical natural law recognizes that, while faith is something that transcends reason, the credibility of those who claim to be agents of divine revelation is reasonably subjected to rational examination. If reason cannot "prove" revelation, those who embrace a particular claim of divine revelation still ought to be willing and able to show why it is not unreasonable to do so.

Universalism

The liberal tradition tends to be universalistic, rather than particularistic. For example, it proclaims that all human beings have a dignity rooted in their equality, and that there are certain fundamental human rights. Equality and rights are not features confined, in principle, to only certain nations. Whatever the prudential considerations that may delay recognition of these rights under some circumstances, in principle they should be acknowledged throughout the world.

Natural law shares this universalistic perspective, since it is committed to certain principles that are rooted, ultimately, in human nature. Among these are human equality and fundamental rights. Some allowances have to be made for certain differences in circumstances. This is one reason why, traditionally, natural law theory has not held, for example, that only one form of government is legitimate. In this regard, natural law holds views similar to such liberal thinkers as Locke, who recognized that the governed could consent to different forms of government,[39] and Mill, who recognized that there were certain civilizational prerequisites for representative government to be possible.[40]

At the same time, however, natural law theory holds up certain standards that legitimate governments at least should strive to realize, as circumstances permit. Thus, for example, broad popular participation in government will not always be possible, but insofar as it gives the broadest scope to citizens' efforts to exercise some of their important capacities, including the capacity to deliberate and make decisions regarding the common good, it is a desirable goal that should be pursued.

This examination of the tendencies of liberalism recognizes that there will be points of tension between natural law and liberal tendencies. At the

---

[39] John Locke, *The Second Treatise of Government*, Peter Laslett, Ed. (New York: Mentor, 1965), Chap. X, p. 399–400.
[40] John Stuart Mill, *Utilitarianism, Liberty, and Representative Government*, Ernest Rhys, Ed. (New York: E.P. Dutton and Company, 1910), p. 178.

same time, it suggests that there is also a good deal of similarity, and no outright incompatibility. Natural law proponents will find many liberal tendencies congenial. Other tendencies they will feel the need to cabin and direct in certain ways, in order to make them reasonable and beneficial. In this they are not fundamentally different from other liberals, who have the same experience of willingness to accept some principles quite readily, while accepting other principles only if they are understood in certain ways (as, for example, contemporary egalitarian liberals will feel the need to constrain economic liberties, or communitarian liberals will feel the need to constrain individualism).

WHAT LIBERALISM OFTEN FAILS TO SEE

I said earlier that, given my description of the core of liberalism, "people of sound judgment and good will, including natural law theorists, should be willing to be considered liberals." That is true, but, at the same time, I also want to say that they should be uncomfortable about being *simply* liberals. (Perhaps that is why I say that should be "willing" rather than "eager" to be considered liberals.) If liberalism has grasped much of the truth about political life, it has also found it difficult to embrace some of that truth, or perhaps has even simply missed some of it.

Influence of the Regime

The first problem with liberalism is that it fails to recognize sufficiently the influence of "the regime," a notion that is so central to classical political philosophy.[41] (This blind spot is tied up with liberalism's view that political life is conventional – man-made – rather than natural.) The vision of political life in the liberal tradition is that it exists to establish a framework for the protection of individual rights. Government should remove the barriers to individual "pursuit of happiness." Even when it acts positively (e.g., in modern liberal economic redistribution), this is viewed simply as providing means to self-development, not actually determining or shaping the direction of that development – it is providing means rather than dictating ends. But classical natural law theorists (as well as postmodernist theorists) correctly doubt that liberalism can avoid shaping ends as well as means.

---

[41] The notion of the "regime" – which combines politics and sociology and economics and culture – is particularly central to and well set out in the work of Leo Strauss.

Jeremy Waldron defends liberalism against a more modern form of this criticism:

> Sometimes liberals are accused of taking the beliefs and preferences of individuals as given and hence of ignoring the fact that forms of society may determine forms of consciousness and the structure and content of preferences. But liberals need not be blind to the possibility of preferences changing, either autonomously or along with changes in social structure and social expectations. Provided this possibility of change is in principle something that people as they are can recognize in themselves and take into account in their reflective deliberations, then it can be accommodated perfectly well in a liberal account of freedom.[42]

The confident "can be accommodated perfectly well" may distract us from the tenuousness of the assumption on which it rests. Liberals can recognize, Waldron says, that people's ends may be chosen due to "changes in social structure or social expectations," that is, due to the shape and tone and influences of the communities of which they are a part. This should not bother liberals, however, as long as "in principle" people "as they are" can recognize this fact and take it into account in their reflective deliberations. Waldron appears to assume that this condition is not problematic. It seems to me deeply so.

The force of the "in principle" is not clear. Is this to be opposed to "in practice"? If it refers merely to the theoretical *possibility* that some people, some of the time, may recognize social and political influences on their lives, that is certainly true, but it's not clear how that constitutes a defense of liberalism against the charge that liberal citizens often do not – perhaps even typically do not – recognize the way that living in a liberal society subtly forms their preferences. How likely, in fact, are people to recognize such influences? Waldron appears to go beyond just theoretical possibility when he specifies that it must be people "as they are." So that is the question: *do* (not just "can") people, as they are, recognize the extent to which their preferences – their ends, their goals, their assumptions about what is good in life – are shaped by the social ecology of liberalism?

This is the kind of empirical question that is very difficult to answer on the basis of anything other than our own experience with human beings. On the basis of my experience, I am simply puzzled that Waldron seems so confident that this condition is met. The people I have dealt with in the course of my life, the students I have taught – even, I confess, some of

---

[42] *Liberal Rights*, p. 41. Waldron, in an omitted footnote, cites Rawls's use of this argument against utilitarianism.

the scholars with whom I have interacted – have not *consistently* demonstrated this awareness and control over such influences in their "reflective deliberations." It *is* common to see reflection and critical awareness with respect to a certain range of issues – especially the ones that are more subject to controversy in our society at a given time – but this is compatible with little or no reflection of other broad attitudes toward life (especially where there is a broad social consensus). In fact, I am impressed over and over again with how many people seem simply to absorb many of their most important attitudes toward life from their surroundings, the culture or subcultures of which they are a part, with relatively little or no critical distance from those influences. (Some simple examples: assumptions about what is the "minimum" standard of living for a "decent" human life, broad dating and courtship patterns, ideas about the "right" size for a family, the notion that a church is a "voluntary association," which areas of thought can attain genuine certitude.) The idea that people "as they are" engage in a high level of self-critical analysis, then, strikes me as an extraordinarily optimistic assessment. It seems to be a very good example of a kind of romanticism that is at the heart of much modern liberalism.

But someone might say, "so what if liberalism shapes people, as long as its shapes them well?" Should we be bothered about the way liberalism shapes people?

I should point out immediately that much of that influence is quite beneficent. For example, liberalism, on the whole, encourages people to be tolerant and peaceful, to be active in pursuit of opportunities, and to have an awareness of their own dignity and rights. We can, and should, recognize the many ways in which liberalism shapes people for the good. It is easier to do so when we look at non-liberal societies – whether in history, or in the post-9/11 world – and see the suffering and insecurity occasioned by intolerance and inhumanity. Tocqueville observes this trenchantly in his chapter on "how customs are softened as social conditions become more equal," in which he describes letters from an aristocratic woman to her daughter indulging in "cruel jocularity" regarding certain "horrors" in the punishment of commoners.[43] For this, and many other reasons, Tocqueville rightly decides in the end that, despite the defects of modern democracy, of which he is clearly aware, a "state of equality is perhaps less elevated, but it is more just; and its justice constitutes its greatness and its beauty."[44]

---

[43] *Democracy in America*, Vol. II, Book III, chap. 1 (Phillips Bradley, Ed., p. 165).
[44] Democracy in America, Vol. II, Book IV, chap. 8 (Ibid, p. 333).

But this decision in favor of liberal democracy – a good and right decision – is not the last word. Having made that decision, it is still necessary to
recognize the limits and defects of liberal democracy, in order to mitigate
them. Or, as Tocqueville says at the end of *Democracy in America*:

> For myself, who now look back from this extreme limit of my task and discover
> from afar, but at once, the various objects which have attracted my more attentive
> investigation upon my way, I am full of apprehensions and of hopes. I perceive
> mighty dangers which it is possible to ward off, mighty evils which may be avoided
> or alleviated; and I cling with a firmer hold to the belief that for democratic nations
> to be virtuous and prosperous, they require but to will it.

I want to turn, then, to ask now about some of the more problematic
aspects of liberalism, and about three tendencies in particular, relative to
truth in general, to religion, and to family.[45]

Liberalism and Truth

The first problematic tendency of liberalism is to emphasize freedom at
the expense of an emphasis on truth about ultimately realities. The claim
to know the truth about human purposes has so often been associated
with abridgment of freedom that liberals are understandably cautious,
not to say suspicious, of truth claims about human ends. The post-
Reformation religious wars (international and domestic) are the most
commonly invoked example, from Hobbes and Locke to Rawls, and in
the contemporary world their place is admirably filled by figures such as
the Ayatollah Khomeini and Osama bin Laden (with whom contemporary
liberals lump the dreaded "Religious Right" in America). This suspicion of
dogma is compatible with an acceptance of certain truth claims, above all,
the claims of modern science and liberalism's "procedural" principles.[46]

---

[45] These are topics that I hope to develop more extensively in the sequel to this book.
[46] For an example of the procedural principles, see Oliver Wendell Holmes, Jr.'s ode to
freedom of speech – replacing the "fighting faiths" of the past with a faith that the
marketplace is the best test of truth: "Persecution for the expression of opinions seems
to me perfectly logical. If you have no doubt of your premises or your power, and want
a certain result with all your heart, you naturally express your wishes in law, and sweep
away all opposition. To allow opposition by speech seems to indicate that you think the
speech impotent, as when a man says that he has squared the circle, or that you do not
care wholeheartedly for the result, or that you doubt either your power or your premises.
But when men have realized that time has upset many fighting faiths, they may come to
believe even more than they believe the very foundations of their own conduct that the
ultimate good desired is better reached by free trade in ideas – that the best test of truth is
the power of the thought to get itself accepted in the competition of the market, and that

(Indeed, the prestige of modern science and its methods – its status as the most credible form of knowledge – helps to account for the widespread doubt that moral philosophy can attain any certitudes.)

Over time, it seems that the citizens of liberal democracies tend to move from "tolerance of other people" to "relativism about ideas of the good." The virtue of nonjudgmentalism, taken even to the point of a kind of principled agnosticism, eclipses the virtue of wisdom.[47] Some people consider this skepticism (more or less qualified) as one of liberalism's attractive features, but those who believe, like natural law theorists, that human beings are very much worse off when they do not understand the most fundamental truths about human life are concerned about the tendency of freedom to overshadow truth so dramatically.

John Stuart Mill exemplifies the curious tendency of liberals to emphasize truth, while subtly undercutting it. Mill squarely bases his justification of a very broad understanding of liberty of thought and discussion precisely on its superiority in attaining truth:

> But the peculiar evil of silencing the expression of an opinion is, that it is robbing the human race; posterity as well as the existing generation; those who dissent from the opinion, still more than those who hold it. If the opinion is right, they are deprived of the opportunity of exchanging error for truth: if wrong, they lose, what is almost as great a benefit, the clearer perception and livelier impression of truth, produced by its collision with error.[48]

But a careful reflection on some of Mill's arguments raises serious questions about whether truth is really the ultimate justification for free speech. In the middle of three sections of his argument, he takes up the question of whether liberty of discussion should be protected *even if it is granted that the received opinion is, in fact, true.* When discussing the Catholic Church's policy, at that time, of prohibiting the reading of books contrary to true faith and morals without special permission (for those who have the duty to defend those teachings) he says

> This discipline recognises a knowledge of the enemy's case as beneficial to the teachers, but finds means, consistent with this, of denying it to the rest of the

---

truth is the only ground upon which their wishes safely can be carried out." *Abrams v. U.S.* 250 U.S. 616, at 630 (1919). Holmes never explains why faith in free speech is not simply one of those "faiths" that will be upset like all the others.

47 The widespread hold of nonjudgmentalism on the contemporary American mind is emphasized (and regarded too benignly) in Alan Wolfe's *One Nation After All* (Viking, 1998).

48 John Stuart Mill, *On Liberty*, chapter two, paragraph one (online at http://www.bartleby.com/130/2.html).

world: thus giving to the élite more mental culture, though not more mental freedom, than it allows to the mass. By this device it succeeds in obtaining the kind of mental superiority which its purposes require; for though culture without freedom never made a large and liberal mind, it can make a clever *nisi prius* advocate of a cause.

What comes across here, I think, is that knowing the truth and being an effective defender of the truth is inferior, for Mill, to "having a large and liberal mind."[49]

What exactly this lovely-sounding phrase ("a large and liberal mind") means, in this context, is not very clear. Remember that, in this section of his argument Mill is *conceding* that the received opinion is true and that the select defenders of that truth are free to examine a wide range of other (false) beliefs to discover why they are false and to confute them. Yet Mill is clearly contemptuous of them for lacking something – but what?

It is hard to resist the conclusion that Mill is subtly going back on his assumption of truth, that he is demanding a sort of permanent tentativeness of opinions on broad philosophical and moral questions. This may not be required regarding other questions – on mathematical questions, he says earlier in chapter two of *On Liberty* (paragraph 23) "there is only one answer," and his *Auguste Comte and Positivism* suggests that he shares a similar view with respect to settled scientific questions – but it seems to apply to "subjects infinitely more complicated, to morals, religion, politics, social relations, and the business of life" (paragraph 23).

In the final analysis, I think that, outside of "scientific knowledge," Mill attributes greater value to being open-minded, curious, studious, intellectually sophisticated – all qualities concerned with the *process* of thinking rather than the *truth value* of the thought – than to knowing the truth. In doing so, he represents a typical tendency of modern liberalism.

Liberalism and Revealed Religion

The second tendency, somewhat related to the first, is the tendency of liberal democracy to undermine revealed religion. We saw earlier, in an account of the history of liberalism, that one of the broad "tendencies" of liberalism, as a tradition of "enlightenment," has been toward secularism or rational religion. Part of this, as Tocqueville argued, was due to the "accidental" (i.e., historical, and not necessary) social and political connections between representatives of established churches based

[49] Ibid., paragraph 25.

on revealed religion and non-liberal regimes, especially continental European monarchies. But there are other, deeper factors as well, which are also noted by Tocqueville.

Tocqueville is well known for his statements about the importance of religion in America. Indeed, he called it "the first of their political institutions," even though he also emphasized the separation of Church and State (one of the primary reasons, he said, for the "peaceful dominion of religion).[50] But there is another side to Tocqueville that is less noted.[51] In particular, it is interesting to note that at the end of *Democracy in America*, in his recommendations for how to prevent democratic despotism, he says nothing about religion. I think the explanation for this is that Tocqueville was aware of the tenuous status of revealed religion in modern liberal democracy.

Tocqueville thought that liberal democracies would be suspicious of tradition, and that the "philosophical method" of Americans would be to rely on themselves. But this strikes at the heart of a certain kind of religion: namely, revealed religion, which rests precisely on the "handing down" ("traditio") of the message that has been revealed to mankind by a God who has intervened in a particular moment of human history. Tocqueville recognized that the natural tendency of modern liberal democracy was the more diffuse and indefinite religion of pantheism.

Tocqueville likewise recognized that liberal democracies would incite and cater to the human desire for physical well-being. So powerful was this tendency that "the heart, the imagination, and life itself" might be given to the pursuit of physical gratifications, "till, in snatching at these lesser gifts, men lose sight of those more precious possessions which constitute the glory and greatness of mankind."[52] He specifically pointed out that one of the advantages of religion was its tendency to curb or moderate this desire. But a moment's reflection shows that this can be turned around: if religion can benefit democracy by acting *against* one of its strongest tendencies, democracy can undermine religion by propagating that tendency.

For these and other reasons, Tocqueville, I think, had some doubts about how efficacious a restraint on liberal democracy religion might be in the long run. I think that American history bears out those concerns. Those who take a more benign view of that history point out the surprising

---

[50] *Democracy in America*, Vol. I, chapter 17, pp. 305, 308.
[51] For a fuller discussion of this point (and more extensive citations), see my "Tocqueville and the Religious Revival," *This World* (Winter/Spring 1982) No. 1, pp. 85–96.
[52] Tocqueville *Democracy in America*, Bradley, Ed. Vol. II, p. 132.

strength of religion in America, especially when compared with Europe.[53] Although this strength should not be ignored, closer attention to the character of that religious belief raises serious questions. In many respects, traditional Christian beliefs, seem to have been modified to accommodate liberal democratic tendencies. Nowhere is this seen more clearly than in the progressive decline of marriage as an institution in American society, a process in which many churches as well as religious believers have simply accommodated dramatically changing sexual mores.

Why is liberal democracy's tendency to undermine revealed religion a "problem"? If liberalism is characterized by an elevation of reason, might not a decline of belief in revelation be one of its beneficial effects, as many liberals, historically, have thought?

There are two answers to this question. First, liberal democracy itself depends for its well-being on religion. This familiar argument was made by Washington, in his Farewell Address, where he argues that liberal democracy depends for its well-being on morality, and that religion is at least an essential component in the foundations of social morality. It is also made by Tocqueville throughout *Democracy in America*, which argues that the freedom of the political world is possible within a fixed moral framework that religion provides.

A second reason why the undermining of revealed religion is a problem is that refusal to consider carefully the claims of revelation is itself illiberal. There is much to be said for reason, but contemporary liberals themselves are often among the first to emphasize its limits. (What Rawls says about "the burdens of reason" suggests such limits.) One position that an honest exponent of reason would consider is that reason's own capacity may be limited, and that claims of a divine revelation might just be correct. Reason might point beyond itself to faith. (I will discuss this point more fully in the next chapter.)

My purpose here is not to prove anything about revealed religion and whether it does, in fact, provide the answers to life's questions, but simply to argue that it is incumbent on all rational people to take the question of revealed religion seriously. Insofar as liberal societies tend to undermine revealed religion, indirectly but powerfully, by some of the attitudes and habits of mind that they encourage – a distrust of certain kinds of knowledge, individualism, materialism – they divert their citizens from confronting some of the most important answers to the profoundest questions of human existence.

---

[53] *Unsecular America: Essays by Paul Johnson*, ed. Neuhaus (Eerdmans, 1986).

Liberalism and the Family

A third problematic tendency of liberalism is the undermining of the stability of the family. Some scholars argue that the family is just as strong as it has been in the past, but has simply assumed new forms.[54] It is certainly true that we should resist the tendency to view the history of the family with an unjustified nostalgia. There were plenty of problems with families in the past, including an excessive rigidity in social gender roles, toleration of spousal abuse, sexual "double standards," and many informal as well as formal ways of "breaking up" a family (desertion being one frequent form).

Nonetheless, it is wrong to think that there have *not* been recent dramatic changes that have greatly weakened the family in performing its essential functions, most importantly, the raising of children.[55] In the past there were many violations of the ideal of marriage and family, but today the notion that there is an ideal or norm is itself under assault. As Elizabeth Fox-Genovese has written,

Today, if we credit our senses, we are witnessing a concerted attempt by a portion of the elite to deny the value of the norm. In its place we are offered marriage as the personal fulfillment of the individual, who must be free to switch partners at will. And we are offered family as "families" – whatever combination of people choose to live together on whatever terms for whatever period of time. It is possible that adults may survive this madness, although one may be permitted to doubt. It is doubtful that any significant number of children will survive it, as the mounting evidence of their distress amply warns.[56]

And, while it is also true that many of the forces undermining the family are part of modernity in general, there seem to be reasonable grounds for finding in liberal democracy itself tendencies contrary to stable family life, such as excessive individualism, affluent materialism, and doubt about absolute substantive moral principles.[57]

It does not follow from my analysis that, because the influence of the regime is so great, and in some cases this influence is not benign, we ought

---

54 One example is Stephanie Coontz, *The Way We Never Were: American Families and the Nostalgia Trap* (Basic Books, 1992) and *The Way We Really Are: Coming to Terms with America's Changing Families* (Basic Books, 1997).

55 Elizabeth Fox-Genovese "Thoughts on the History of the Family," in *The Family, Civil Society, and the State*, Christopher Wolfe, Ed. (Rowman and Littlefield, 1998), pp. 3–11.

56 Ibid., pp. 10–11.

57 The general topic of marriage, family, and sexuality is another one I hope to take up in more detail in the sequel to this book.

to abandon liberalism. The alternatives, after all, might be worse. I, for one, certainly have no desire to return to the Greek polis or the Roman republic. Medieval Christendom might seem to some people (especially some Catholics and other natural law thinkers) to be more attractive, but I would warn such people not to romanticize the actual once-existent forms of that ideal either. As Tocqueville suggested about the aristocracy of the *ancien regime*, one can be distracted by the high points so much that one fails to see the enormous amount of human misery and injustice.

What I would say, instead, is that natural law theorists should help people as much as we can to be more self-critical about aspects of liberalism that are less attractive. We should remind our fellow citizens, for example, of the sobering passage with which Tocqueville concludes his discussion of the "advantages" of democracy in America, in which he notes the deep tendency of liberal democracy to gravitate toward the "middling state of things," the down side of which is mediocrity.[58] And we should also try to "high-tone" liberalism to the extent that we can – for there is a wide range of forms of liberalism, and some of them shape people in much better ways than others.

There is distinguished precedent, I think, for this approach to the question of liberalism. It parallels closely Aristotle's handling of the topic of democracy in his *Politics*.[59] An examination of his account of the various forms of democracy would find that he describes a range of democracies that are on a spectrum from less to more democratic. The democracy he considers best is one that would be at the somewhat less democratic end of that spectrum. (The same would be true of oligarchy.) Underlying his judgment is the principle behind the "mixed regime": the recognition that any form of government has its own defects, and benefits from an infusion of the principles of other forms of government. Just as democracy is best when it is a moderate democracy, liberalism is best when it is a moderate liberalism.

RECONCILING NATURAL LAW AND LIBERALISM:
WHY DOES IT MATTER?

Why does it matter whether there is some phenomenon called "liberalism" and whether it is a good thing or a bad thing that natural law has much in common with it? It may be said that this discussion is primarily a semantic

---

[58] *Democracy in America*, Vol. I, chapter 14, pp. 252–53.
[59] *The Basic Works of Aristotle*, McKeown, Ed. (Random House, 1941). Book IV, chapter 4, pp. 1212–1213.

game – people fighting over whether they or others fall within a category that can be defined in very different ways – and that what matters is not semantics and names, but substance. So why shouldn't we talk about substantive principles and not worry about whether this or that person or institution or principle is "liberal," or "conservative," or whatever.

There is some truth to this. "Liberalism" is a term that has been used to cover such a broad range of thinkers and programs that it might be wondered whether it is that useful a term at all. And, in the final analysis, what matters is not whether a particular principle or political practice is "liberal," but whether it is good. John Finnis, for example, points out that arguments about whether something is compatible with liberalism

enmesh the would-be theorist in the shifting contingencies of political movements or programmes which, taken in their sequence since the term 'liberal' emerged in political use in the 1830s, hav[e] virtually nothing significant in common and, as movements, no principle for identifying a central case or focal sense. The only sensible way to deal with philosophical claims framed in terms of liberalism, liberal political institutions, etc., is to treat them as rhetorical code for 'sound', 'true', 'warranted', 'just', or the like; one translates accordingly and carries on with the consideration of the arguments or claims on their merits.[60]

But the discussion about liberalism is, I think, useful. Peter Berkowitz has some valuable observations in this regard:

Several reasons justify the effort to give liberalism its due. First, liberalism clarifies the contemporary intellectual scene by providing a framework which reveals that what appear to be rival and incompatible schools of thought in fact share a formal structure and governing moral intention. Second, giving liberalism its due means a substantial gain in self-knowledge, both for those who think of themselves as liberals and for those who do not recognize the liberalism of their ways. Third, the liberal tradition has untapped resources for understanding more precisely how to defend, and sustain a political life that rests upon, the premise of natural freedom and equality, a premise whose power not many would wish to deny and whose authority few can honestly resist.[61]

By his first point, Berkowitz means to point out that an understanding of liberalism demonstrates the similarities that get glossed over or lost in discussions of the differences between liberal and communitarian writers, and liberal and post-modernist writers. I would add that discussions of the differences between liberalism and contemporary natural law theory can also obscure what they have in common. Likewise, by his second

---

[60] "Is Natural Law Theory Compatible with Limited Governmnent" in *Natural Law, Liberalism, and Morality*, R. George, Ed. (Clarendon Press, 1996), p. 22, n.38.

[61] Berkowitz, p. 161

point, Berkowitz suggests that it is important for communitarians and postmodernists to recognize their own liberalism, and I add that the same is true for advocates of natural law. By his third point, Berkowitz argues that the liberal tradition has resources that are often overlooked today, and I would argue that those resources are sometimes principles that classical liberals inherited from pre-liberal thought and practice, based on forms of natural law, and which they did not consider incompatible with liberalism, but rather supportive of it. That is, not only is it true that natural law thinkers are often more liberal than they know, but also liberal thinkers (especially the more moderate ones) are often more rooted in natural law than they know.[62]

In the end, it matters whether natural law theorists should consider themselves liberals because, if they don't, they may not think and speak as clearly about themselves and others as they should. This is bad for at least two reasons. First, they won't understand the truth about themselves. And second, they will be less able to defend their own principles persuasively to others who value liberalism greatly.

At the same time, it matters that liberals be aware of what they owe to natural law, so that they can be self-critical liberals who are aware of the balance of strengths and weaknesses in liberalism and can help others to share that awareness.

---

[62] A recent form of this argument can be found in Thomas West's Witherspoon Lecture for the Family Research Council (2001): "Vindicating John Locke: How a Seventeenth Century 'Liberal' Was Really a 'Social Conservative'."

10

Natural Law Liberalism and Religious Liberty

Having given a general description and defense of the possibility and desirability of natural law liberalism, I would like to offer one example of how natural law liberalism "cashes out" on a particular topic. The topic of religious liberty seems particularly appropriate, not only because of its intrinsic importance, but also because it has been a central issue and a central problem in the history and development of natural law.

What I hope to show in this chapter is that natural law liberalism provides a distinctive ground for the principle of religious liberty. It rejects more traditional forms of natural law teaching on the subject, which excessively curtailed the scope of religious liberty. It also rejects contemporary liberal understandings of the grounds for that freedom, since they tend to rest essentially on some important element of skepticism, as to either the existence of religious truth or its knowability by human beings. In a way that neither of those approaches does, it protects a broad form of religious liberty while maintaining a firm belief in the existence and intelligibility of religious truth.

PRELIMINARY NOTE ON "RELIGION"

Before I turn to the stance taken by natural law liberal public philosophy toward religion in general, I need to point out a significant problem in discussing any question regarding "religion," namely, the absence of any very satisfactory definition of it.

Most people throughout history have subscribed to some form of religious belief. (Only in relatively recent times have agnosticism or atheism, based on scientific naturalism, been publicly embraced by significant parts of some societies.) The forms of religious "belief," however, have been extraordinarily varied, to the point where it is difficult even to define the term "religion." One can distinguish between religions with clear-cut deities (e.g., Hinduism) and those with vaguer "forces" (pantheism); those that involve immanent gods (e.g., animism) and those with a transcendent God (e.g., traditional Judaism); and those that are based on reason (e.g., Deism) and those that claim a particular divine revelation (e.g., Judaism, Christianity, Islam). Is it really possible to fit all these sorts of belief – systems into a single over-arching category?

Paul Griffiths gives powerful reasons for doubting the utility of any "neutral" or "scientific" definition of religion.[1] He recognizes that we customarily think of "religion" as a genus with various species (Christianity, Judaism, Islam, Buddhism, and so on), in the same way we think of "currency" as a genus with species like dollars, pounds, euros, and so on. But, while we have few arguments about what constitutes currency, there is deep and often passionate disagreement as to what constitutes religion.

One way to respond to the question, Griffiths argues, is to adopt the approach of Pastor Thwackum (a character in Fielding's *Tom Jones*): the Church of England is true religion, which provides us with the essential characteristics of the genus, and other religions are religions insofar as they share those characteristics. This is a frankly theological use of the term "religion." (Griffiths argues, rightly I think, that the founders of American government had such a definition of religion, based on Protestant Christianity.)

The other approach is found in scholars of contemporary "religious studies," who want

an understanding of religion not derived from the self-understanding of some church, without theological commitments, sufficiently subtle and interesting to permit interesting intellectual work to be done, and capable of being agreed upon by a community of scholars sufficiently large to make possible the development of a discipline with religion as its central topic. But no such understanding has yet been found. . . .[2]

(I think that what he says of religious studies scholars could also be said of most judges, political scientists, and legal scholars.)

---

[1] Paul Griffiths, "The Very Idea of Religion" in *First Things* 103 (May 2000): 30–35 (and also the correspondence about it in subsequent issues).
[2] Ibid., p. 31.

Griffiths points out that the word "religion" had little significance among pre-Christian thinkers, and that it became more widely used after Augustine as referring to public and communal worship, with Christian worship being the preeminent or full sense of the term (the Thwackum-like essential characteristics of the genus) and other religions being measured in those terms. With the splintering of Christianity in the Reformation, and with European discovery of other, non-European cultures with their own religions, the idea of religion as a generic category grew. But "[o]ver these intellectual moves, too, Parson Thwackum's spirit hovers: 'religion' means 'things like Christianity' and "[e]ven in the analyses of religion offered by such resolutely anti-Christian figures" as Hume, Kant, and Hegel "'religion' is analyzed by a process of abstraction from features of Protestant Christianity."[3]

In the final analysis, our choices are limited: we can dispense with the notion of religion entirely (dividing its former content among other disciplines such as history, literary studies, anthropology, and cultural studies), or we can adopt a theologically inspired definition of religion (i.e., a definition of religion based on certain theological commitments). The latter category would include the Pastor Thwackums of the world (those who consider a particular religion paradigmatic). But it would also include those, like contemporary social scientists, who adopt a purely "naturalistic" view of religion (one that would "rule out appeal to or use of God as an explanation of anything") – though the latter don't "seem to see that [their] own uncritical presentation of naturalism as though it were obviously true, or obviously to be adhered to by students of religion in a public university, makes it seem formally and functionally indistinguishable from the confessional commitments" they reject.[4]

Griffiths' argument about the difficulty of defining religion, taken together with the sheer diversity of what is customarily included among "religions," yields this conclusion: almost anything that is said in contemporary discussions about, for example, "politics and religion" is likely to be either (1) untrue, because it would apply, not to "religion" in general, but, at most, only to some particular religions, or (2) uninteresting, because what would apply to all religions would be so general or so thin as to be useless.

My way of dealing with this problem will be frankly to confess that I operate on a certain theological understanding of religion that is rooted in

[3] Ibid, pp. 32–33.
[4] Ibid, p. 34 and p. 35.

and shared by the major revealed religions of the Western world (Judaism, Christianity, and Islam) as public and communal worship of a transcendent God. Such a view does not deny that there are other kinds of religion, but it does see those other religions largely in terms of what they share or do not share with those revealed religions.

Particularly central to my discussion will be the dichotomy[5] between "natural theology" (which is based on reason) and "revealed religion" (which claims to transcend the limits of human reason in various ways). I make no pretense that this is a "neutral" choice, as if there were some neutral framework (i.e., one that took no stance on any religious propositions) for understanding religion. Any framework of analysis "privileges" certain religions and philosophical views that use or are more or less compatible with such a framework. The very distinction between natural and supernatural religion is deeply rooted in Western history, and especially in Christianity (particularly in theology or philosophy that traces its roots in some way back to the great Thomistic synthesis that shaped late medieval Christianity), as well as in American history. Again, as Griffiths points out, this general observation about the impossibility of religious neutrality emphatically includes modern philosophical systems that are naturalistic, atheistic, or agnostic. It is impossible to understand modern secularism without understanding it as (in part) a culmination of increasingly rationalistic religious views, which themselves were historically a development first arising within, and over time increasingly against, western Christianity.

NATURAL LAW AND RELIGION

In discussing natural law and religion, I use natural law in a broad sense that includes not only natural law ethics, but also the philosophical anthropology and metaphysics associated with the classical natural law teaching of Thomas Aquinas. While historically these were all integrated in Thomas under the direction of theology, I will generally seek to confine my discussion to those parts of his thought that appeal to reason rather than revelation for their grounding. What I will say here, for my purpose of providing a background to a discussion of the natural law liberal view

---

[5] My use of the term "dichotomy" is not meant to imply any necessary incompatibility or hostility between natural theology and revealed religion – in principle, while different, they could still be quite harmonious. That is certainly the classic natural law position.

of religious liberty, constitutes a brief description of the natural law perspective on religion rather than a defense of it.

Natural Religion

The greatest representatives of natural law have argued that our knowledge of God comes from two sources: our reason and God's revelation. Thomas Aquinas situates natural law within the broader context of the eternal law – natural law is "man's participation in the eternal law" – in the *Summa Theologiae*, his one systematic discussion of natural law. This discussion of law can be separated from the context of revealed theology in that work: natural law is not necessarily a doctrine of revealed religion.[6] It is more questionable whether it can be separated from a natural theological context. On this point there is considerable debate among contemporary natural law thinkers.

Proponents of the "new natural law" theory of Germain Grisez, John Finnis, Robert George, and others propose a view of natural law that is rooted in a notion of practical reason that is very distinct from theoretical reason. Practical reason begins with a search for the good, identifies various basic human goods, affirms a moral principle that one ought to seek the integral good of oneself and all others, and employs various principles of practical reasoning to arrive at concrete moral decisions. This practical knowledge is not derived from theoretical knowledge (in fact, it is more likely the source of important theoretical knowledge about human beings), and there is no recourse at any point to the notion of a lawgiver. This may be one factor in the lack of enthusiasm for the term "natural law" in this camp. (None of this is to say that the new natural law is, in principle, hostile to an ultimate divine source of all things, including human nature and practical reason. John Finnis, for example, has given a powerful defense of such a view.[7] It simply does not regard such a source as an essential part of ethics.)

---

[6] I am not asserting here that it is possible to understand Thomas's full doctrine on natural law without any advertence to its context in theology. I only claim that there is an intelligible and defensible natural law teaching that can be discussed without reference to revealed theology, for purposes of discussing political and moral affairs with those who do not accept revelation.

[7] See his "Telling the Truth about God and Man in a Pluralist Society: Economy or Explication?" a paper delivered at the conference "How Naked a Public Square? Reconsidering the Place of Religion in American Public Life, Princeton University, October 22–23, 2004.

More traditional forms of natural law theory do not think that the notion of a lawgiver for natural law can be dispensed with. This does not mean that natural law, in order to be law, must be reduced to a species of divine positive law or will or command. A "thinner" notion of promulgation through man's nature suffices to meet Aquinas's own requirement of promulgation as an essential feature of law. But an ordinance of reason is more plausible if it is ordained by someone, and promulgation is more plausible if it is promulgated by someone. A fuller account of natural law and practical reasoning, then, will account for its origins and give greater sense to the notion of a natural *law*.[8]

Aquinas's natural law teaching cannot be divorced from his discussion of man's natural knowledge of God and eternal law. The notion of a lawgiver who is the source of the law, by being the source of human nature itself, is not only a teaching of divine revelation, he maintains, but a truth accessible to human reason (moving from creatures as effects to their cause), as he elaborates in his *Summa Contra Gentiles* (especially Books One and Two and Three, on God and Creation and Providence).

This teaching about natural knowledge of God is not peculiar to medieval natural law. It is also a characteristic feature of early or classical liberalism. Locke, for example, appeals to the fact that human beings are the "workmanship of God," in his argument against suicide.[9] Commentators on Locke often focus on the way in which his religion – Christianity reduced to a religion of reason – seems reductionist relative to previous forms of Christianity, contracting the scope of religious truth. This truth should not obscure the fact that Locke firmly rejects atheism and grounds his thought in religion at various points of his writing.[10]

A natural theology can also be seen in the arguments of the Declaration of Independence that Americans are entitled to assume a separate and equal station to which the laws of nature "and of nature's God" entitles them, and that men are endowed "by their Creator" with certain inalienable rights. While this language – the God and the Creator – would have been interpreted by most Americans as referring to the Christian God they worshiped, the language itself seems to rely on a natural theology accessible to reason, rather than only on revelation accessible to faith

---

[8] See, for example, Russell Hittinger, *The First Grace: Rediscovering the Natural Law in a Post-Christian World* (Wilmington, Delaware.: ISI Books, 2003), especially chapter 2.

[9] John Locke, *Two Treatises of Government*, Laslett, Ed. (New York: Mentor, 1965), p. 311.

[10] I take no stance on Locke's private religious beliefs, a much debated issue. Here I simply deal with what he says on the face of his writings.

(and it was certainly understood in that more limited way by significant founders, such as Jefferson himself).[11]

This "natural" knowledge of God does not take the form of rigorous philosophical knowledge, of course. Recall the discussion in Part I (in my analysis of Stephen Macedo's use of "public reason") of the sort of knowledge of ethical principles that natural law describes. Most people consider murder wrong, although they are not particularly able to construct a powerful ethical argument against it. Their "natural law" knowledge that murder is wrong is quite strong and quite true, though often inarticulate. Others (the "wise," Thomas calls them) are better able to provide sophisticated intellectual defenses of this natural knowledge.

Likewise, most people know that a divine source of being and meaning (God) must exist, although they would have to leave sophisticated intellectual arguments for it to others. Their inarticulate knowledge is not based on self-evidence, as the knowledge of precepts of the moral law is. It requires an argument, in this case from effects back to a cause, for example, one that moves from the existence of beings whose existence is contingent to the existence of a being whose existence is necessary. But this is an argument that most people are capable of, even if in an inarticulate form. And yet, like precepts of the natural law, this natural knowledge of God's existence is also capable of being obscured by corrupt customs and passions.

Revealed Religion

Revealed religion is different in fundamental ways from natural religion. While the unity of truth means that valid truths of reason about God would be confirmed by revealed religion, there are also other truths about God that exceed the capacity of reason. Reason itself shows that human beings have no direct access to God that would enable them to know the divine essence directly, in itself.

---

[11] The Declaration also includes references to divine Providence and the Supreme Judge of the world. While classical natural law argued divine Providence can readily be known through reason (see Thomas Aquinas, *Summa Contra Gentiles* (Notre Dame: University of Notre Dame Press, 1975), Book Three), it is less clear whether God's judgment of the world can be. Still, it is likely that those who framed and read the Declaration thought that God's judgment could be known through reason. (Moreover, there is an ambiguous reference in the last line of Locke's *Second Treatise on Government*, chapter 3, "Of the State of War": "Of that I my self can only be Judge in my own Conscience, as I will answer it at the great Day, to the Supream Judge of all Men" (Laslett, Ed., p. 323). The ambiguity arises because this statement follows a discussion of an Old Testament passage.)

Of course, natural law – based on reason – cannot itself speak to the strict truth of revealed religion. Insofar as revealed religious truths exceed the scope of reason, they are known to be true on a different basis: namely, the word of another who is trustworthy. Many human truths of day-to-day life are, in fact, based on faith (the word of others), some of which can be confirmed by direct knowledge (e.g., the belief that England is an island) and others of which cannot be so confirmed (e.g., historical truths, like the fact that Julius Caesar once existed). Truths about the nature of God are of a different order, in that unaided human reason (and so the word of other human beings as well) cannot reach them.

Reason has some role to play relative to claims of divine revelation. For example, reason may provide probable arguments of greater or lesser strength for the credibility of claims of divine revelation, and it can refute allegedly demonstrative arguments that are incompatible with divinely revealed truths (i.e., it can show that arguments that appear to contradict divine revelation are not demonstrative or compelling). But they cannot ultimately prove the truth of revelation insofar as divine revelation claims to include elements that are in principle beyond discovery through reason.

The part of this brief summary of the appropriate stance of reason toward divine revelation that I want to emphasize is the openness to claims of divine revelation that reason should embrace. Given (1) our natural knowledge of God, as the necessary being that is the explanation for the actual existence of all the contingent beings we see; and (2) our awareness of the limits of reason, especially in the face of what we experience as a natural human desire to know much more about reality – especially our own origin, reason, and destiny – than our intellects can achieve; and (3) the existence of claims to divine revelations that have at least some reasonable motives of credibility (e.g., in terms of their capacity to generate powerful intellectual systems and to help found and shape broad cultures and civilizations), the appropriate stance of the human mind should be at least to consider such claims open-mindedly. Countervailing factors raise doubts about such claims (e.g., the existence of evil, and especially the many evils perpetrated by those who have subscribed to revealed religions), and these factors also require an open-minded examination. My point is not that reason requires acceptance of claims of revelation (even the most reasonable ones). It is only that there is nothing in reason that, in principle, requires a rejection of the possibility of revelation, and in fact there are good reasons to examine such claims seriously and without prejudice.

This position has been powerfully restated in our time:

The truth comes initially to the human being as a question: Does life have a meaning? Where is it going? At first sight, personal existence may seem completely meaningless. It is not necessary to turn to the philosophers of the absurd or to the provocative questioning found in the Book of Job in order to have doubts about life's meaning. The daily experience of suffering – in one's own life and in the lives of others – and the arrays of facts which seem inexplicable to reason are enough to ensure that a question as dramatic as the question of meaning cannot be evaded. Moreover, the first absolutely certain truth of our life, beyond the fact that we exist, is the inevitability of our death. Given this unsettling fact, the search for a full answer is inescapable. Each of us has both the desire and the duty to know the truth of our own destiny. We want to know if death will be the definitive end of our life or if there is something beyond – if it is possible to hope for an afterlife or not...

No one can avoid this questioning, neither the philosopher nor the ordinary person. The answer we give will determine whether or not we think it possible to attain universal and absolute truth. This is a decisive moment of the search. Every truth – if it really is truth – presents itself as universal, even if it is not the whole truth. If something is true, then it must be true for all people and at all times. Beyond this universality, however, people seek an absolute which might give to all their searching a meaning and an answer – something ultimate, which might serve as the ground of all things. In other words, they seek a final explanation, a supreme value, which refers to nothing beyond itself and which puts an end to all questioning. Hypotheses may fascinate, but they do not satisfy. Whether we admit it or not, there comes for everyone the moment when personal existence must be anchored to a truth recognized as final, a truth which confers a certitude no longer open to doubt....

The search for truth, of course, is not always so transparent nor does it always produce such results. The natural limitation of reason and the inconstancy of the heart often obscure and distort a person's search. Truth can also drown in a welter of other concerns. People can even run from the truth as soon as they glimpse it because they are afraid of its demands. Yet, for all that they may evade it, the truth still influences life. Life in fact can never be grounded upon doubt, uncertainty or deceit; such an existence would be threatened constantly by fear and anxiety. One may define the human being, therefore, as the one who seeks the truth.

It is unthinkable that a search so deeply rooted in human nature would be completely vain and useless. The capacity to search for truth and to pose questions itself implies the rudiments of a response. Human beings would not even begin to search for something of which they knew nothing or for something which they thought was wholly beyond them. Only the sense that they can arrive at an answer leads them to take the first step. This is what normally happens in scientific research. When scientists, following their intuition, set out in search of the logical and verifiable explanation of a phenomenon, they are confident from the first that they will find an answer, and they do not give up in the face of setbacks. They do not judge their original intuition useless simply because they have not reached their goal; rightly enough they will say that they have not yet found a satisfactory answer.

The same must be equally true of the search for truth when it comes to the ultimate questions. The thirst for truth is so rooted in the human heart that to be obliged to ignore it would cast our existence into jeopardy. Everyday life shows well enough how each one of us is preoccupied by the pressure of a few fundamental questions and how in the soul of each of us there is at least an outline of the answers....

Nonetheless, there are in the life of a human being many more truths which are simply believed than truths which are acquired by way of personal verification. Who, for instance, could assess critically the countless scientific findings upon which modern life is based? Who could personally examine the flow of information which comes day after day from all parts of the world and which is generally accepted as true? Who in the end could forge anew the paths of experience and thought which have yielded the treasures of human wisdom and religion? This means that the human being – the one who seeks the truth – is also the one who lives by belief.

In believing, we entrust ourselves to the knowledge acquired by other people. This suggests an important tension. On the one hand, the knowledge acquired through belief can seem an imperfect form of knowledge, to be perfected gradually through personal accumulation of evidence; on the other hand, belief is often humanly richer than mere evidence, because it involves an interpersonal relationship and brings into play not only a person's capacity to know but also the deeper capacity to entrust oneself to others, to enter into a relationship with them which is intimate and enduring...

From all that I have said to this point it emerges that men and women are on a journey of discovery which is humanly unstoppable – a search for the truth and a search for a person to whom they might entrust themselves. Christian faith comes to meet them, offering the concrete possibility of reaching the goal which they seek.[12]

The point of this long excerpt does not concern the truth per se of Christianity, but merely this more simple, and yet fundamental, point: reason itself, prior to any belief in divine revelation, has adequate grounds at least to examine, carefully and with an open mind, claims of divine revelation. This point helps prepare us to see that a natural law conception of the common good will include the promotion of precisely this search for religious truth.

NATURAL LAW, THE COMMON GOOD, AND RELIGION

Unlike contemporary liberal theorists, who start from the fact of inevitable and deep differences of opinions about the good, and ask how to manage

---

[12] John Paul II, *Fides et Ratio* (1998), nos. 26–33.

the potential conflict arising from different goals,[13] natural law political theory starts with the idea of the common good.

The Common Good and Truth

The common good has two interrelated dimensions: the quality of the common life of the community itself, and the quality of the life of the members of the community. An example of a common life is a sports team. Its good is measured, not by cumulating or "adding up" the quality of individual actions or the benefits accruing to each of its members, but by evaluating the integral action of its members acting as a whole, and its results, especially whether the team wins or loses.[14] That is why, in principle, it is easy to imagine, say, a basketball team whose individual members have basketball skills – dribbling, shooting, rebounding – that are superior to the individual skills of another team's members, but that is still a worse team. It is not just the individual skills, but the relationship among them, and especially their integration, that counts.

At the same time, the quality of the common life is not something that subsists apart from the activity of its members. The team wins or plays well, as a "whole," but the action of the team is not something separate from the (joint, interrelated) actions of all its members. The skills of teamwork itself are skills found *in* the members of the team.

The common good of a human community is necessarily a human good, a good for the kind of being man is. This human good is man's ultimate end, or happiness. There are various dimensions of this good. It includes goods shared with other substances, especially the preservation of existence. It also includes goods shared with other animals, especially preservation of the species through procreation and education of the young. And it includes, above all, the distinctive human activity of reason.

This good of reason does not itself consist in a single activity, since there are various forms of rational activity, no one of which completely

---

[13] For a good example, see John Rawls, *A Theory of Justice* on the "burdens of reason."

[14] The actual relation between the external result (winning or losing) and the quality of the activity itself (how well the team played) is complex. While the point of the game itself is to win, the point of playing the game is somewhat broader, and is concerned with the skillfulness of the play rather than simply winning or losing. Anyone who has experienced both the satisfaction of playing well in losing a hard-fought game against a good opponent, and the boredom of winning a comparatively easy victory against an inferior opponent will understand why. But this does not affect the point I make in the text, since the evaluation still focuses on the quality of team play, not individual components thereof.

constitutes man's perfection. These forms include theoretical or speculative reason (whose end is knowing), practical reason (whose end is doing or making), and the activity of other faculties that participate in reason, such as morally virtuous activity, including acts of temperance and fortitude. (Note that the first two categories of goods, shared with substances generally and with animals, are meant to be subject to, and permeated with, reason, in human beings.) No one of these should be pursued exclusively, as even contemplation, arguably the highest rational activity, pursued exclusively would quickly result in a man's death, and would prevent the achievement of other genuine goods, such as skill or excellence in physical activity or play.[15] Man's ultimate good, then, even if summed up in the phrase "rational activity," is a richly diverse set of goods.

One aspect of the human good is knowledge. All men, as Aristotle noted, desire to know. But while all knowledge is good in itself, some knowledge is much more important than other kinds. Knowing the overall character or structure of reality, of the universe and its parts, and especially the place of man within it – his origin, nature, good, and destiny – has a special eminence within the category of knowledge. At the same time, that eminent knowledge – precisely because it is so comprehensive and complex – is particularly hard for men to achieve.

Knowledge or truth – especially about the most important matters – is an end in itself; it is a very high good, closely tied to the very distinctive human capacity of reason. Reason is valuable not merely as an instrument to identify means to ends that are extrinsic and simply given, but as a way of grasping and contemplating the truth about reality, as an end in itself. Those who do not attain this end (i.e., those who are not growing in such knowledge and have not attained some significant understanding of the broad outlines of reality – for no one could ever reasonably claim full knowledge of the truth), to that extent, lack an important element of a good and happy human life.

Alexis de Tocqueville noted that human action depends on this kind of knowledge, since our actions all have to be traced back to some much broader notions of human destiny, and he notes an important implication of this fact:

---

[15] An important feature of natural law theory is the recognition that perfection is not always found in the existence of what is highest, but in the rich diversity of various levels of existence. Just as the universe is more perfect for including material substances, plants, animals, human beings, and angels, and not just the higher forms of being, so a more perfect common good of a human community includes not just contemplation or any other single activity, but rather a wide and diverse range of activities.

If man were forced to demonstrate for himself all the truths of which he makes daily use, his task would never end. He would exhaust his strength in preparatory demonstrations, without ever advancing beyond them. As, from the shortness of his life, he has not the time, nor, from the limits of his intelligence, the capacity to act in this way, he is reduced to take on trust a host of facts and opinions which he has not had either the time or the power to verify for himself, but which men of greater ability have found out, or which the crowd adopts.[16]

There is hardly any human action, however particular it may be, that does not originate in some very general idea men have conceived of the Deity, of his relation to mankind, of the nature of their own souls, and of their duties to their fellow-creatures. Nor can anything prevent these ideas from being the common spring from which all the rest emanates.

Men are therefore immeasurably interested in acquiring fixed ideas of God, of the soul, and of their common duties to their Creator and to their fellow men; for doubt on these first principles would abandon all their actions to chance, and would condemn them in some way to disorder and impotence.[17]

The question is not whether man will have dogma or belief, but only what that dogma or belief will be.[18]

This brings us, inevitably, back to the religious question. Revealed religion, as we have seen, claims to provide a special source (genuine though limited) of knowledge of the broadest and most important aspects of the comprehensive truth about reality. A great deal rides on whether, or in what respects, a particular religion, or no religion, is true. (The "truth" may be, of course, that different religions have, in different degrees, particular and sometimes overlapping aspects of truth. The most comprehensive truth, therefore, would be the perspective of the person who sees accurately what elements of truth the various religions have. And part of the truth about human life might be that human beings are simply incapable of ascertaining much of the truth about the general character of reality. But that itself is a particular truth claim.)

Those people who have more accurate ideas of at least the general outlines of the truth about reality, either through a true religion or through

---

[16] *Democracy in America*, Part Two, Book One, chapter 2 (Phillips Bradley, Ed., p. 8).

[17] Ibid., p. 20.

[18] This applies, of course, to modern dogmatic secularism and atheism, which is as much a matter of "belief" – rather than strict "knowledge" – as religion is, for the vast majority of those who hold the one or the other. The beliefs of dogmatic secularists generally rest on their willingness to accord credibility to a certain set of authorities, namely, the priesthood of modern scientists, though the equations of modern scientists are every bit as obscure to the average person – including the average intellectual – as any divine revelation. I am not saying that all scientists are dogmatic skeptics or atheists. But it is generally true that today's dogmatic skeptics or atheists claim some variant of "modern science" as their ultimate framework for understanding reality.

the truth of no-religion, are, to that extent, better off or more humanly fulfilled or happier. They have achieved a very significant aspect of the human good. Those whose beliefs about reality (however sincere) are significantly erroneous (e.g., those who believe that there is a god, if in fact no god exists; or those who do not believe in God, if in fact He does exist) are, to that (very serious) extent, worse off or humanly stunted or unhappier. They suffer a great evil. (When this is not understood, often it is because people make the mistake of identifying "happiness" with "subjective satisfaction," which is quite different.)

This is not the way many people habitually think about these matters of truth today, at least regarding what are considered questions of "value" or opinion rather than of "fact." They focus simply on the right to believe whatever you want, with sincerity being the key virtue. What counts is the free and honest search for truth, rather than truth itself. That right may be a genuine right, and sincerity may be a great virtue, and the never-completed search may be central to human life. (I think all three of these propositions are true and important.) But it should also be recognized that one can exercise that right, and be truly sincere, and deeply engaged in the search, and still be in a very (objectively) unhappy state, that is, a state of false belief, thinking that you are "living in" the real world, when "your" world is really quite different from the real one.

If the truth does matter this way, those who have responsibility for ensuring the common good – those who exercise political power (and so, in a democracy, everyone) – should, to the extent they can, promote the pursuit of and attainment of truth. This can be done in various ways: equipping people (directly or indirectly) with the intellectual skills to pursue deeper understanding (e.g., basic skills of thinking, reading, writing, and speaking, and more advanced knowledge of the principles and methods of various sciences and arts); inculcating through education an understanding of various truths, which can serve as a foundation for the pursuit of wider and deeper truths; and protecting people from obstacles to the pursuit of truth (e.g., vices and passions that distort human perception of the truth, and specious presentations of falsehoods as truth).

The Common Good, Truth, and Religious Freedom

Given this background, let us suppose a people who are committed to a natural law liberal philosophy and, in addition, generally (although not unanimously) share a common understanding of the broad outlines of reality, and, specifically, a certain revealed religion, say, Christianity. (In what follows, much of what I say may apply to other religions but, as I have suggested, the use of a concept as amorphous as "religion" is often an obstacle to careful analysis, and so it is more useful to focus on a particular religion.) The substantive conception of the common good in such a society – the shared good of the community, realized through and in the activity of its members – would include belief in and practice of this religion (though that leaves open the important question of whether that would involve direct government sponsorship of such religious activity). Would such a community guarantee a broad form of religious liberty, that is, freedom of religious *belief*, and also freedom of religious *practice* insofar as it is compatible with the rights of other citizens?

A religion of the sort that gives prominence to virtues such as faith and charity, like Christianity, would seem necessarily to embrace a fundamental, core principle of religious liberty. Belief and love, in order truly to be belief and love, must be free. Moreover, from a natural law perspective, a good human life is a life in accord with reason, which is a life of human excellence or virtue, and virtue resides, not in external acts, but in the will.

Compulsion ordinarily acts only on bodies and external acts and, since it is usually unable to reach the will, it is unable to "make" someone virtuous.[19] Religious acts of adoration, love, repentance, thanksgiving, and so forth, require freedom. A religion that values such acts, then, must not merely grudgingly concede religious freedom, but emphatically embrace it, as a necessary precondition for religious acts.[20]

And so the following might be said about religious liberty:

It is in accordance with their dignity that all human beings, because they are persons, that is, beings endowed with reason and free will and therefore bearing

---

[19] In certain cases, compulsion can go deeper, and actually determine the will, as in the case of "brainwashing" – coercion so systematic and compulsive that it does seem to bring about a change in the will. But it does so at the price of a person's identity: it is doubtful that one could say that the "person" who is the source of post-brainwashing consensual acts is truly the "person" who was initially subjected to the brainwashing.

[20] Note how this is a good example of a question that should *not* be approached by asking generic questions about the stance of "religion" on the necessity of freedom in religious belief. Different religions may have quite different conceptions of what forms of religious acts are acceptable to the Deity, and for some religions, this may include coerced acts. Some forms of Islam, for example, seem to emphasize Allah's absolute sovereignty over everything, and therefore to attribute value to external, compelled acts of submission.

personal responsibility, are both impelled by their nature and bound by a moral obligation to seek the truth, especially religious truth. They are also bound to adhere to the truth once they come to know it and to direct their whole lives in accordance with the demands of truth. But human beings cannot satisfy this obligation in a way that is in keeping with their own nature unless they enjoy both psychological freedom and immunity from external coercion. Therefore, the right to religious freedom is based not on subjective attitudes but on the very nature of the individual person. For this reason, the right to such immunity continues to exist even in those who do not live up to their obligation of seeking the truth and adhering to it. The exercise of this right cannot be interfered with as long as the just requirements of public order are observed.[21]

Note that the right to religious liberty is not a right to believe whatever one chooses to believe – since human beings have an obligation to pursue and adhere to the truth – but rather a right *against being compelled* to adhere to any religious views (even true ones); it is an immunity from coercion. Moreover, since the right (in that sense) to follow one's conscientious views includes the right to profess them, and since human beings are naturally social creatures, rights of religious expression, including public worship and proselytism, seem to be included within this general right to religious liberty, subject to the requirement of public order.[22]

If natural law theory argues that a broad form of religious liberty is based on the dignity of the human person, one might reasonably ask, why did it take so long to establish a solid principle of religious liberty in Western civilization, the source of natural law thought? The answer to that question is complex, I think, and I will make no effort to give a complete answer here.[23] At least part of the answer is that Christians have often not lived up to their professions of belief, and have given in to temptations to take the "shortcut" of using political power to obtain their goals.[24] While some of this persecution was not on grounds of religious

[21] "Declaration on Religious Liberty" *(Dignitatis Humanae)*, in *Vatican Council II*, A. Flannery, Ed. (Northport, NY: Costello, 1996) #2, p. 553.
[22] *Dignitatis Humanae*, #3 (p. 554). There is some dispute as to the breadth of the term "public order," but I think it is clear that the Council used it in a relatively limited way, as comprehending the rights of other people, public peace, and public morality. Most importantly, the term was *not* intended to justify suppression of religious proselytism by non-Catholics in "confessionally Catholic" countries.
[23] Two works that may provide some elements of the answer are P. Brown, "St. Augustine's Attitude to Religious Coercion" in *The Journal of Roman Studies*, Vol. 54 (1964), pp. 107–116, and Charles Journet, *The Church of the Word Incarnate* (New York: Sheed and Ward, 1955), chapter VI.
[24] These are acts for which John Paul II went so far as to ask forgiveness: "While we praise God who, in his merciful love, has produced in the Church a wonderful harvest of

heterodoxy *per se*, but rested on political grounds (i.e., the politically seditious activities of nonbelievers or heretics[25]), there is no question that straightforward persecution of religious dissidents in medieval and early modern societies in which natural law was influential was widespread.

Moreover, great representatives of the natural law tradition defended certain forms of coercion regarding religion. Thomas Aquinas argued against forced conversions and defended the basic religious freedom of Jews and Muslims: "Among unbelievers there are some who have never received the faith, such as the heathens and the Jews: and these are by no means to be compelled to the faith, in order that they may believe, because to believe depends on the will."[26] But he also explicitly maintained that heretics could be treated differently, since they had made religious promises to which secular authorities could hold them: "On the other hand, there are unbelievers who at some time have accepted the faith, and professed it, such as heretics and all apostates: such should be submitted even to bodily compulsion, that they may fulfill what they have promised, and hold what they, at one time, received."[27]

On the basic issue of compelled religious belief and practice, I think that – despite the failure fully to employ them – the tradition of classical natural law had readily available to it the intellectual resources necessary to defend a strong position of religious freedom, especially in

---

holiness, missionary zeal, total dedication to Christ and neighbor, we cannot fail to recognize the infidelities to the Gospel committed by some of our brethren, especially during the second millennium. Let us ask pardon for the divisions which have occurred among Christians, for the violence some have used in the service of the truth and for the distrustful and hostile attitudes sometimes taken towards the followers of other religions." (Homily for the Day of Pardon, March 12, 2000). See also the report of the International Theological Commission "Memory and Reconciliation: The Church and the Faults of the Past" (December 1999), especially section 5.3. "The Use of Force in the Service of Truth."

25 An awareness of this concern informs Peter Ackroyd's biography, *The Life of Thomas More* (London: Chatto & Windus, 1998). It was also a key feature (but only one) in St. Augustine's call for the secular authorities to suppress the Donatists in the late fourth century. But for a complex summary, see P. Brown (above, n. 23).

26 *Summa Theologiae*, II–II, Q. 10, a. 8. Aquinas also says that human rulers should imitate God, in permitting certain evils, such as the rites of unbelievers, "lest, without them, greater goods might be forfeited or greater evils ensue." II–II, Q. 10, a. 11. Moreover, at least partly on natural law grounds, he argues that the children of unbelievers should not be taken and baptized against their parents' will. II–II, Q. 10, a. 12.

I say "basic" religious freedom, however, because nothing that Aquinas says would prevent civil disabilities being placed on non-Christians, so even this religious toleration is quite limited.

27 *Summa Theologiae*, II–II, Q. 10, a. 8.

Aquinas's phrase (quoted above) "because to believe depends on the will." "Compelled belief" is no belief at all, but simply external submission to avoid punishment.

There is another aspect of the issue of religious freedom, however, that may be more difficult to deal with.

The More Serious Argument for Limiting Religious Liberty

Another important factor explaining the regrettable historical delay in recognizing the full breadth of religious liberty in the West and in natural law theory was the existence of a more serious intellectual argument for curtailing it in significant respects – an argument concerned not with religious belief per se, but with its public expression and its impact on others. The point of suppression, according to this rationale, was not to compel individuals to adopt true religious belief, but to protect those who hold true religious beliefs from those who seek to spread false ones.[28]

Thoughtful contemporary liberals like Jeremy Waldron and Brian Barry have understood that this is the stronger theoretical argument for curtailing religious liberty, one that is not as easily dismissed as the argument for direct religious compulsion.

Waldron argues, in a discussion of Locke's *Letter Concerning Toleration*:

Suppose the religious authorities know that there are certain books that would be sufficient, if read, to shake the faith of an otherwise orthodox population. Then, although again people's beliefs cannot be controlled directly by coercive means, those who wield political power can put it to work indirectly to reinforce belief by banning everyone on pain of death from reading or obtaining copies of these heretical tomes. Such means may well be efficacious even though they are intolerant and oppressive; and Locke, who is concerned only with the rationality of persecution, provides no argument against them.[29]

---

[28] After Aquinas says that unbelievers who have never received the faith should not be compelled, because faith depends on the will, he goes on to add: "nevertheless they should be compelled by the faithful, if it be possible to do so, so that they do not hinder the faith, by their blasphemies, or by their evil persuasions, or even by their open persecutions. It is for this reason that Christ's faithful often wage war with unbelievers, not indeed for the purpose of forcing them to believe, because even if they were to conquer them, and take them prisoners, they should still leave them free to believe, if they will, but in order to prevent them from hindering the faith of Christ." *Summa Theologiae*, II–II, Q. 10, a. 8.

[29] *Liberal Rights* (New York: Cambridge University Press, 1993), chapter 4, p. 109.

Similarly, Barry points out that

The persecutor may be less concerned with converting existing heretics than with preventing them from gaining new adherents from the ranks of the currently orthodox, and for this purpose it may well be sufficient to prohibit all outward manifestations of the heretical belief. Even more importantly, the persecutor may well consider that, in the great scheme of things, saving the souls of the present generation of adults is of trivial significance compared with what is at stake in saving the souls of their descendants. And here the historical record is extremely clear. Most of the contemporary adherents of Islam are the descendants of people who originally adopted it at the point of a sword, but the quality of their faith today is no less for that. The same goes for many Protestant and Catholic areas in Europe. The effectiveness of coercion in producing genuine belief over the course of a few generations is beyond question.[30]

This approach is not immediately subject to the critique that it tries to coerce an assent that must be free. It focuses, rather, on the protection of third parties. It can be understood on the analogy of the obligation of society to protect the public health by quarantining people with a serious contagious disease. (It is an example of what Dworkin calls "critical paternalism," discussed above in Chapter 5.) If society has the obligation to protect people from germs that threaten their physical life and health, how much more, it might be said, does it have the obligation to protect people from falsehoods about the most important truths that provide the framework for human life.

One response to this argument for limiting religious freedom is that it fails because the distinction between "(private) religious practice" and "public worship and proselytism" is problematic. Those who view religion as a purely personal and private aspect of life might accept such a distinction, it might be said, but those who consider public worship and proselytism as an integral aspect – even an essential duty – of their religion cannot. For them, "proselytism" is not something "extra," icing added to the cake, that comes "after" practicing your religion. It is a constituent element of religious practice itself. Thus, the reasons that ground a right to believe and practice religion (privately) also ground a right to proselytize.

This response is true, but it doesn't prove a right to religious proselytism, because even the right to religious practice is not unqualified. When religious *practice* affects the rights of others, it is generally recognized that the state can legitimately impose limits (as in the obvious case of

---

[30] "How Not to Defend Liberal Institutions" in *Liberalism and the Good*, R. Bruce Douglass, Gerald R. Mara, and Henry S. Richardson, Eds. (New York: Routledge, 1990), p. 48.

human sacrifice[31] and in cases such as lifesaving transfusions for children of parents religiously opposed to them). Restricting rights of religious proselytism is justified on these familiar grounds (protecting the rights of others), although this application of the general principle (i.e., to protect people's adherence to religious truth by prohibiting contrary speech) is less familiar.

At the same time, it must be pointed out that, even if the motive of suppressing religious actions is not to compel religious belief, but only to protect the rights of others, such suppression may still have some of the same distorting effects as direct religious persecution: it creates incentives not to act conscientiously on one's religious belief in order to avoid penalties associated with non-conforming religious activity. A person whose religious beliefs call for him to evangelize, but who does not evangelize in order to avoid punishment for doing so, fails to act with integrity – and the government action has encouraged this, even if its motive was simply to protect third parties. At the least, this has to "count against" such government action.

Another response to this defense of government power to suppress false religious proselytism would invoke the weaknesses of the analogy of protecting (physical) public health. There is a key difference, it will be said, between the putative harm of false religious proselytism and harms that involve the direct violations of others' rights: namely, that the harm to others caused by false religious proselytism (i.e., their falling away from true religious belief) can only occur with the active concurrence of the persons harmed – they have to *choose* (freely) to adopt the false religious beliefs proposed to them.

Even conceding that difference, however, that is all the more reason, an advocate of restrictions on religious proselytism might argue, to prevent people from facing such temptations to do something freely that will seriously harm themselves – to prevent them from having an opportunity freely to choose the false belief they are misled into considering true.

Moreover, a better analogy in these matters would be the duty of governments to prohibit the distribution of medical drugs that do not actually accomplish what the distributors claim they do, even if the distributors sincerely believe such drugs do work and the buyers agree. (One thinks

---

[31] Perhaps I shouldn't say "obvious" so readily. Not all forms of human sacrifice are non-consensual – think of certain accounts of Euripides' Iphigenia and Jephthah's daughter – and those liberals who defend the absolute right of the individual over his or her own life (including a right to suicide) would seem to be logically committed to accept the right of voluntary or consensual religious human sacrifice.

of the example of a supposed, controversial cancer-mitigating drug that government regulators have clear and compelling grounds to consider ineffective.) Where governments are sure that the drugs do not have the desired effects, might they not feel compelled to prohibit their distribution?[32] The advocate of restrictions on false religious proselytism would claim the same authority.

But, again, the proposed analogy could be challenged. There is no positive virtue in taking, out of ignorance, a medical drug that does not accomplish what it is supposed to do. But a person who responds to a false religious argument by embracing it is actually performing a formally virtuous act: embracing the truth as he sees it.

Nonetheless, the response would be that this formally virtuous act would be materially harmful to the person who performed it (it might not be a morally bad act, but it would still be an act that harmed him, by leading him away from religious truth), and it would be doing someone a favor to prevent him from facing the occasion that made such harm possible.[33]

So questions remain (e.g., those raised by Waldron and Barry) about the coherence of belief in the obligation of society to promote the common good, including religious truth, the greatest of human goods, and the recognition of broad religious liberty, including not just false religious belief, but also false religious proselytism.[34] The principled arguments for religious liberty we have so far noted seem to work well for the narrower version of religious liberty (no compelled belief), but not so well regarding the broader version (no restriction of religious proselytism).

---

[32] I say "might," because I recognize that liberals could very well split on this question, some upholding such government prohibitions (on the grounds that encouraging false hopes or expectations is harmful), others not (on the grounds that, as long as the drugs are not actually harmful – and perhaps even if they are – people should be free to try dubious or illusory, or harmful, remedies that they consider worthwhile).

[33] Note that I have avoided including in this dialectic the argument that we don't know what the religious truth is. That is because I am trying to explore, in this chapter, whether it is possible to come up with a solid argument for a broad form of religious liberty that doesn't rely on skeptical religious premises.

[34] I should note that the issue of religious proselytism on which I am focusing here could be extended to include other issues. For example, the narrower view of religious liberty might permit suppression of "public" worship, since even the existence – the "example" – of public worship might affect other people's religious ideas, and therefore be considered a way of propagating religious views indirectly. Likewise, advocates of this narrower view might also consider civil disabilities justifiable – preventing those who do not adhere to religious truth from participating in political decisions – on the grounds that they would undermine the social commitment to religious truth.

Should a natural law liberal, then, adopt the narrower or the broader view of religious liberty? The arguments above, and the historical record, lead some liberals to believe that natural law theory is committed, in principle, only to the narrower view, although there may be pragmatic reasons for basing public policy on the broader view in some circumstances. Such liberals view the post-Reformation embrace of policies of religious toleration by traditional religious believers/natural law advocates as a response to the less-than-ideal circumstances of the modern world (i.e., religious pluralism) – but a response that leaves open the possibility that, if conditions were to change (and their religious beliefs were adopted by most citizens), the policy of toleration would be dropped. That is, the historical post-Reformation doctrine of religious liberty among religious believers (as opposed to Enlightenment figures like Locke) is thought to have been merely "tactical" rather than "principled." This approach is the one that John Rawls referred to, pejoratively, as a mere "modus vivendi."[35] (It also corresponds to a well-known position within Catholic theological circles, still influential as late as the mid-twentieth century.[36])

This leaves us with the question: Is there a compelling natural law argument for the broader form of religious liberty (including public worship and a right to proselytize) that is consistent with the beliefs that there is a knowable religious truth, which all should pursue and to which they should adhere, and that the political community has an obligation to promote the comprehensive common good, including religious truth?

PRINCIPLED VS. PRUDENTIAL ARGUMENTS FOR A BROAD SCOPE OF RELIGIOUS LIBERTY

Contemporary natural law theorists do assert the compatibility of a belief in the existence and intelligibility of religious truth, the obligation of human beings to pursue it and live in accord with it, the political community's responsibility (where circumstances permit) to promote religious truth as part of the common good, and a full acceptance of a broad understanding of religious liberty, including the right to proselytize.

The first step toward an adequate doctrine of religious liberty is to recognize the inadequacies of a traditional natural law position that

---

[35] Rawls, *Political Liberalism*, pp. 147ff.
[36] See John Courtney Murray, *The Problem of Religious Freedom* (Westminster, Md.: The Newman Press, 1965); see also the description and discussion of this position in Edward Goerner's *Peter and Caesar* (New York: Herder and Herder, 1965), pp. 153–72.

combined a "principled" position protecting only a narrower form of religious liberty (that belief not be compelled) with a pragmatic or "prudential" position embracing a broader form of religious liberty (including religious proselytism), but only under some circumstances ("tactically").

Principled and Prudential Arguments in General

As it turns out, the line between "principled" and "prudential" arguments becomes much less clear on analysis. We normally say that an argument for a liberty is "principled" when it is universal, when it holds always and everywhere, and not just in some circumstances. This is usually because the liberty is rooted in some aspect of human nature itself, and denial of it is incompatible with respecting that aspect. An argument for liberty is "prudential," on the other hand, when it does not hold universally, always and everywhere, but only in some circumstances. This is usually because there is nothing in human nature that demands such a right, but the balance of its benefits and harms makes it desirable (or not) in given circumstances.

An example of a principled argument would be the rule against (genuinely) coerced confessions (e.g., against physically compelling a person, through the infliction of pain), to confess to a crime he may or may not have committed. This is a principled argument because it doesn't depend on particular circumstances, but on our conviction that it is always wrong to physically compel someone to accept personal guilt for an action he did not in fact commit.

An example of a prudential argument would be the traditional right against self-incrimination in Anglo-American legal systems – that is the right not to be a witness against oneself in court – which was based on the appraisal of the benefits (more reliable testimony, greater respect for individual dignity, fewer temptations for law enforcement authorities to act improperly) relative to the harms (less information in the process of ascertaining the facts accurately) in the sort of adversarial legal system that is characteristic of common law countries. The arguments here are not principled arguments, which hold universally, since different legal systems, such as the civil law systems of continental Europe that deny the right to refuse to answer questions in the course of criminal investigations, are generally acknowledged to be compatible with universal moral principles (e.g., respect for human dignity).

These distinctions may become clearer by looking at another example, the use of torture in investigations of criminal conspiracy. The absolute proscription of torture in such criminal investigations is based on the principle that the deliberate infliction of great pain on a person, against his will and for the benefit of others, as a means to coerce him to give information, is inherently incompatible with the dignity of human beings. This argument is principled because it maintains that there is an *essential* connection between the absolute prohibition and the dignity of the person, and so it holds universally, not only in certain circumstances.

Another, more prudential, argument against torture would be that information obtained through torture is unreliable. This is less principled and more prudential because the reliability of such information actually varies a good deal with the circumstances. In some cases, such information may be quite reliable. For example, if a person under torture reveals the hidden whereabouts of the murder weapon he used, and the weapon is found, the information could be judged quite reliable.[37] One might still use such an argument to defend a policy of absolutely proscribing torture as a criminal investigation tool, on the grounds that, more often than not (or at least often enough, relative to the benefits gained), information obtained that way would be unreliable. But such an argument would be highly vulnerable to exceptions being carved out in those cases where the benefits seem very great (e.g., when the goal is to discover weapons of mass destruction that may be used imminently) and/or the harm not so great (e.g., when the person being tortured is considered to be a despicable person). The possibilities of abuse and error in the use of torture are other prudential arguments against it.[38]

Prudential Arguments Regarding Religious Liberty

We have already seen a principled argument that provides solid grounds for at least one aspect of religious liberty: namely, the principle that religious acts should be free, and therefore compelled religious acts are of no value. But we have also seen that this argument does not respond to the more sophisticated challenge to religious liberty aimed, not at private belief, but at public worship and proselytism based on religious error.

[37] A good example of the reliability of a coerced confession can be found in *Ashcraft v. Tenn.* 322 U.S. 143 (1944), which went on to hold that voluntariness, rather than reliability, should be the test for admissibility of confessions.

[38] The case of torture is actually more complex, since the very definition of torture is not easy to come by. (At what point, for example, does sleep deprivation constitute "torture"?) My point here is that, on my understanding of natural law, at least certain unambiguous instances of torture are absolutely prohibited, no matter what "benefits" they might be thought to achieve.

One way of responding to this challenge might be to concede that there is no "principled" argument to uphold a universal right of those who have erroneous religious views to worship publicly or to proselytize. They have a right against attempts to compel them to believe religious truth, but they have no right to engage in acts whose natural effect may be to draw others away from the truth. There are, however, it could be argued, very powerful "prudential" arguments in favor of recognizing rights to public worship and proselytism, under at least some – or even many, or most – circumstances.

What are some examples of these prudential arguments against restricting public worship and proselytism? One is that, given the wide variety of human beings and human societies, the abuse of the power to suppress public proselytism of error will often – perhaps typically – do more harm than the proper use of it will do good. That is, such a power would likely more often be employed to suppress truth than to suppress error. For example, a natural law-oriented Christian tempted to adhere to the narrower notion of religious liberty (hoping that Christian countries would restrict non-Christian proselytism) might observe that there are many Islamic countries today, in which those same restrictions on proselytism are used to prohibit the public practice of Christianity, and they might well conclude that, on balance, Christianity would benefit more from universal recognition of a broader notion of religious liberty than from a narrower one. (But their judgments about this might be affected by their perceptions or expectations regarding how much political power Christians actually have, or are likely to have, in various countries around the world.)

Another example is the danger that a civil power invoked to aid religion – that is, even a "friendly" civil power supportive of religious truth – may overstep its bounds and try to influence religion (possibly in good faith) in ways that distort it. For example, the Roman emperor Constantine, having provided protection to the Christian religion, then went on to try to provide a muddled political compromise to resolve the Arian controversy, which jeopardized orthodox Christian teaching on the divine nature of Christ. (This recalls the line from *The King and I*, in which the king wonders: "If I join with other nations in alliance, if allies are weak am I not best alone; if allies are strong with power to protect me, might they not 'protect' me out of all I own?")

Similar concerns arise for natural law-oriented religious believers today regarding the net benefits and harms of public aid for religiously affiliated schools. The schools may benefit from such aid, in important ways, but they are also thereby subjected to various regulations, some of which may distort or obstruct their religious mission. The nature and scope of the regulations, and the likelihood of their expansion, may determine whether the aid is worth the danger of the strings attached to it.

These can be considered "prudential" arguments because they both show that the full range of religious liberty (including the right to proselytize) should be required in *some* situations, rather than requiring that religious liberty be fully recognized in *all* situations. For example, in a certain civilizational context, it might appear very unlikely that public power will be used to advance error rather than truth, and so a supporter of religious truth might argue that full religious liberty is not necessary there. Likewise, there may seem to be very good reasons to believe that a friendly civil power *will not* overstep its bounds and distort the religion it is helping, thus making full religious liberty seem unnecessary.

That is, it might be possible to avoid the potential harmful effects of limiting full religious liberty in some given (ideal) set of circumstances, and in such a situation the prudential reasons underlying religious liberty would be absent, and so – the argument goes – suppressing certain important aspects of religious liberty – such as proselytism – for those who hold untrue religious beliefs could be justified.

The "Principled Prudential" Argument

I think a more adequate understanding of the argument for the broad form of religious liberty is that – in addition to the principled argument for the central core of religious liberty (the rejection of coerced religious belief) – there is a "principled prudential argument" for natural law advocates to adhere to an even broader view of religious liberty that would include religious proselytism.

The problem with what I have called prudential arguments for a broad religious liberty, as I have laid them out so far, is that it takes much too narrow a view of "prudential" considerations, in two ways. First, the evaluation of each argument for and against broad religious liberty must consider not just the circumstances at a given time, but the general impact over human history of *ever* adopting a policy of narrowing religious liberty. (Call these "long-term prudential arguments.")

For example, genuine prudence does not merely require that we ask "what are the chances *now or in the foreseeable future* that civil power will be used to advance truth rather than error?" True prudence would require us to see that there will inevitably be *many* times in human history when a civil power aiming to advance religious truth will instead advance religious error, and therefore religious truth will benefit more from *universal* civil policies of broad religious liberty than it would from alternate policies of broader and less broad religious liberty, chosen according to the circumstances.

Second, and even more importantly, the evaluation of the overall argument for and against broad religious liberty must consider the *cumulation* of various long-term prudential arguments. So far I have mentioned two such arguments: the unlikelihood that government support for religion will actually benefit religious truth, rather than religious error, and the likelihood that civil powers "friendly" to a true religion may ultimately intervene in religious affairs in ways that may undermine religious truth. There are many others as well, and it is the cumulation of these arguments that creates, in the final analysis, a compelling case for a consistent, unwavering policy of broad religious liberty.

Among many arguments, the one I find particularly powerful is the fact that a policy of prohibiting and punishing public worship and proselytism by adherents of religious error can (very understandably) engender in the victims and their religious compatriots a hatred and an obstinacy which will constitute very great obstacles to proselytism on behalf of religious truth.

Many of us – perhaps especially liberals, who are so committed to universal principles and therefore a form of cosmopolitanism – sometimes find it hard to understand the power of historical and ethnic ties, for example, those associated with nationalism. We tend to be perplexed, for instance, when we see that certain groups of people hate other groups based on events that occurred decades or centuries ago. But the fact is that such loyalties and hatreds exercise enormous power over many men.

Powerful testimony to this tendency can be found in history: Greek Orthodox resentment of the West for the sack of Constantinople eight centuries ago, the ethnic hatreds that rent Yugoslavia, Protestant and Catholic Irish bloodletting – the list is endless. These hatreds can also be found in various literary masterpieces. One example can be found in *Les Miserables*, which portrays the deep hatred of religion by French Revolution republicans – based in great part on the association of religious leaders with the oppression of the *ancien regime*. As Tocqueville pointed out, the Church had benefitted from the support of its social alliance with the monarchy, but it paid a price for doing so:

As long as a religion rests only upon those sentiments which are the consolation of all affliction, it may attract the affections of all mankind. But if it be mixed up with the bitter passions of the world, it may be constrained to defend allies whom its interests, and not the principle of love, have given to it; or to repel as antagonists men who are still attached to it, however opposed they may be to the powers with which it is allied. The church cannot share the temporal power of the state without being the object of a portion of that animosity which the latter excites.[39]

Another literary example is the Spanish novel *The Cypresses Believe in God*, peopled with characters who represent the extremely broad range of political opinions on the eve of the Spanish Civil War – and the extraordinarily deep hatred of so many of the different groups for each other.[40]

That is to say, religious believers must concern themselves with creating the conditions for persuading others about religious truth. Those conditions are not simply a matter of trying to "win a debate" – as if mere argument were the conclusive factor in bringing people to accept broad and complex truths about reality. People are inevitably affected by the character of the "messenger" who claims to bring truth – they want to see the attractiveness of the lives lived by those who embrace a certain belief. It is unrealistic to ask human beings to find attractive a message communicated by men who are persecuting them.[41] One only has to look at the religious hatreds occasioned by persecution, and how the Inquisition and Galileo live on as perpetual motifs in the criticism of the Catholic Church.

So genuine prudence would tell us to look at much more than whether suppression in *today's* particular circumstances of those who propagate religious error will create hatreds that may now, or for the foreseeable future, be obstacles to their willingness to listen to religious truth. It

---

[39] Alexis de Tocqueville, *Democracy in America*, Phillips Bradley, Ed. (New York: Alfred A. Knopf, 1972), Vol. 1, chap. 17, p. 310.

[40] Jose Maria Gironella, *The Cypresses Believe in God*, trans. Harriet de Onís (New York, Knopf, 1955).

[41] To give one testimony to this observation: "The Catholic Church is not confined to a particular territory and she has no geographical borders; her members are men and women of all regions of the world. She knows, from many centuries of experience, that suppression, violation, or restriction of religious freedom have caused suffering and bitterness, moral and material hardship, and that even today there are millions of people enduring these evils. By contrast, the recognition, guarantee and respect of religious freedom bring serenity to individuals and peace to the social community; they also represent an important factor in strengthening a nation's moral cohesion, in improving people's common welfare, and in enriching the cooperation among nations in an atmosphere of mutual trust." John Paul II, "Message to the Heads of State signatories of the Final Act of Helsinki" (September 1, 1980), no. 6 (available at: http://www.vatican.va/holy_father/john_paul_ii/messages/pont_messages/1980).

requires, instead, that we recognize that, in the course of human history, suppression of religious rights will inevitably create very long-term obstacles to the willingness of very many people even to consider conversation with those groups who have been their persecutors.

A whole set of arguments focuses on the effect of persecution on the religious believer himself. For example, there is the great difficulty of maintaining a Christian spirit in the midst of the strife occasioned by efforts to suppress propagation of false religious ideas. So often in history, Christians, who are supposed to love their neighbors, have ended up looking pretty indistinguishable from the people of the world who seek vengeance for offenses against them and their families. (Think only of the Crusades.)

Moreover, it is only too likely that the use of material weapons (including government coercion) to fight unbelief may inadvertently lead to a decreased emphasis on the primacy of spiritual resources (prayer, good example, preaching). This has often happened in countries with established religions. One thinks of the Anglican Church in England, for instance (or the Lutheran Church in Scandinavia, or the Roman Catholic Church in other parts of Europe), which is still the official church of the nation, but is a religion practiced by hardly anyone there today.

There is also the argument that "unsuccessful persecution" only increases or exacerbates opposition, and that we are now far past the day when persecution can be successful in cutting off the circulation of ideas permanently. In the modern world, technological and political and social developments guarantee that unorthodox ideas will in fact be circulated in society. (The last years of communism exemplified this problem: fax machines, photocopiers, and cellular phones made it increasingly difficult to prevent the diffusion of heterodox ideas and the building up of communities based on them.)

Moreover, the refusal to permit heterodox ideas to be spoken or published is likely to inhibit substantially the effective response to them as well. Therefore, the only way effectively, in the long run, to combat hostile ideas is to confront them publicly and make effective arguments against them.

Reliance on persecution to suppress opposing (false) ideas can also encourage people to think that the persecution is being used as a substitute for effective arguments. It seems to bespeak a lack of self-confidence in the truth's defenders as to their ability to demonstrate its truth. Even if that is not true – for example, it may reflect, not a lack of confidence in the ability of the truth's defenders to make an effective argument, but rather a lack of confidence in many peoples' ability to see the truth through the fog of specious arguments – this may be a case where people's (mis)perceptions are as influential as the truth.

It is not just one of these arguments, but their cumulation and convergence that constitutes a compelling case for the broad form of religious liberty. These so-called "prudential" considerations – taken together, and viewed, as they should be, over the full range of human history and circumstances – cease to be "merely prudential" arguments and constitute an overwhelming and, in fact, *principled* case for universally (in time and place) protecting the full scope of religious liberty.

This ethical/political argument is analogous to an epistemological argument put forward by John Henry Newman, in his *An Essay in Aid of a Grammar of Assent*. Dealing with the concept of "moral certitude" there, Newman argues that the mind does attain genuine moral certitude by attending to cumulating and concurring probabilities. This is a form of "concrete" reasoning in which the mind reaches the conclusion that "it can be no other way"

by the strength, variety, or multiplicity of premises, which are only probable, not by invincible syllogisms, – by objections overcome, by adverse theories neutralized, by difficulties gradually clearing up, by exceptions proving the rule, by unlooked-for correlations found with received truths, by suspense and delay in the process issuing in triumphant reactions, – by all these ways and many others . . . [42]

In many matters, it is the "cumulation of concurring probabilities" that leads the human mind to certitude (the certitude "appropriate to the subject – matter," as Aristotle would say[43]). So it is, in ethical/political reasoning, that a cumulation and convergence of what appear to be merely prudential arguments can arise to a universal principle.

This combination of a purely principled argument against coerced religious belief and a "principled prudential argument" for the broader rights of public worship and religious proselytism is compatible with the full recognition of religious truth. It requires no skepticism or agnosticism about the capacity of human beings, in principle, to know religious truth, and neither does it require or support an enthusiastic embrace of "religious pluralism" for its own sake. In fact, throughout, it recognizes the distinction between religious truth and error, and the desirability of all human beings attaining to religious truth. At the same time, it goes beyond any sort of "tactical" embrace of the full scope of religious liberty only for

---

[42] John Henry Newman, *An Essay in Aid of a Grammar of Assent* (Garden City, NY: Doubleday, 1955), p. 254.
[43] Aristotle, *Nichomachean Ethics*, Book I, chapter 3 (McKeon, Ed., p. 936).

some circumstances, which would hold in reserve some (supposed) "ideal" that accords a narrower scope to religious liberty. It leads to the conclusion that there are sound reasons to recognize the full scope of religious liberty always and everywhere. That is why it is not a "merely prudential," but a fully principled case for religious liberty.

11

A Natural Law Public Philosophy

In this book I have argued that natural law and liberalism, despite historical tensions to the contrary, are really fundamentally harmonious, and that natural law theory can provide the best foundation for a public philosophy. What would a public philosophy rooted in or guided by the principles of natural law look like, especially one that would be applicable to the circumstances of contemporary American society? In this concluding chapter, I want to give a preliminary outline of a natural law public philosophy for America.

THE FOUNDATIONAL PRINCIPLE: THE DIGNITY
OF THE HUMAN PERSON

The most fundamental principle of a public philosophy, on which all others ought to rest, is the dignity of the human person. This dignity is rooted in certain distinctive human qualities, especially intellect and free will, the human capacity to know the truth and to love and choose the good. In these fundamental capacities, all human beings are equal.

These capacities, the sources of human dignity, are not always lived up to. Part of the "philosophical anthropology" at the foundation of a public philosophy, in fact, must be the recognition of the capacity of human beings to act either in accordance with or contrary to the source of their dignity, especially by misusing their intelligence and freedom to do wrong. Nonetheless, each human being remains capable of acting freely to attain the good, and therefore never definitively forfeits human dignity.

THE ORIGINS AND END OF GOVERNMENT: THE COMMON GOOD

The purpose of government is to serve the common good of the political community, which encompasses the physical, moral, and intellectual well-being of the people. The common good must be understood in light of the goods toward which human persons are inclined by nature, in all their diversity and richness. The benefits involved in the common good should be shared in by all, but it is not merely the sum total of individual goods (as the "common good" of a sports team transcends the individual talents and activities of its members).

Government is "natural," rather than "artificial," because it flows spontaneously from lesser communities as an essential means for achieving the common good. (In this regard, a natural law public philosophy follows Blackstone's Aristotelian account of the origins of government rather than Locke's.)

This overall account leaves open the question of how government should be particularly constructed (the form of government) in order to achieve its objective. That will depend to a considerable degree on the particular character and circumstances of a nation. Nonetheless, it can be said that it is desirable that conditions be such that popular participation is an important element of the form of government, as an important barometer of the impact of political rule on the citizens of the community and as an important stimulus to the development of their intellectual and moral capacities.

THE LEGITIMATE SCOPE OF GOVERNMENT: LIMITED GOVERNMENT

There are many important limits on the scope of legitimate government action.[1] First are the restraints of the moral law itself, such as not to lie, steal, or murder. (Applying these principles in the political world is not always easy, but the separation of politics from morality is unacceptable.)

Among the moral limits on government would be included the obligation to respect the consciences of the citizens, so that religious liberty is a fundamental principle of just governments. (There are still, of course, just limits to religiously motivated *actions*, even when they are based on conscience.) Such a view of religious liberty is perfectly compatible with the notion that there is a fundamental duty to pursue the truth about God

---

[1] For an interesting discussion of this topic by a contemporary natural law thinker, see John Finnis's contribution to *Natural Law, Liberalism, and Morality*, ed. Robert George (Clarendon Press, 1996), pp. 1–27.

and to act in accordance with it. In fact, that duty is precisely the basis of the right.

A second set of limits is made up of those which flow from the importance of government "fostering" the common good and the development of its citizens, which precludes government *substituting* its own activity for their initiative and their own efforts to identify and achieve a choiceworthy set of particular goods. Among other implications, this principle, known as subsidiarity, entails an appropriate decentralization of government functions (one form of which is American federalism). Moreover, the same principle impelling higher governments to leave to lower levels of government the functions that they are capable of handling adequately, will often also require governments in general to achieve their goals through support for, or to leave various social functions to, voluntary associations and to families.

POLITICAL AUTHORITY

Political authority is natural, and those who exercise political power legitimately, acting within their proper powers and in the pursuit of the common good, should be respected and obeyed.

In a well-founded and well-developed polity, the people should have a share in rule and, in a democratic republic such as the United States, the requirement of the consent of the governed should apply not only to the form of government (e.g., the general character of the constitution), but also to regular accountability of public officials to the citizenry (e.g., through elections). The desire to limit the potential abuse of government prudently leads Americans to embrace the principle of separation of powers, which provides for different parts of government, often selected in different ways, with different legitimate powers, to provide a wholesome check on political power in general.

The obligation to obey the law derives, not merely from popular will, but from the duty and right of government to foster the common good. (This is one way of saying that the demands of the common good bind "the people" in their collective capacity, as much as it does public officials themselves.) Even when government falls short of successfully attaining this goal, the importance of political stability normally calls for citizens to obey the laws. But there are limits to the obligatory character of law, in particular, when laws command citizens to do things that are morally evil, and when the entire character of the government is so contrary to the fundamental principles of justice that citizens may justly alter or abolish it.

CITIZENSHIP

A nation must have some principles and rules that determine who will be citizens. The presumption ought to be that all adults residing permanently in a nation, who are willing and able to accept the responsibilities of citizenship, ought to be able to become citizens. (These responsibilities presume some preparation in the form of education regarding the principles and history of the nation.) It will also be necessary to establish rules determining who will be permitted to reside in the nation, in particular, rules regarding immigration. Those rules will consider the many particular circumstances regarding whether the integration of potential immigrants will advance or impede the common good. Again, the presumption ought to be in favor of a generous willingness to welcome others.

POLITICAL AND PERSONAL RIGHTS OF CITIZENS AND PERSONS

One central feature of a sound public philosophy is the protection of rights, both political and personal. The rights of citizens to life and personal liberty are fundamental constituents of the common good. Freedom of speech, freedom of religion, freedom of association, and certain rights regarding legal procedure were enshrined in the Constitution, and have generally been broadened over time. These rights are derived from the goods toward which human beings are naturally inclined, as means to ends, and it is in light of those goods that reasonable limits on and regulation of rights is appropriate.[2]

RELATIONSHIP OF THE POLITICAL COMMUNITY TO OTHER COMMUNITIES: CIVIL SOCIETY

Besides the relationship of the general government to states given in the principle of federalism, government has important rights and duties vis-à-vis other forms of community. It should provide support for and encouragement to the basic "cell" of society, the family, which should have a privileged place in the legal and social structure of society. The stability of marriage should be supported by a strong legal bond. Parental rights in

---

[2] See Robert George's *Making Men Moral*, chapter 5, for an outline of a "natural law" defense of civil liberties. For an example of how the ends of rights determine some of their reasonable limits, see Francis Canavan, *Freedom of Expression: Purpose As Limit* (Carolina Academic Press and The Claremont Institute for the Study of Statesmanship and Political Philosophy, 1984).

the upbringing and education of children should be recognized as primary. Interventions by government into family life are sometimes justified, however, when the essential well-being of some of its members are seriously and immediately threatened.

Society should encourage and facilitate the formation of voluntary associations, as these associations contribute greatly to the goods of friendship and individual development that are part of the common good.

"Natural" groups in society, such as ethnic or racial groups, and their individual members should be protected from invidious discrimination and assured of equal participation in the political community. (The extent to which the political community will formally acknowledge political rights for groups will vary with the character and circumstances of a given nation.) Their rights to maintain their language and culture should be protected, as itself a contribution to the common good, by means consistent with the common good (which may require measures to prevent a kind of group isolationism that could threaten social divisions and unrest, e.g., a requirement to learn the country's major language[s]).

Different economic and occupational groups (business and labor, manufacture and commerce and agriculture, professions and services) should have the right to organize and participate in political and social life. Their pursuit of their own self-interest ought to be consonant with a fundamental commitment to the common good (just as the common good should not be considered to be merely a majority or aggregate good, but must consider the good of all the citizens).

THE ECONOMIC SYSTEM AND THE RIGHTS
AND DUTIES OF PROPERTY

The importance of property rights is and has always been an essential element of both natural law theory and American public philosophy. Indeed, in the founding era in particular, many would have said that the protection of property (broadly understood) was the great function of government. It is impossible to maintain the security and independence, the self-rule and self-reliance, of republican citizens in the absence of private property.

Yet, sound public philosophy has always recognized that property carries with it certain social responsibilities, in varying degrees. One way of looking at this matter is to understand that property provides human beings with the means to pursue the various goods toward which they are inclined by nature and that, in some sense, all the resources of the world exist to facilitate the development of all human beings. Accordingly, a just economic system will attempt to make available to everyone in society the resources needed to act well. This principle entails certain obligations (which can be enforced by political authority, where appropriate) on the part of those who have more than enough property to meet their needs, in a world where many people, through no fault of their own, lack the necessary resources for self-development, and often even the most elementary necessities of life. (The qualification – through no fault of their own – is important, for ordinarily people should be expected to provide for themselves and their families by their own work and efforts.)

Another element of the economic life of a nation is the fundamental human activity of work. By work, human beings provide for the support of themselves and their families, develop their own talents and abilities, and make a contribution to the common good of the community. The political community should foster an economic system that provides effectively for the employment of its citizens. (The best way to accomplish this is a complicated empirical question.) Those who have the power and responsibility to shape workplaces should keep in mind the priority of persons over things, so that the production or provision of goods and services is harmonized as well as possible with the growth and development of those who work. (Among other things, this suggests that economic activities ought to be regarded as cooperative undertakings, with due respect for the rights and responsibilities of all participants.)

EDUCATION

Among the most important aspects of the common good is education. Education ranges from the basics of literacy (reading, writing, and arithmetic) and skills necessary for employment, to the political education necessary for the proper fulfillment of our duties and rights as citizens, to moral, intellectual, and spiritual development.

The responsibility for this important task is shared by parents, teachers, the political community, and religious communities. Political and religious communities exercise their important roles especially by facilitating the efforts of parents to educate their children, whether by means of public or religiously affiliated schools or by supporting private educational initiatives of parents.

CULTURE AND ENTERTAINMENT

Issues of culture play an important part in the life of a nation (and indeed may be thought of as an important form of "education" extended beyond basic schooling). Institutions of higher education will have a great impact here, as will a multitude of cultural institutions and activities, such as those involving literature and drama, music, and art. And in modern democratic communities, "popular culture," for example, as found in television, radio, and movies, may constitute a significant part of the "common" life of the community. Especially given the greatly increased leisure time available to citizens under modern economic conditions, entertainment must be regarded as a very important part of the national life, with great import for the common good. While, in general, cultural activities will arise as the free initiatives of groups and individuals in society, there is room for public promotion of culture and also for public restrictions on elements that debase the culture (e.g., pornography).

THE SHARED UNDERSTANDING OF THE COMMUNITY REGARDING ITS HISTORY

One of the sources of community is a shared understanding of a nation's past life. This constitutes a kind of "collective memory" of the political community. Indeed, education in the nation's political principles, and the "handing on" of the traditions that have been constitutive of a given nation's ideals and culture is an important requirement for maintaining a "common" life. This education should foster a proper pride in the nation's distinctive path in pursuing the common good, but it can and should recognize occasions on which it has not lived up to its ideals and responsibilities. (For example, an education in American history will recognize the ideals of liberty under law and equal rights and the distinctive contribution of American political life to self-government, while recognizing that it has taken great efforts over time to achieve civil rights for black Americans, and that this is still an on-going process.)

Not surprisingly, the effort to define the public philosophy at any given time is often fought out through competing visions of the history of the nation and their relationship to present debates. The lens through which a people looks at its past will often shape its present and its future.

RELATIONSHIP OF THE NATION TO OTHER PEOPLES AND THE WORLD

As to its guiding principles, the foreign policy of a nation ought not to choose between (much less oscillate between) an idealism unattached to national interest and a realism devoid of concern for what might be called the "international common good" (still inchoate) and the good of other nations. Its primary aim should always be to provide for the independence, the security, and the well-being (as essential constituents of the common good) of the nation itself. But this legitimate and appropriate focus on national self-interest does not mean that the nation is exempt from important moral considerations similar to those that govern the action of individuals. In particular, nations must conform to certain fundamental moral norms, such as not waging unjust wars against other nations even when it might appear to be in the narrow self-interest of the nation to do so – and they ought even to be willing to act benevolently for the good of other nations, when such action would achieve important goods for other nations or people without "excessive" costs for the acting nation. No doubt, application of these principles is frequently difficult (e.g., what constitutes "an excessive cost," may be difficult to discern), but that is often the case in the lives of individuals too.

Relations among nations ought to be regulated, not by mere power, but according to principles of justice. In principle, it would seem desirable that, where the common good of nations requires coordinated activity, this activity be regulated by principles that are clearly established and stable, and therefore, juridical principles. Given the great differences among nations and peoples (a pluralism far deeper even than the "deep pluralism" of Western liberal democracies), however, such a juridical order seems unlikely in the foreseeable future. Were an international consensus on fundamental principles sufficient for a juridical order to be achieved, however, even then any such order would have to place great emphasis on subsidiarity.

Moreover, a candid recognition of the depths of differences among different peoples and cultures and political systems in the world today, as well as a prudent concern for the dangers of political power exercised over large portions of the globe, would also counsel caution in international juridical undertakings, and reliance on relationships of voluntary cooperation to cover many areas of common concern.

RELATIONSHIP OF THE POLITY TO THE TRANSCENDENT ORDER

In a pluralistic society, religious establishments are neither possible nor desirable. Nevertheless, this does not require so strict a notion of establishment as to preclude public recognition of God and his providence, which is, in fact, legitimate and desirable. Traditionally, Americans have recognized the existence of God and his providence – particularly his providence in regard to this nation – by such symbols as Thanksgiving

Day proclamations, the use of "In God We Trust" on coins, the inclusion of "under God" in the pledge of allegiance, and religious invocations at public events. Recognition of God does not require a nation to claim or believe that its activity is based on any special, divine authority.

Such recognition of God and his providence has several justifications. First, it is "true," and therefore society, which has benefitted from that providence, ought in justice to recognize it. Second, it is both true and "useful" as the essential foundation for other important elements of the public philosophy. Perhaps most importantly, the recognition of God as the author of Creation provides the most solid ground for the dignity of all human persons and their "inalienable rights." Those rights can be viewed as important sources of moral limits on the action of government and other citizens.

CONCLUSION

It is important to recognize the limits of any public philosophy. The above principles of a natural law public philosophy should not be expected to provide a specific resolution for all, or even most, of the vast number of particular questions that arise in the life of a political community. Such decisions must always be governed by prudence, in light of the widely varying characteristics of different political communities and of the historical circumstances in which they find themselves. These decisions are not, however, simply ad hoc judgments. They are prudent applications of more general principles that provide essential guidance in such decision making. Much of the disagreement about specific questions in political life can be traced to fundamentally differing conceptions of public philosophy. That fact is particularly clear at a time when there is a widespread sense that we find ourselves in the midst of "culture wars" that are particularly resistant to reasonable discussion and resolution.

Describing the more determinate implications for contemporary American public life of a natural law liberal public philosophy is a task for another book. In that work, I hope to deal with issues such as the grounds for human dignity; the relationship between the quest for religious truth and political life; the basis for, and limits on, freedom of thought and discussion; the standing of the institution of marriage in law and social norms regarding sexuality; and rights and duties of property and principles of economic life.

If much remains to be said, we can say at this point, after an examination of contemporary liberalism, of the broad expanse of the liberal tradition, and of natural law theory in its classic and contemporary forms, that natural law liberalism is a realistic foundation for public life that provides a much needed alternative to contemporary versions of liberalism. Contemporary liberalism lacks adequate foundations (a fact that may seem unimportant in times of prosperity, but may be dangerous in more troubled times), attempts to transform an important means (autonomy) into an ultimate political end, truncates our understanding of public reason, and unfairly marginalizes and even threatens important liberties (such as parental rights, and freedom of speech and association) of many citizens, especially those with religious and traditional moral beliefs.

Rather than continue down the dead-end street of contemporary liberalism, we need to explore ways of understanding, articulating, and applying natural law liberalism. Natural law liberalism is more respectful of a human reason that is not merely instrumental, a reason that, for all its limits, is capable of knowing the human good. It has a deeper sensitivity to the social nature of human beings, and to the importance of the "moral ecology" in their growth and development. At the same time, it recognizes the importance of personal liberty and the limits of law. Natural law liberalism embraces the strengths of liberalism – its concern for human equality and rights – while recognizing and helping alleviate its more problematic tendencies, especially its tendency to promote materialism and individualism at the expense of developing man's higher intellectual and moral capacities. Natural law liberalism therefore gives to us, who are already committed to liberal democracy, a better account of the foundations and essential requirements of liberalism. And it will also help us to give a more persuasive and attractive defense of a richer and nobler liberalism to the world's many non-liberals.

Index

Made in the USA
San Bernardino, CA
26 September 2014